STRINDBERG

TWENTIETH CENTURY VIEWS

The aim of this series is to present the best
in contemporary critical opinion on major
authors, providing a twentieth century perspective on their changing status in an era
of profound revaluation.

Maynard Mack, *Series Editor*
Yale University

STRINDBERG

A COLLECTION OF CRITICAL ESSAYS

Edited by

Otto Reinert

Prentice-Hall, Inc. *Englewood Cliffs, N. J.*

A SPECTRUM BOOK

PRENTICE-HALL INTERNATIONAL, INC. (*London*)
PRENTICE-HALL OF AUSTRALIA, PTY. LTD. (*Sydney*)
PRENTICE-HALL OF CANADA, LTD. (*Toronto*)
PRENTICE-HALL OF INDIA PRIVATE LIMITED (*New Delhi*)
PRENTICE-HALL OF JAPAN, INC. (*Tokyo*)

Contents

STRINDBERG

Introduction[1]

by Otto Reinert

I

Who would have thought I'd ever find the ocean small, the horizon narrow!

—Letter to Verner von Heidenstam,
1885

It's hardly possible to have anything to do with him. But I don't care, and I see that you don't either. After all, he is August Strindberg.

—Knut Hamsun in a letter, 1895

. . . after forty-one years of experience I no longer dare to have views on anything, for the moment I make up my mind to fight for this or that I feel tied, and then I no longer grow, and it is still my joy in life to feel how I am growing.

—Letter to Georg Brandes, 1890[2]

Strindberg is the artist as neurotic, and criticism must begin by coming to terms with the life and the personality that were both source and subject of one of the most remarkable imaginative achievements in modern literature. We think of him as that other brooding Scandinavian genius, more original than Ibsen, perhaps, but also less accessible—paradoxically so, since of the two Strindberg seems to have had much the shorter "distance between the blood and the ink." [3] It rarely occurs to us to search the reticent Ibsen's conventional public

[1] The editor wishes to thank Miss Aden Ross, a graduate student at the University of Washington, for help in the selection of essays and for her comments on an early draft of this introduction.

[2] The translations from Swedish in the Introduction are the editor's.

[3] The phrase is an anonymous Swedish critic's quoted by Robert W. Corrigan in his Introduction to *A Dream Play and The Ghost Sonata* (San Francisco: Chandler, 1966), p. ix.

life for the originals of his dramatic fictions, but between us and a
clear perception of Strindberg's work stand the thrice-married misogynist, the suspicious and ungrateful friend, the paranoid hater of
dogs and lesbians, the frustrated gold-maker, and the receiver of mes-
sages from the occult in cloud formations, names of hotels, and crossed
twigs in the road. Because Strindberg's real and projected selves are
so indistinct, we have until recently had more about Strindberg "the
possessed" than about Strindberg "the maker." [4]

Today, the new orthodoxy in Strindberg criticism is that everything
that matters about him is present in his writings and that their faithfulness to the outer facts of his life is an issue that can be left for
biographers to settle. "My new plays," said Strindberg of his chamber
plays, "are the usual mosaic from my own and other lives, . . .
neither autobiography nor confession. Whatever does not conform
with the facts is poetry, not lies." [5]

To the extent that this attitude discourages trivial source-hunting
among the records of Strindberg's eccentric and chaotic life, it was
long overdue and has released critical energies that have yielded important new insights. But there is something circular about the argument on which it rests. Granting that an author's life is critically
relevant whenever it can illuminate his work (the new Strindberg
critic says), in Strindberg work and life are so manifestly congruent
that the relevant biography can be inferred from what he wrote, and
what cannot be inferred is *ipso facto* irrelevant.

But the critic's problem of what to do with Strindberg's biography
is not quite so easily disposed of. *The Bond* is a powerful play whether
or not we know that it was based on Strindberg's ugly divorce from
his first wife. Yet our knowing or not knowing affects our response
not just to the play itself, but also to the mind that made it. For all
the verifiable autobiography in it, *The Son of a Servant* can be read
as a Tainean novel about the influence of heredity and environment
on a hypersensitive temperament. Yet its autonomy as fiction affects
its status as autobiography. A biographer may use it and Strindberg's
other works to support his view that Strindberg, the bourgeois artist-
intellectual, can serve as a touchstone for his age, victimized and
driven to *Angst* by a hostile society and his own divided allegiances.

---

[4] Göran Lindström, "Strindberg Studies 1915–1962," *Scandinavica*, II (May, 1963),
50. Lindström distinguishes three phases in Strindberg scholarship: genetic studies
(comparative and ideological), studies of Strindberg's "psychic peculiarities," and
"unbiased analysis of Strindberg's craftsmanship." Chronologically, however, the
divisions are not altogether so sharp as Lindström seems to suggest.

[5] *Brev* [*Letters*], selected and edited by Torsten Eklund (Stockholm: Aldus/Bon-
niers, 1965), p. 228 (April 2, 1907).

And a critic who chooses *not* to disregard the stresses in Strindberg's literary and marital career from which his works erupted is not necessarily failing to mind his proper business. The old conundrum about writers—"Does the life explain the work or the work the life?"—usually poses a false choice. The alternatives are particularly crude in the case of someone like Strindberg, who wrote his life and lived his imagination more fully than just about any other major author we can think of. Among moderns, perhaps only Kafka is an expressionist in the same radical sense. And both, significantly, are writers whose bizarre inscapes have become familiar landscapes of the modern consciousness and whose private nightmares have become common myths.

After Shakespeare's, no playwright's world is so inclusive as Strindberg's. But while Shakespeare's world is so densely and variously populated and so omnivocal that the playwright himself eludes discovery, over much of Strindberg's there hovers, like some unaccommodated residue of private psychic matter, a monotone of petulance with life. Strindberg lacks Shakespeare's generosity of spirit and his intelligence of imagination. "Transmutation," Robert Brustein observes, "—the conversion of existing material into something higher—is the goal of all his activity." But the conversion is never complete. In Strindberg's alchemical laboratory in Paris in the 1890s, the raw material almost, but not quite, turned into gold. And when the alembic of his art has done what it can to transmute inferno into elysium and private into universal experience, we may feel that the carbon and the sulphur of his private hellfires still remain what they were.

Since poverty was not the least of Strindberg's many difficulties, he sometimes wrote just for a living. It is striking how often money is a major plot motif in his works. There were, happily, other times when he delighted in the sheer exercise of his creative powers and artistic skills. But there was hardly a single extended period in his productive life when writing was not also a therapeutic effort to sublimate psychic pain. Words for Strindberg could punish and vindicate, conjure and exorcise. No wonder his creativity did not always keep up with his industry. The standard collected edition of his works in Swedish runs to fifty-five volumes. In addition, there are two volumes of posthumously collected pieces and eleven volumes of letters, with more to come. He wrote fifty-eight plays; fifteen novels and autobiographical seminovels; more than one hundred short stories, sketches, and fairy tales; three volumes of verse; a number of historical works and pseudoscientific treatises; and a multitude of essays and articles on chemistry, botany, politics, economics, philosophy, religion, philology, drama, music, and art. He painted (well enough to sell some pictures), composed music, played the piano and the guitar, and was a competent amateur photographer.

But next to Leonardo's or Goethe's, Strindberg's achievement over a wide range of intellectual and artistic activity appears less universal than simply versatile—shallow and sometimes silly, and frenetic rather than grand. As a belated polyhistorian he may have been doomed to be an anachronistic failure; already the fragmentation of human knowledge had gone too far. But that does not keep the versatility from being something that Strindberg partisans are more inclined to apologize for than to glory in. He expended his extraordinary gifts indiscriminately on ephemera, esoterica, and personal vendettas and on sublime visionary parables, brutal transcripts of actuality, and lovely childlike legends. One understands why critics have felt both tempted and obliged to turn to the life in order to bring light and shape to the huge, heterogeneous canon—to discover its core and continuity not in the works but in their creator.

But Strindberg was as "characterless" a character as any he ever created—a "soul complex" multiply motivated, a dark chaos past finding out. Like the child Johan in *The Son of a Servant,* he went through life "afraid and hungry" and ridden with guilt, his nerves painfully exposed.[6] He thought of himself as having been born, like Johan, in some sense prematurely: unwanted by his parents and with an incompletely developed will. The few happy scenes in his plays come not in his comedies, which are realistic and acerbic, but in his fairy-tale plays. They are a nostalgic mind's wish fulfillments, regressions to some ideal childhood, some secure family harmony, that destiny had cheated him of. The child of an ex-menial and a burgher descendant of a déclassé aristocratic family, he felt socially homeless and was always uncomfortably conscious of social class and manners. Drawn to the masses by instinct (or by loyalty to the mother he lost in early adolescence), he contemned them by intellectual conviction. He lived on the defensive. He came to hate whatever he loved because loving threatened his feeble sense of self; he saw a vampire in anyone having emotional claims on him. He desired nothing more ardently than the bliss of quiet domesticity with wife and children (though his own were not to cry at night and their diapers had to be kept out

[6] When his friend Verner von Heidenstam, tired of Strindberg's endless expostulations with life, told him in a letter in 1886, "I believe your vitality is just a matter of your enormous fretfulness," Strindberg replied: "Fretfulness is the quality of a nervous system more finely organized than others and therefore better equipped to do what it is supposed to do. A chronometer is more fretful than a turnip, but who cares as long as it records hundredths of seconds." *Brev,* p. 87 (June 23, 25, 1886).

of his sight), but he could never resolve the traditional dilemma of seeing woman both as madonna and as corrupting temptress and latent prostitute. His wife had to be both sensuous and virginal, motherly and submissive, a housekeeper and a soul companion. That a man and a woman who want nothing more than to live together in love invariably end up torturing one another seemed to him another move in the cruel game "the powers" play with the poor human pawn.

His intellectual development was as volatile as his emotional life, as if ideologies after a while turned as menacing as women and friends. At one time or another, Strindberg occupied just about every political, philosophical, and religious position available to a late-nineteenth-century intellectual, sometimes returning to positions he had violently abandoned earlier. By the time he was fifty his youthful social radicalism appeared to him the bastard offspring of sentimentalized Christianity and crass materialism. In the meantime he had been a Rousseauistic progressivist, an apolitical skeptic, and (in the late 1880s) an enthusiastic believer in Nietzsche's *Herrenmoral*. Even in the seventies he had offended his liberal friends with his views on the woman question. He admired Bismarck's Germany for keeping women in their place and men masculine. In the nineties he sided with the anti-Dreyfusards. But at sixty he was once again a political liberal and wrote newspaper polemics in support of social democracy and women's suffrage and property rights.

After the stern and joyless pietism of his childhood, he moved in the late 1860s and the 1870s through Unitarianism and Darwinistic agnosticism, arriving at atheism in the late 1880s. The paradoxes of Kierkegaard's pseudonymous personas took him to a moral impasse (he discovered Kierkegaard's religious stage only later). Kant's moral imperatives left him wondering whether it was he who was stupid or Kant who was muddled. His intellectual despair was deepened by Buckle, whose relativistic approach to history convinced him that "doubt is the beginning of truth." The dictum that "consciousness is pain" in von Hartmann's radical critique of rationalism in *Philosophie des Unbewussten* (1869) confirmed his own sense of life, and von Hartmann's world-weariness reinforced his childhood lessons in Christian *contemptus mundi*.

During the Inferno crisis in the mid-1890s—a nervous breakdown which in Strindberg, characteristically, took the form partly of near-suicidal terror and partly of ecstatic, semimystical epiphanies—he once again changed his ideological furniture, abandoning atheism when the powers began to persecute him. Roman Catholicism attracted him, but he never converted, and he tried theosophy only until he dis-

covered that the leader of the cult was a woman, Mme. Blavatsky.
Even after the Inferno crisis he kept "blindly following" the mystic
Swedenborg, "my Virgil who guides me through hell." [7] The author of
Legends rejects Christ the Redeemer because the notion of an innocent's vicarious atonement for *his* sins insults his pride. Yet, two years
later that notion is the theme of the first of the royal histories, *The
Saga of the Folkungs,* where the death of King Magnus's young, innocent son Erik atones for the crimes of his ancestors. And in his
last years Strindberg defined his religion as "confessionless Christianity."

This is clearly the story of a mind vainly seeking sanctuary in a
continually disappointing multiverse, and Strindberg's years of exile
and wandering seem allegorical. [8] Seeking his own identity, Strindberg
kept finding his protagonists among the God-obsessed heroes of Biblical myth. Johan in *The Son of a Servant* is obviously Ishmael, "the
bondwoman's son," disinherited and cast out in the desert, "his hand
against every man and every man's hand against him." The story of
A Madman's Defense, the other major work of pre-Inferno semiauto-
biography, is the story of Samson, shorn of his strength in the whore's
lap, treacherously given into the hands of his enemies. The nameless "Unknown" pilgrim, the most frequent authorial mask in the post-
Inferno years, is Cain, becoming an envious fratricide only when
God arbitrarily turns away from his offering; Job, the innocent victim
of God's conspiracy with Satan; Saul of Tarsus, coming to blinding
awareness on the road to Damascus that He whom he persecutes is the
God his soul has secretly sought; and Jacob, wrestling with the Lord
who smites his hip. It is the Jacob figure who speaks the Hunter's
last words in Strindberg's last play, *The Great Highway*:

> O Everlasting One! I won't let go your hand,
> Your hand so hard, till you bestow your blessing!
> Bless me, and bless your whole mankind,

[7] *Samlade skrifter av August Strindberg,* ed. John Landquist, 55 vols. (Stockholm:
Albert Bonnier's förlag, 1912–20), XXVIII, 294.

[8] Gunnar Brandell has commented on the relationship between Strindberg's psychological development and his changing ideological stances: "The crisis that followed the *Married* trial [1884] and the Inferno crisis [1894–97] are the great turning
points in Strindberg's life. The former led him to atheism, the latter back to a
belief in God. Between them they define the beginning and the end of the natural-
istic-pessimistic period in his life, comprising a little less than a decade. . . . Psychologically, the naturalistic phase coincides with his paranoia. Up to the *Married*
crisis, his personality had been predominantly hysterical . . . ; after the Inferno
crisis it becomes predominantly schizoid, and world-alienated autism is one of its
strongest features." *Strindbergs Infernokris* (Stockholm: Albert Bonniers förlag,
1950), pp. 43–44.

Who suffer, suffer from your gift of life!
But first bless me, who suffered most—
Whose greatest pain was that I could not be
The man I always wanted to become!

There is hardly another passage in all Strindberg that better expresses at once his own colossal egoism ("But first bless me, who suffered most") and his pathetically vulnerable sense of selfhood. Strangely, or rather not so strangely, the two were inextricable.

Strindberg's personal tragedy was that he was forever reaching out for what it is not in the power of life to grant. All he wanted was professional fulfillment, the world's love and respect, sexual passion forever renewable, family happiness, peace of mind, and supernatural reassurance that human existence has meaning. It would never have occurred to him that this way of describing his desires is in any sense funny. There are humor and wit in Strindberg, although mostly of the sardonic sort, but even his self-ironies have a Promethean ring. A lifetime of suffering taught him that his demands on the ultimate were preposterous, but he never learned to reduce them. And yet, for an author who so single-mindedly sought catharsis of his existential discontent, it is remarkable how seldom erring artistic tact betrayed him into whining self-pity.

Strindberg's embarrassing versatility is therefore neither lunatic hubris nor meretricius fickleness responding to literary fashions. As no religious creed and no philosophical system for long could still his metaphysical hunger or mediate between his sense of personal guilt and whatever agent was responsible for burdening him with it, so no single literary form sufficed for the expression of his riven self. Without the mystic's temperament, he had a mystic's impulse toward some single, comprehensive experience of reality, an *"Anschluss mit Jenseits"* ("union with the beyond"),[9] and with all his insecurities, conflicts, and phobias—his whole impossible personality—he still possessed some reservoir of resilience that allowed him to adapt his creativity to his turning quest. His seascape paintings were expressionistic renderings of his inner storms. His music symbolized the harmony he never attained. His attempts to transmute metals have been discredited, but they were part of his yearning for monism: he sought empirical confirmation of his intuitive conviction that all elements are basically one. An amateur chemist, working with crude equipment and neither competent nor patient enough to verify his find-

---

[9] *Samlade skrifter*, XLI, 138. The phrase appears in *Black Banners* (1904, first publ. 1907) in one of the discussions of religion among a group of friends who have withdrawn from the corrupt city to an island outside Stockholm.

ings, he was a religious poet seeking in experimental science proof
that all is in all. He attributed souls to flowers and to rooms in which
human lives had been lived intensely. He never succeeded in obliter-
ating his image of the world process as a whirling chaos, though he
tried at different times to accept both the orthodox believer's cosmos
of unalterable law and the Romantic's dynamically evolving universe.

Obsessed with religion and desperate for some kind of teleology,
Strindberg turned from nihilism to occultism, but the peace of certain
faith continued to elude him. He can never decide whether he is the
vilest of sinners or the most persecuted of innocents and whether the
world is God's or Satan's or a Manichean battleground. "Man is both
innocent and responsible," says Adolf in *Creditors.* "Innocent before
Him who no longer exists, responsible to himself and to his fellow
men." This is Strindberg the atheistic moralist of the eighties. But the
author of the Inferno books a decade later fears that the demonic appearance of the world may conceal only nothing, that he may be living
in a metaphysical void where his moral urges are irrelevant because
man-made morals are no substitute for the departed numen. "I burn
with the desire to accuse myself and defend myself both at the same
time," cries the narrator in the *Wrestling Jacob* section of *Legends.*
"But there is no court, no judge, and I consume myself here in my loneliness! " [10] Strindberg's hell was a state of rebelliousness against the
world not for being evil, but for quite possibly being absurd.

II

> This, then, is what my life adds up to: a sign of warn-
> ing, an example for the improvement of others, an
> object for general amusement that proves the noth-
> ingness of fame and honor and teaches youth how
> not to live. I am the proverbial laughing-stock who
> thinks himself a prophet but stands exposed as a
> cheat. But it was the Almighty who tricked the false
> prophet into speaking, and the false prophet does not
> feel himself accountable, for he has only played the
> part he was assigned.
>
> Epilogue to *Inferno,* 1897

Writing to Harriet Bosse, his third wife, in 1905, two years after
their separation and about a year after their divorce, Strindberg described his state of mind:

[10] *Samlade skrifter,* XXVIII, 364.

My disharmonies lacerate me; my loneliness drives me out to seek other people, but after even the best of meetings I withdraw wounded and find myself inwardly worse. I feel shame without reason, remorse without having sinned, disgust with myself without knowing why. . . .

I struggle upwards but go downwards. I want to see life as beautiful, but only nature is; I feel pity for people but can't respect them and can't love them, for I know from myself what they are. My only comfort now is in Buddha, who tells me in so many words that life is a phantasm, an inverted image, which we shall see righted only in another existence. My hope and my future are both on the other side; that is why I find life so difficult. Everything breaks and mocks. Everything should be viewed at a distance—everything! [11]

An entirely different self-analysis appears in *Alone*, the last and most mellow of Strindberg's autobiographical books. It was written in the early summer of 1903, when Strindberg already realized that his marriage with Miss Bosse was breaking up. In its anticipation of a loneliness not yet actual, *Alone*, like the other autobiographies, is a work of semifiction, its narrative voice somewhere between that of a diarist and that of a fully fictionalized character. But the generic ambiguity of the book rather increases than diminishes its relevance to a study of Strindberg's creative psyche.

It was Strindberg's habit during his last years to take an early-morning walk through the streets of Stockholm in order to recharge his batteries for the day's writing (the electrical metaphor is Strindberg's own). Back at his desk, he turned the "power" he had picked up outside from "the alternating and direct currents of disharmony and harmony" to his "various uses":

. . . I live and I live multifariously the lives of all the people I describe. I am happy with the happy, evil with the evil, good with the good. I creep out of myself and speak with the tongues of children, of women, of old men; I am king and beggar; I am raised high, a tyrant, and the most despised, the oppressed hater of tyrants. All opinions are mine, and I confess all creeds. I live in all ages, and my own self has ceased to exist. This is a state that brings indescribable happiness.[12]

In the letter to his ex-wife, the anguished self watches itself disintegrate into warring antitheses; in the passage from *Alone*, it happily annihilates itself at esthetic distance. The act of the histrionic imagination restores the poet's self to the wholeness broken by the mocking deceptions that are all actuality is. If the world outside is illusionary, the mind can claim for its fabrications at least an equal degree

[11] *Brev*, pp. 222–23 (October 4, 1905).
[12] *Samlade skrifter*, XXXVIII, 155–56.

of reality. Our imagination makes possible "our highest achievement . . . the concealment of our vileness." [13] That so subjective a writer as Strindberg found his fullest voice in drama, the most objective of literary genres, is not really a paradox: his capacity for unhappiness was matched by his ability to objectify his inner warfares. From his own guilt and pain he extrapolated the whole human condition.

He came to think of his own life as a drama. "Going over in my mind what my life has been," he wrote in 1901,

> I wonder whether all the horrible things I have experienced have been staged before my eyes to enable me to become a dramatist and depict all mental states and all possible situations. I was a dramatist at twenty, but if the course of my life had run smoothly, I should have had nothing to write about.[14]

The same idea still haunts him in a letter to a friend six years later: "Sometimes my whole life seems to me as if it had been staged for me, to make me suffer and write." [15] There are hints in such passages from Strindberg's last years that he succeeded in enduring his life to its natural end only by denying it any other reality than that of a tragic script put together by unknown powers who had cast him in the part of both protagonist and spectator-scribe.[16] Quite early in his career he began to hate watching performances of his own plays. There are even hints that he was aware of some such psychological defense mechanism in himself.

I intend the drama metaphor as a tool for critics, not as the kind of statement of fact a psychiatrist might make about Strindberg or as moral endorsement of a paranoiac's stratagem for self-justification. I submit that the literary critic best comes to terms with Strindberg's intrusive life by treating his works as imaginative analogues to it and that their ubiquitous authorial presence is not that of the real-life August Strindberg, his anguish subverting his art, but of a meta-character created by a self-dramatizing imagination brooding on the

---

[13] *From an Occult Diary: Marriage with Harriet Bosse,* ed. with Introduction and Notes by Torsten Eklund, trans. by Mary Sandbach (New York: Hill and Wang, 1965), p. 76 (September 3, 1904).

[14] *From an Occult Diary,* p. 19 (January 25, 1901).

[15] *Brev,* p. 228 (April 2, 1907).

[16] Even Strindberg's last recorded words, "All is atoned for," sound like the curtain speech in a passion play. I am not impugning the "sincerity" of his last known thought. I am suggesting that in his final moments of consciousness he discovered the shaped meaning of his troubled life. He "saw" it the way one "sees" the perfectly imaged content of a successful work of literature.

parabolic meaning of the strange life of August Strindberg. The character is that of an appalled Everyman in a world of evil illusion, victim and witness both, now accepting the mystery that human suffering is chastisement for known and unknown sins, now indicting the inscrutable chastisers for their injustice. Like his maker, he is metaphysician, scientist, and social satirist, sensualist and ascetic, polemicist and penitent, denier and affirmer, seeking an answer to the great riddle in unending dialectics among his many selves. He is the ruthless naturalistic prober in the battle-of-the-sexes plays of the 1880s and early 1890s, to whom the man-woman relationship prefigures a vital but terrible dividedness at the very center of all life. But his presence is nowhere felt more distinctly than in the expressionistic pilgrimage plays, with their echoes of Indra's Daughter's "Pitiful mankind!" from *A Dream Play* (Strindberg's own "most beloved drama, the child of my greatest pain").[17] His is the controlling vision that holds their surrealistic episodes together, the "single consciousness" of "the dreamer," "governing all the characters,"[18] as he dramatizes his dream in sorrowful pilgrimages and sordid little domestic scenes. The aging Strindberg thought of death as an awakening into reality, and the dreamer's dream is Strindberg's own nightmare experience of the world as a penal colony and of all men as criminals guilty of the crime of existence. The metaphor is the last and most radical of the many imaginative strategies by which Strindberg's private petulance became large compassion, his estrangement fellowship. His kindred spirits among the moderns are Dostoyevsky, Kafka, and Gide.

III

> Yes, that is the secret behind all my narratives, short
> stories, fairy tales—that they are all dramas.
>
> Letter to Emil Schering, 1907

Non-Swedish—or at least non-Scandinavian—audiences and readers know only a small part of Strindberg's vast production. His international fame rests on half a dozen plays or so, about evenly divided between naturalism and expressionism. The situation is certainly not ideal; *Inferno* and *Legends* are in their way as great works of art as *To Damascus* and *A Dream Play*, and not to know *The Red Room, The Natives of Hemsö, The Scapegoat,* and the best of the short stories

[17] *Brev*, p. 229 (April 17, 1907).
[18] "Memo," prefatory to *A Dream Play*.

is to miss much of Strindberg and much superior fiction.[19] But neither
is it quite absurd. With his sense of life as conflict, even Strindberg's
nondramatic works tend toward drama in their explosive confronta-
tions in stageable settings. The climaxes in his fiction are very often
scenes of dialogue, and Strindberg's dialogues are always, in Erik
Hedén's perfect choice of epithet, "drastic." [20] And though the small
handful of his famous plays do not adequately represent his dramatic
range, they begin to suggest it.

Strindberg's lyrical and satirical nondramatic verse does not translate
easily, and its largely occasional nature reduces its interest for non-
Swedish readers. For all Strindberg's skill in music and despite the
fugue-like form of the chamber plays, the symphonic orchestration of
some of his historical and expressionistic plays, and his dramatic use of
musical leitmotifs (Beethoven and Mendelssohn in *To Damascus,*
Haydn in *Easter,* Bach in *A Dream Play* and *Charles XII*), his verse,
including his dramatic verse, is not particularly musical, and only a
few of his plays and novels have anything resembling a musical structure.

But even outside of Sweden there is growing recognition of Strindberg's achievement in prose fiction. His range here is hardly less than
in drama, and even the most summary comment must do more than
recognize the Dickensian quality of Strindberg's eccentrics (he never
attempted Dicken's mystifying intrigues) and the influence of Balzac,
"the great vizard," whose comprehensive and tolerant objectivity
Strindberg himself—rather surprisingly—acknowledged had taught
him how to "look at life with both eyes" and to submit to fate's
ministrations of bitter medicine.[21]

Strindberg was a superb storyteller when he chose to be. Among the
novels, *The Natives of Hemsö* and *The Scapegoat* are good examples;
and among the short stories, "A Doll's House" and "The Child," two
antifeminist stories from *Married* I and II, respectively (one playful,
the other grim, in keeping with the general character of the two collections), and the funny and tender "Dance at the Tailor's" from *Life in
the Skerries.* But his narrative talent was for anecdote and fable rather
than for slow and broad epic development, and he did not always

[19] Thanks to the work of Sprinchorn, Johnson, Paulson, Meyer, Sprigge, and
others, most of Strindberg's important writings in the various genres have in recent
years become available in faithful and readable English. I have listed most of the
successful translations in section IB of the selected bibliography, without presuming
to judge their relative merits.

[20] Erik Hedén, *Strindberg: liv och diktning* (Stockholm: bokförlaget Nutiden,
1921), p. 487. But, curiously, Strindberg's one attempt to dramatize one of his own
novels, *The Natives of Hemsö,* produced one of his weakest plays (1889).

[21] The tribute appears in *Alone. Samlade skrifter,* XXXVIII, 147.

choose to practice it. There are expository passages of political, economic, and scientific theory not just in the autobiographies, whose decorum of epics of the mind can accommodate them, but also in more conventional novels, such as *By the Open Sea* (Inspector Borg's Lamarckian reflections) and *Black Banners* (the theosophical discussions among the cloistered intellectuals), where they appear as almost detachable excursions, slowing the narrative and biasing the psychological analysis. Strindberg is quite likely to parade his knowledge of botany and geology in the middle of lyrical descriptions of the Swedish landscape he loved best, the islands in the Baltic southeast of Stockholm. His characters are sometimes just mouthpieces or pawns in a polemic, and even the most memorable of them are alive without much complexity. He was not much concerned with theories of genre and exercised his craftsmanship on style rather than on structure, becoming—unintentionally—an experimenting innovator in fiction because his lean and agile prose could respond so precisely to his changing enthusiasms and phobias.

Strindberg's fiction includes the acid vignettes on the vanity of human wishes for wedded happiness in *Married* and the fevered monologues of a modern Job in the Inferno books, the episodic social and topographical panorama of *The Red Room* and the claustrophobic hallucinations in *The Roofing Feast*. But the variety is not incoherence. Both the robust and sunny peasant realism in *The Natives of Hemsö* and the vicious attacks on thinly disguised real-life models from the contemporary Stockholm intelligentsia in *Black Banners* rise at times to a mode of grotesquerie, hilarious in the former and demonic in the latter. Both *The Natives of Hemsö* and *By the Open Sea* are naturalistic demonstrations of the destruction of exceptional individuals by the ethnic and physical forces of the alien environments they enter and seek to control. They are, except for their near-tragic endings, rustic versions of the story of Arvid Falk in *The Red Room,* a young naïf who tries to make his way as a writer but ends by selling out to the bigoted hypocrites in Stockholm's subliterary establishment. In *The Scapegoat,* the same wry and scrupulous realism that makes some of the short stories and some of the episodes in *The Red Room* reminiscent of Maupassant's and Chekhov's manner of understated irony insinuates large allegorical meaning through close and keen observations of small-town life. In its approximation of a stream-of-consciousness technique, *The Roofing Feast* (like *The Scapegoat,* a long novella) is generically akin to the impressionistic-expressionistic records of a morbidly susceptible mind's responses to its environment in the autobiographies. *A Madman's Defense* treats the theme of *Married* in the form of painful personal apologia, and there are scenes in *Inferno* that rival both *Married* and *The Red Room* in their persuasive realistic detail of narrative and description. Strindberg recollected his sojourn in hell with considerable detachment, and the single consciousness of the narrator gives artistic unity to his interior kaleidoscopes. In general, Strindberg's development in fiction followed that of his drama. *Married* belongs to the period of his naturalistic tragedies of sex. Borg's destiny in *By the Open Sea* has something in common with the Captain's in *The Father*. The Inferno books anticipate, and *The Roofing Feast* is a late contemporary of, his dramatic expressionism. Both scene and mood in *Alone* are those of *Storm,* the first of the chamber plays.

More and more, as our perspectives in modern drama lengthen, Strindberg's major plays appear as the most seminal single body of plays of the last hundred years—visual, dynamic (if not always linear), speakable, and disturbingly relevant to an age of accelerating fragmentation of personal and communal integrities. This is not quite the same as saying that he is the greatest of the modern playwrights of the older generation. In different ways, both Ibsen and Chekhov are better builders of solid and subtle dramatic structures than Strindberg. If he still seems historically more indispensable than either of the other two, it is because his dramatizations of the awful human impasse seem more powerfully contemporary than Ibsen's anatomies of middle-class marriage or Chekhov's determination of the limits to which minute domestic realism can be carried without shattering in a miscellany of genre pictures. However idiosyncratic its origins in Strindberg's psyche and circumstances, his existential despondency and the theatrical images he found for it have been authenticated by modern sensibilities.

Strindberg's dramatic career falls into four main phases.[22] The first covers the nine years between 1872 and 1881, when he wrote and rewrote *Master Olof,* trying to satisfy both his own artistic integrity and theatrical producers who, while admitting the power of Strindberg's play about the sixteenth-century Swedish religious reformer and his inner conflicts, refused to accept it because it broke with received notions about its historical figures. The difficulties Strindberg had getting *Master Olof* produced contributed to the growth of his persecution complex.

The second phase is the period of the naturalistic plays from 1886 to 1889, followed by a series of naturalistic one-acters, ending with

---

[22] After 1881, the longest hiatuses in Stringberg's dramatic productivity were those between *Sir Bengt's Wife* (1882) and *Comrades* (or *Marauders*) (1886–88); between *The Bond* (1892) and *To Damascus* (1898) (the Inferno years intervening); and between three abortive "world-historical dramas" (1903) and the first of the chamber plays (1907).

The Bond in 1892. Nearly all of these reflect Strindberg's monomaniac obsession with his problems in his first marriage. They are increasingly concentrated in form—the fifteen-minute monologue *The Stronger* represents the logical conclusion of this development—partly in deference to the naturalistic theory that act divisions and time elapsing off-stage weaken verisimilitude, but also because for Strindberg the essence of human relationships was in swift, catastrophic encounters. By traditional definition, Strindberg's protagonists in these plays are nontragic, but in any argument over whether or not there can be such a thing as tragedy of determinism—unheroic man victimized by ruthless mechanistic forces—*The Father, Miss Julie,* and *The Bond* are strong support of the affirmative. What is at least equally significant about these plays is the way Strindberg's conscious intention of being a kind of social scientist is compromised by his biases, by his casual observation of plausibility of plot and situation, and by his concept of human motivation as being a matter of erratic whims and obsessions rather than of fixed psychological law. This is why the traditional division of Strindberg's play-writing career into a naturalistic and an expressionistic period is too facile. It obscures the essential continuity of his dramatic imagination, of which his dialogue also is evidence. There is more lyricism in the language of the naturalistic plays and more realism in the language of the lyrical and expressionistic plays than the conventional view of two distinct groups of plays recognizes.

The culminating phase in Strindberg's drama is the period of four years from the spring of 1898 till the spring of 1902 when he wrote eighteen plays, of which all but four or five are major items in his canon and which represent all his four major dramatic genres: realism, history play, expressionism, and lyrical allegory. From the viewpoint of literary history, the Inferno years may be considered a fortunate interlude in Strindberg's life, an apparently sterile but actually highly germinal period that was followed by his astonishing psychological recovery and an equally astonishing burst of dramatic creativity. Criticism can only despair of encompassing in a single descriptive definition an achievement that includes all the great history plays, *To Damascus* and *A Dream Play, The Dance of Death, Easter,* and *The Bridal Crown*. But even in the apparently most realistic of these plays, *Crime and Crime* and *The Dance of Death,* there is a core action of religious symbolism akin to that in the two modern mystery plays *Advent* and *Easter* and in *The Saga of the Folkungs,* Strindberg's most Shakespearean history. Strindberg's naturalistic world view did not survive the Inferno experience.

The final phase is marked by the four chamber plays he wrote in 1907 (he added a fifth and rather different one in 1909) in order to provide his Intimate Theater in Stockholm with a repertory suitable to its small stage and its limited technical and financial resources. These are plays that seek "the intimate form, a small subject intensively treated, few characters, large vistas, free fantasy, simple but not too simple, no elaborate apparatus. . . ." [23] A shimmer of cosmic mystery plays over even their realistic scenes. Their small plots probe behind the façades of middle-class apartment houses for the ugly pain of interlocking iniquities within. Because surfaces deceive, drama has become disclosure. But rather than sit in moral judgment on the exposed sinners, the dramatist uses the images of fire (in *The Burned House* and *The Pelican*), a gathering thunderstorm (in *Storm*), and the collapse of houses in both a literal and a figurative sense (in *The Ghost Sonata*) to symbolize larger conflagrations and more apocalyptic tremors.

Most of Strindberg's plays do not lend themselves to careful plot analysis—another reason for finding his dramaturgy peculiarly "modern." Their unit of meaning is the immediate crisis in the individual soul; we recall single scenes and speeches more easily than whole actions. Even the justly famous first act of *Gustav Vasa* is not much of an exception. One by one the king's enemies are summoned to his presence, while the uneasy conversation between his emissary and the peasant leaders who remain build a brilliant crescendo that ends only when the king's messenger opens the door and throws three bloody coats into the room. But only in the climax of his last act does Strindberg again use this manner of tightening tension through a chain of events in incremental repetition. Generally, the cohesiveness of his plays is an emotional climate rather than plot causality. He seems less interested in ideas than in the swiftness of the associative process. His characters are exhibits of passional caprice rather than integrated psychologies gradually revealed and accounted for. Strindberg believed in a drama of Man rather than of individual men and quarreled with the old humor comedy because he felt that its stereotypes falsified the reality of the human flux. Even realistic case studies of unusual individuals like Miss Julie and Jean are representatives of their sex and class, and the Captain in *The Father* is without a surname the better to stand for all fathers.

Strindberg's recurrent dramatic motifs define rather than explain the human situation: the ambiguities of childhood guilt, the uncertainty of identity, sex as the fatal mutual attraction of two hostile

---

[23] From a letter Strindberg wrote to a playwright friend in 1907. Quoted in August Falck, *Fem år med Strindberg* (Stockholm: Wahlström & Widstrand, 1935), p. 31. According to Falck, the director of the Intimate Theater, the passage describes the technique of the chamber plays "in a nutshell."

species whose struggles serve some mindless life force, vampire figures that drain others of their vitality, endless household drudgery, disgust with physicality, the eternal return of the same sorrows and frustrations, myths of expiation of personal and collective sin. He discovered archetypes in the kitchen and in his own family squabbles and overdrawn bank accounts. He dispensed with traditional patterns of action, because such patterns presupposed stable laws of causality and character continuum. He writes about souls that break under pressures from somewhere out of a dark chaos. Not plot suspense but the thrust of dialogues in which people catechize one another in words resonant with metaphysics accounts for the palpable dramatic intensity of his best plays. When the Old Man in Scene I of *The Ghost Sonata* tells the Student his version of the story of the old enmity between himself and the Student's father, the Student says:

> It's funny the way the same story can be told so differently.
> *Old Man.* Surely you don't believe I'm telling you what isn't so?
> *Student.* What am I to believe? My father didn't lie!
> *Old Man.* Very true. A father never lies—But I too am a father, and so it follows—

One speaker's subjective truth becomes part of the logic by which the other sustains his aggressive self, and the agreed-on premise deadlocks the dialogue. The brief, stalemated exchange is quintessentially Strindbergian.

This is not the place for detailed commentary on Strindberg's individual plays or on the major groups into which they fall, but the history plays deserve a further word because they are such a large part of the canon, because they are less well known abroad than the naturalistic and expressionistic pieces (in Sweden the best of them are part of the national repertory), and because they represent the most substantial and stageable body of history plays since Shakespeare's.

The comparison is not gratuitous. Strindberg's interest in Shakespeare is evident in the space he devotes to his plays in the *Open Letters to the Intimate Theater,* and the Shakespearean influence on the history plays is quite clear. It takes three forms. First, Strindberg treats historical facts cavalierly: anachronisms of event, style, and characterization abound. Second (and accounting for the anachronisms), he was, as Birgitta Steene points out, trying to distill from his historical sources universal fables of providential moral patterns in the life of the nation and her kings. It is significant that for his sources he preferred early-nineteenth-century historians, with their romantic emphasis on strong, decisive personalities, to authors of more sober and reliable modern studies. Third, his interest was less in the political crises and ideologi-

cal and dynastic issues than in the creation of characters that have stage
life by virtue of psychological details that contribute little to plot or
theme. This was something the Danish critic Georg Brandes had taught
him to admire as Shakespeare's greatest triumph as a historical dramatist. Strindberg admitted to trying to emulate Shakespeare in the presentation of his historical heroes "at home." What is most striking in
Master Olof, Gustav Vasa, Erik XIV, and *Queen Christina* is not the
line of coherent chronicle, which is actually quite weak, but the telling
minutiae by which complex souls define themselves in intimate stage
moments: Olof in agony because of conflicting claims on his conscience;
Gustav's moral scruples nearly subverting the imperious, irascible, and
efficient ruler's purpose; his neurotic son Erik, made will-less and cruel
by lack of love; and Christina, both a self-indulgent little girl and a
consummate actress, manipulating men to satisfy her erotic whims and
religious longings. When Strindberg sacrificed his fascination with
royal characters of divided soul to historical accuracy and inclusiveness, the result was *Gustav Adolf,* an enormous and diffuse national
pageant. On the other hand, in *Charles XII* Strindberg created one of
his most original and memorable history plays through a succession of
semi-independent, semistylized scenes about the weary king who returns from long exile to the ominous silences of the country his wars
have desolated, attended by a counterfeiter, a mordant dwarf, and
specters from the past. The play has none of the realistic, Shakespearean
bustle of the tavern scenes in the Vasa trilogy, but even so it is perhaps
the only one of Strindberg's history plays in which symbolic movement
and nonverbal scenic imagery count for more than dialogue and psychology.

As a theorist of drama, Strindberg is important mainly as the author
of the manifesto of naturalistic playmaking and staging with which he
prefaced *Miss Julie* and for his advice on theatrical production in his
Open Letters. Nowhere does he even begin to formulate a systematic
theory of expressionism, and he never uses that term for the kind of
drama he is credited with inventing: symbolical, dreamlike in its free
and open form, of fluid space and fractured time, and with generic
rather than individualized characters. But then he didn't need to; he
wrote the plays. The Preface to *Miss Julie* is significant, first, because
of its concept of the "characterless character" (Pirandello was to seize
upon this and turn it into a basic premise for his theatricalist relativism), which Strindberg opposes to the conventional humor character of Ben Jonson and Molière, and, second, because of its Darwinian
definition of "the joy of life" as delight in "cruel struggles" for survival. Though twenty years separated them, the only important doc-

trinal difference between the Preface and the *Open Letters* is that Strindberg in the latter advocates simple and visually pleasing stage decor of semiabstract design rather than the illusionistic details he had called for in the former. The post-Inferno pessimist and pseudomystic seeks uncluttered concentration on stage essentials—not verisimilitude, but symbolic beauty.

But there is little in the *Open Letters* to suggest sympathy with Gordon Craig's nearly wordless theater of pure design. Craig sought to reduce the actor to a "supermarionette," just another item in the director-designer's repertory of devices for the creation of atmosphere.[24] In his advice to the actors of the Intimate Theater he sounds much more like Stanislavsky (whom he doesn't mention). The script is primary: "Follow the text . . . ; play the part and no more!"[25] He wants clarity of enunciation ("the spectator has paid for the privilege to hear")[26] and distinctness of gesture and movement. Unless the actor knows and understands the whole play, he cannot understand his own part. He must subordinate his personal vanity to ensemble acting and the total effect. He should draw upon the resources of his own personality in order to induce in himself the almost trancelike state of mind necessary to his "becoming" the character he is impersonating. The director must remain in ultimate control of the production, for only he can make one whole out of the different arts of the theater.

> If we are asked, what does the Intimate Theater try to do, and what is it we intend with the chamber plays, my answer is this: in the drama we seek the strong, significant motif, but with limitation. In our production we avoid all vain artifice, all calculated effects and deliberate occasions for applause, star acting, and solo performance. The author is bound by no particular form, for his subject determines his form. In other words, freedom of treatment, restricted only by the unity of the conception and by a feeling for style.[27]

The *Open Letters* (and August Falck's memoirs of his years of collaboration with Strindberg[28]) are useful reading for those who think of

[24] Strindberg speaks noncommittally of Craig in the last of the *Open Letters* as a man of "peculiar" ideas about the theater. *Samlade skrifter*, L, 290. Character was too real and words were too urgent for Strindberg to be tempted by such extremes of rarefaction.

[25] *Samlade skrifter*, L, 101.

[26] *Samlade skrifter*, L, 46.

[27] *Samlade skrifter*, L, 12.

[28] See footnote 23. In the end, Strindberg broke with Falck (as he sooner or later broke with almost all of his friends) when the latter put on a play by Maeterlinck. Strindberg liked Maeterlinck's plays, but he claimed to have exclusive right to supply the repertory for the Intimate Theater.

Strindberg as an author who simply wrote his neuroses and who was ignorant of, incapable of, or uninterested in the disciplined craft of drama and theater.

IV

> I feel like a supercharged Leyden jar and want only to give off sparks!
>
> Letter to Ola Hansson, 1889

Unlike Ibsen, Strindberg did not really enter the consciousness of critics in the English-speaking world until the centennial of his birth in 1949. Before then, despite occasional flurries of publicity (as when O'Neill acknowledged his debt to Strindberg and when Shaw gave his Nobel Prize money to a project for translating Strindberg into English), the Strindberg literature in the United States was, with some notable exceptions, limited to brief, tentative, and often perplexed remarks in historical surveys and in introductions to the same two or three, usually naturalistic, plays in drama anthologies. The extent of the prevailing ignorance is suggested by a reference in 1941 to *The Dream Play* (the wrong article is symptomatic) as one of Strindberg's "tender fantasies of childhood." Significant recognition remained sporadic; when theater producers did not ignore Strindberg's plays, audiences did; and if the educated layman associated anything at all with the name, it was only to recall a Nordic neurotic, compulsively and prolifically confessing his turbulent life in weird plays.

Since 1949 Strindberg in America has become one of the classics of modern drama, whose plays—we now see—anticipated themes and techniques of the "new drama" of expressionism, theatricalism, and the absurd. In cruelty (not in coarseness) of words between husband and wife, Strindberg's *The Dance of Death* easily matches Albee's *Who's Afraid of Virginia Woolf?* His plays are being staged, and the Strindberg section in international bibliographies grows longer every year. If the old image of the man remains pretty much intact, it is because scholarship has found it to be essentially valid. But instead of being used by philistines as a pretext for dismissing his works as those of a madman, it has turned into an archetype of the contemporary claustrophobic consciousness seeking escape in stage images of shared experience.

American critics, however, still tend to write about Strindberg as if he needed to be "introduced" to a public who without the critic's help must be expected to find his plays incomprehensible and distasteful. Considering the range and quality of Strindberg criticism over the last twenty years, it is surprising that, at least outside of Sweden and perhaps Germany, there is still no general agreement among responsible critics about what the crucial issues in present Strindberg studies are. No genuine debate on the nature and value of Strindberg's artistic achievement has generated. The sheer size and variety of the canon go far toward accounting for another and related characteristic of American Strindberg criticism: a fragmentation of critical effort because of each critic's apparent belief that he is exploring a new area in a new way. The recent literature is rich, but it lacks focus. So much has been done and done so well that there would seem now to be time for a consolidation of critical gains. We need to define, in consensus or controversy, what Strindberg means to us today.

The essays that follow are meant to provide initial material for such stock-taking. The conclusions they collectively suggest have been left implicit; I have not deliberately collocated different views on the same few subjects. I believe it would now be possible to put together a critical symposium on, say, the metaphysics of Strindberg's changing dramatic modes, or on the imagery of his expressionistic plays, or on the style and structure of his fiction, but the present volume is something both more and less.

The essays have been selected with three ends in mind. First, to stimulate students of Strindberg to further study. Second, to represent a reasonable range of Strindberg criticism—chronologically, geographically, in topics discussed, and in critical method. Third, since for Americans Strindberg is still primarily a dramatist and since space is limited, to offer essays that may at least suggest the totality of "twentieth-century views" on Strindberg's plays. I shall try briefly to say what I find most central and distinctive in each essay.

The first four are basically biographical in approach, and the first, Robert Brustein's (of which a little more than the first half appears here), even has a chronological organization. Brustein's argument that autobiography provided both Ibsen and Strindberg with the substance of their plays and that both shared the same romantic rebelliousness on behalf of the embattled self challenges the terms in which the two Scandinavian playwrights are usually contrasted. For Brustein, the clue to Strindberg's fertile torment of soul is his sexual and social dualism: the unresolved conflict between the male and the female components in his make-up and between the domineering aristocrat and the submissive proletarian. Since neither conflict was a stable corollary of the other, Strindberg's doubts about his own identity caught him in a maze without an exit. As a result, his quarrel with God was a much more ambiguous enterprise than Ibsen's. Torn between revolt and submission, he ended in a kind of "melancholy fatalism." In both his pre-Inferno and post-Inferno phases the reality of his own imagination seemed more substantial to him than that of the empirical world. Even *The Father,* commonly labeled a naturalistic play, is in this view an allegorization of the struggle in Strindberg himself between man as both child and lover and woman as both mother substitute and vampire-mistress.

Raymond Williams, too, defines the creative tension in Strindberg as a battle of the soul; that is the sense in which Strindbergian tragedy is "private": an inner *agon*. Unlike Brustein, however, Williams does not see Strindberg's inner struggles as primarily sexual and social. His Strindberg is a victim of hypertrophied awareness of an antinomy built into human existence between death wish and libidinal quest. Tragedy for Strindberg was "in the living process itself," and death was relief from pain that is unbearable because it is inevitable. Strindberg's plays about the man-woman relationship present a "terrible and absurd vision" of the fact that "love and loss, love and destruction, are two sides of the same coin." What for Brustein is Strindberg's "messianic rebellion" becomes for Williams a protest on behalf of an impossible ideal against a natural condition of which the family relationship is emblematic: the child destroys the lovers' illusion of love's permanence, and "the dance of sexual excitement is the dance of death." Walter Johnson's discussion of the dance-of-death motif in the late marital play that takes its title from this motif provides incidental support for Williams's thesis, and both Brustein's and Williams's essays are relevant to Evert Sprinchorn's discussion of the sexual imagery in *A Dream Play.*

R. J. Kaufmann's intricately argued essay asserts the essential unity of the Strindberg canon only to indict the rigidity and narrowness that was the price at which the unity was achieved. Kaufmann's real subject is the quality of Strindberg's mind. He considers the absence of irony in Strindberg a symptom of the playwright's inability to admit life's "organic latitude." A Romantic, mistaking single-mindedness for sincerity, Strindberg was barred from the genuine dramatist's multiplicity of voice and vision. His plays are "petrified situations," intense and perturbing because of their "phobic fertility," but "stalled" as dramas. Invincibly egocentric, Strindberg, "the least philosophical of playwrights," was only a ventriloquist saying over and over again, "I suffer, therefore I am!" Kaufmann's attack approaches obscure ellipsis in some of its self-generating subtleties, and much in Strindberg is safely outside of Kaufmann's target. Those for whom Strindberg is an explorer of unmapped regions of the modern soul and his plays sensitive registers of that soul's broken rhythms will occasionally be exasperated by Kaufmann's essay, but they cannot afford to ignore it. They will even find that it does justice to the fearfully obsessive power of the plays.

With Victor Svanberg's vigorous polemic against Strindberg's anachronistic personality we are moving in a much more open landscape. Svanberg's confident animus reflects the positivistic bias of the progressive liberal of the 1930s, to whom Strindberg's religiosity necessarily appears savagely primitive, his naturalism half-baked and perverted, and his lordly treatment of his first wife outrageous. Like Brustein, Williams, and Kaufmann, Svanberg deals with Strindberg's difficult psyche, but he is much less interested than they in describing the nature of his imagination. He uses Strindberg for dialectical purposes, exposing Sweden's prime cultural exhibit as the pitiful product of the stifling environment in a petty bourgeois home in the Victorian age. Svanberg speaks eloquently on behalf of those who find Strindberg personally and ideologically hateful and who consider admiration of his art a cult of nihilistic decadence. Theirs is not a sophisticated attitude, but it is probably safe to guess that it is a rare student of Strindberg who has never felt its appeal as the gut reaction of provoked sanity.

The next three essays share a common interest in the larger implications of Strindberg's original dramaturgy.

Maurice Gravier deals with Strindberg's contribution to the development of German theatrical expressionism about the time of the First World War. He does so in terms, first, of Strindberg's impatience with the fixity of character in older drama and, second, of the concurrent movement in the graphic arts away from the objectivity of earlier impressionism toward the expression of the artist's own self in color, line, and spatial arrangements. Strindberg's historical importance, Gravier argues, is that he was the first to dramatize the new artistic vision in plays that seek the timeless realities of the human spirit behind fleeting and random surface fragments. Not "character" but "soul," not illusionism but a new "metapsychology" (Freudianism and Jungianism were contemporary phenomena), are for Gravier the essence of Strindberg's influential expressionism.

Pär Lagerkvist, the novelist-dramatist, writing before Gravier, implicitly anticipates the Frenchman's argument in his view of Strindberg as the rescuer of modern drama from the dead weight of Ibsen's scrupulous social detail. That Lagerkvist's use of Ibsen as a straw man commits him to a reductive view of the Norwegian's plays is much less significant than the fact that, like Yeats, he wants a drama that is beautiful rather than verisimilar and evocative rather than analytical and polemical. He sees Strindberg as an innovative liberator because his stagecraft is medieval in its allegorical stylization and Shakespearean in its pageantry and its imaginative range and fluidity. Not surprisingly, Lagerkvist feels that Strindberg's theory of the chamber play represents a deplorable limitation on the rich resourcefulness of staging which Strindberg's own historical and expressionistic drama had invited.

Eric Bentley turns his enthusiastic notes on a Viennese production of *The Bridal Crown* in the early 1950s into a plea for a more open-minded approach to Strindberg staging. His call for a recognition of the spectacular and Dionysiac elements in Strindberg's scripts and for a subtler classification of them than the two categories of raw, tight naturalism or misty and fractured symbolism can supply has, unfortunately, lost little of its relevance.

Gravier, Lagerkvist, and Bentley all see Strindberg as achieving a vital synthesis of poetic dialogue and theatrical spectacle, something like Nietzsche's and Artaud's "total theater" of the senses and the imagination, which has failed to find full expression only because of the inertia of theater producers. The remaining five essays deal with Strindberg's *literary* achievement either in single plays or in single groups of plays.

At the time of its first appearance, Martin Lamm's close and comprehensive analysis of *Miss Julie* was a more original piece of criticism than it is likely to seem today, when its successful combination of carefully informed scholarship and sensitive critical acumen has become an achievement less rare than it was in the early 1920s. A fuller, more balanced, and generally sensible study than Lamm's essay (here slightly abridged) of Strindberg's most representative naturalistic play has yet to appear. Particularly valuable are Lamm's relating the play to transitions in Strindberg's philosophical outlook in the late 1880s and his point that Jean's function as the proletarian superman of the future is highly ambivalent.

Walter Johnson discusses Strindberg's use of the medieval Danse Macabre motif in *The Dance of Death,* perhaps the playwright's most relentless study of a married hell. Strindberg turns the motif into a symbol that serves both as a structural device and as a thematic image, and Johnson argues that his allusive and latently allegorical method amounts to an adaptation of his expressionistic manner to a form that only superficially recalls his earlier naturalism. For Johnson as for Bentley, Strindberg is not one but many.

Birgitta Steene's study of Strindberg's history plays begins with a provocative distinction between the tragic hero as a questioning inner agonizer and the hero of the history play as a public figure and a doer. She then goes on to trace the collapse of Strindberg's projected grand cycle of Shakespearean histories as he gradually moved away from political history as the manifestation of providence toward studies of individual royal characters—a movement from panoramic ritual to focused psychological realism, from "history" to near-tragedy.

Evert Sprinchorn's ingenious Freudian reading of *A Dream Play* hardly exhausts that rich and baffling play, but it does succeed in imposing more than gratuitous order and direction on a play which earlier criticism too often defeatedly dismissed as just a chaos of private phantasmagoria. The specifics of Sprinchorn's analysis supplement both Brustein's locating the source of Strindberg's creative energy in a male-female dichotomy and Williams's argument that Strindberg's centripetal tragic vision was rooted in his prerational sense of the human condition itself as a see-saw between life-seeking and life-denial. The play's framing action images the disharmony in the love relationship, Strindberg's intolerable *crux:* descending, Indra's Daughter is a temptress; ascending, she is a pitying conciliator of man and the deity. In Sprinchorn's cogent reading, Strindberg's most central—if not his most flawless—play becomes a compendious and compelling dramatization of the mythology of sex. And like Lagerkvist and Bentley, Sprinchorn emphasizes the intense visuality of Strindberg's late dramatic manner.

Finally, Brian Rothwell swiftly surveys a number of the verbal and nonverbal images that make for coherence within the individual chamber plays and which link them together as a distinct group within the larger canon. His free-ranging essay may seem a little uncertain of its own function (advice to actors and directors? a new-critical inventory of image clusters? rehabilitation of unduly neglected plays?), but his many perceptions of detail and his awareness of the nature of the dramatic textures build still another persuasive argument that Strindberg's drama fulfills itself only in the configurations of spectacles and dialogues in an actual or imagined theatrical performance.

PART ONE

The Divided Self

August Strindberg

by Robert Brustein

To all appearances, August Strindberg would seem to be the most revolutionary spirit in the theater of revolt. Actually, that distinction must go to Ibsen, but Strindberg is certainly the most restless and experimental. Perpetually dissatisfied, perpetually reaching after shifting truths, he seems like a latter-day Faust with the unconscious as his laboratory—seeking the miracle of transmutation in the crucible of his tormented intellect. The metaphor is precise, for transmutation—the conversion of existing material into something higher—is the goal of all his activity, whether he works in science, turning base metals into gold, or religious philosophy, turning matter into spirit, or in drama, turning literature into music. His entire career, in fact, is a search for the philosophers' stone of ultimate truth through the testing of varied commitments. In his theater, where almost every new work is a new departure, he experiments with Byronic poetic plays, naturalistic tragedies, boulevard comedies, Maeterlinckian fairy plays, Shakespearean chronicles, expressionistic dream plays, and chamber works in sonata form. In his religious and political attitudes, he covers the entire spectrum of belief and unbelief, skirting positivism, atheism, socialism, pietism, Catholicism, Hinduism, Buddhism, and Swedenborgian mysticism. In his scientific studies, he ranges from Darwin to the occult, from naturalism to supernaturalism, from physics to metaphysics, from chemistry to alchemy. His literary work is one long autobiography, whether it takes the form of confessional novels, misogynistic short stories, revolutionary verses, anguished letters, scientific treatises, theatrical manifestoes, or short plays, full-length works, double dramas, and trilogies. More than any other dramatist who ever lived, Strindberg writes *himself,* and the self he continually exposes is that of alienated modern man, crawling between heaven and earth, desperately trying to pluck some absolutes from a forsaken universe.

Because of his restless Romanticism, and particularly because he initiated an alternative "antirealistic" theater in opposition to Ibsenist "realism," Strindberg has generally been regarded as Ibsen's antimask, the nonconformist Bohemian in contrast with the stolid, practical bourgeois. At first sight, indeed, the two Scandinavians do seem separated by a much wider gulf than the boundary that divides their two countries. Compare *Pillars of Society* with *A Dream Play.* The one, tightly structured and carefully detailed, proceeds from the daylight world of domestic problems, casual discourse, and social awareness; the other, shadowy in outline and fluid in form, emerges out of a chimerical world of fantasy, delusion, and nightmare. Yet, these two plays are extreme examples of each man's art; and the contrast between the two playwrights, while unquestionably strong, has been somewhat overemphasized at the expense of their similarities. As a matter of fact, both are part of the same dramatic movement, sharing certain general traits which have rarely been explored.

Undoubtedly, Strindberg himself is largely to blame for this unfair emphasis, since he had a tendency to define himself *against* Ibsen, and spent most of his career directly or indirectly attacking what he thought to be the older man's themes and forms.[1] His hostility is understandable. When Strindberg came to artistic maturity, Ibsen was considered the master dramatist of Europe—and like all figures of authority to Strindberg, he was therefore ripe for attack. Yet, Strindberg never understood Ibsen very well, and his antagonism often seems to be based on rather willful misconstructions of the Norwegian's work. It is clear, for example, that while Strindberg was obsessed with the conflict between the sexes, this subject hardly interested Ibsen, except as a metaphor for a wider conflict between man and society. But since Strindberg had come to regard art (and life) as a battleground in which there was no room for subtlety or neutrality, he became convinced that Ibsen was the fervent champion of his hated enemy, the emancipated woman.

The play that convinced him was, of course, *A Doll's House.* For in spite of the fact that, in early years, Strindberg had identified deeply with Ibsen's Brand, he always preferred to couple Ibsen with this more domesticated work, which he called "sick like its author." Here

[1] Ibsen was perfectly aware of Strindberg's antagonism towards him, and kept a portrait of Strindberg on his wall: "I cannot write a line," he remarked, "without that madman standing and staring down at me with his mad eyes." Later, he told an American writer about the source of his interest in Strindberg: "The man fascinates me because he is so subtly, so delicately mad."

he found the seedbed for that "Nora-cult" of feminism which he saw
infecting Scandinavia like a loathsome pestilence; and ignoring the
complexity, ambiguity, and essentially nonsexual character of *A Doll's
House,* he simply concluded that Ibsen was the leader of the other
side, fomenting plots to undermine masculine domination. As a result of this initial misunderstanding, he mistakenly interpreted *Ghosts*
as a treacherous attack on Captain Alving, a dead man no longer able
to defend himself against character defamation;[2] he assumed that *The
Wild Duck* was a libel on his family life, thinking that Ekdal's doubtful paternity of Hedvig was meant to suggest that he, Strindberg, was
not the father of his own child; and he found in *Hedda Gabler* and
The Master Builder (two plays which did not support his convictions
about Ibsen's feminism) conclusive evidence that Ibsen had fallen
under his spell and changed his views. Throughout his life, Strindberg was subject to severe paranoiac symptoms, in which fears of
persecution alternated with delusions of grandeur; and while his
ability to transform these symptoms into art constitutes one of the
most thrilling triumphs of modern drama, his paranoiac tendencies
hardly qualify him for objective evaluations of other people's work
and motives. Yet, it is Strindberg's view of Ibsen's subject matter,
coupled with that tiresome characterization of Ibsen as a mouthpiece
for social problems in realistic form, which dominates most comparisons of the two dramatists.[3]

If these assumptions are correct, and Ibsen is merely the champion
of bourgeois realism and the emancipated woman, then the gap between the two men is unbreachable. Since the assumptions are quite
wrong, let us attempt to close the gap a little. Where do Ibsen and
Strindberg join hands in the theater of revolt? Quite clearly, in their

---

[2] See *The Father,* Act I, where the Doctor says: "And I should like you to know,
Captain, that when I heard Mrs. Alving blackening her late husband's memory, I
thought what a damned shame it was that the fellow should be dead." Either the
Doctor or Strindberg did not attend to *Ghosts* very carefully, because, before the
end of the play, Captain Alving's blackened memory has been partially white-
washed again.

[3] Pär Lagerkvist's comments are typical. In order to praise Strindberg, Lagerkvist
has to attack Ibsen, exploding all the rusty artillery of anti-Ibsenist criticism:
"Ibsen, who was long the modern writer *par préférence* because he exhaustively
plodded through all the social, sexual, and mental-hygienic ideas and ideals which
happened to come up for discussion, merely weighs us down with his perfectly consummated and fixed form, impossible of further development . . ." ("Modern
Theatre: Points of View and Attack," *Tulane Drama Review,* Winter 1961, p. 22).
[See the excerpt from Lagerkvist's article in this volume, pp. 90–96.] At this
point, it grows tiresome to repeat that Ibsen's forms are far from fixed, and his
basic subject matter has very little to do with social, sexual, or mental-hygienic
"ideas."

basic artistic attack. Both are essentially autobiographical writers, exor-
cising their furies by dramatizing their spiritual conflicts; both are
subject to a powerful dualism which determines the changing direction of their themes and forms; and both are attracted to the more
elemental aspects of human nature. But above all, both are Romantic
rebels whose art is the unrelieved expression of their revolt.

In the beginning of his career, in fact, Strindberg's point of departure is almost indistinguishable from Ibsen's. "I am Jean-Jacques's
intime when it comes to a return to nature," he writes to a friend in
1880. "I should like to join him and turn everything upside down to
see what lies at bottom; I think we are so much entangled, so terribly
much regulated that things can't be put right, but must be burnt up,
blasted, and then begun afresh." Two years later, at the age of thirty-
three, Strindberg puts these sentiments into verse form. In a poem
called "Esplanadsystemet" ("The Building Program"), he envisions
the young razing everything to the ground, while a respectable pillar
of society looks on with disapproval:

> "What! This is the spirit of the times! Demolishing houses!
> Dreadful! Dreadful! What about constructive activity?"—
> "We're tearing down to let in light and air;
> Don't you think that constructive enough!" 4

Even as late as 1898, in *The Road to Damascus* [*To Damascus*], Part II,
Strindberg—through the mouth of the Stranger—is still expressing his
determination to "paralyze the present order, to disrupt it," envision-
ing himself as "the destroyer, the dissolver, the world incendiary."

In these images of demolition, the destructive fantasies of a total
revolutionist, Strindberg joins Ibsen in his uncompromising revolt
against modern life. Finding common roots in Rousseau and the Romantics, each hopes to redeem mankind from spiritual emptiness
through desperate remedies: Strindberg by clearing away rotten build-
ings, Ibsen by torpedoing the Ark—both by unremitting warfare on
all existing social, political, and religious institutions. The negative,
individualistic, and essentially antisocial quality of these attacks exposes their metaphysical sources. Both playwrights begin as messianic
rebels, animated by strong religious needs, and determined to war on
the God of the old while advancing towards something new. Strindberg's early plays—works like *The Freethinker, The Outlaw,* and

---

4 I am indebted to Evert Sprinchorn for calling my attention to this untranslated
poem. The translations I have used in this chapter are those of Elizabeth Sprigge,
except for that of *Miss Julie,* which is by Professor Sprinchorn, and [*To*] *Damascus*
by Graham Rawson. I have rendered the *Inferno* passages myself from the original
French.

Master Olof—are often strongly reminiscent of Ibsen's *Brand* and *Emperor and Galilean* in their rebellion against God, sometimes even embodying open attacks on God as the author of madness and the father of evil. In the epilogue to *Master Olof*, for example, it is God who maliciously introduces misery into the world ("The creatures who live [on Earth]," He declares, "will believe themselves gods like ourselves, and it will be our pleasure to watch their struggles and vanities"), while it is Lucifer, the rebellious son who, Prometheuslike, tries to bring good to man, and is outlawed for his pains.

Strindberg's identification with Lucifer, rebelling against a mad, merciless, mechanical Will, is quite clear throughout the first phase of his career. In his opposition to established authority, Strindberg also identifies with related figures like Cain, Prometheus, and Ishmael— all rebels against God—willingly, and sometimes rather theatrically, embracing their pain and torment as well. Like Ibsen voluntarily exiled from his native land, Strindberg wandered over Europe, alienated from the world of men even when most honored there. "Born with nostalgia for heaven," he writes in *Inferno*, "I cried even as a child over the filthiness of existence, finding myself homeless among my parents and society." He often describes himself as a pariah—"a beggar, a marked man, an outcast from society" (*Inferno*)—outlawed from paradise, his brow marked with the sign of the rebellious son. Strindberg's admiration for religious rebels presses him well beyond the usual revolutionary postures to an embrace of Satanism, under the spell of which he practices black arts, worships the occult, and studies the transmigration of souls, pursuits which he considers dangerous and diabolical. As the Confessor says, in [*To*] *Damascus*: "This man is a demon, who must be kept confined. He belongs to the dangerous race of rebels; he'd misuse his gifts, if he could, to do evil." Strindberg's flair for self-dramatization leads him to exaggerate his demonic activities, for they were really harmful to nobody but himself (he suffered severely from sulphur burns). But there is no doubt that he thought himself pledged to Lucifer by a kind of Mephistophelian pact.

This seems like a much more radical form of rebellion than anything found in Ibsen. But as Strindberg implies in *Inferno* ("Ever since childhood," he writes, "I have looked for God and found the devil"), his revolt against authority is really the reverse of his desire for authority, just as his Satanism is actually an inverted form of Christianity. In consequence of this shaky posture, Strindberg's revolt is always a little nervous and uncertain, rather like the act of a man in constant dread of retribution. And while Ibsen's messianism remains consistent, Strindberg's is gradually tempered by his fears of divine revenge from an omnipotent power. Even when he considers himself a freethinking atheist, these fears are never far from the surface. He became an unbeliever, as he declares in *Inferno,* when "the unknown powers let slip their hold on the world, and gave no more sign of life." But when these "unknown powers" do begin to appear to him in the nineties, his messianism becomes less and less defiant, until he finally becomes convinced that the powers are personally guiding his destiny, and revealing themselves to him in every material object.

Even then, however, vestiges of his messianic defiance remain. He wishes to do the will of these nameless authorities, but even in his moments of submission he "feels rebellious and challenges heaven with doubts." Reflecting on the wayward history of his beliefs, he even begins to blame the powers for his own spiritual uncertainty:

> You have directed my destiny badly; you have brought me up to chastise, to overthrow idols, to stir up revolt, and then you withdraw your protection from me, and deliver me over to a ridiculous recantation! . . . When young I was sincerely pious, and you made me a freethinker. Out of the freethinker you made an atheist, and out of the atheist a religious man. Inspired by humanitarians, I advocated socialism. Five years later, you showed me the absurdity of socialism; you have made all my enthusiasms seem futile. And supposing that I again become religious, I am certain that in another ten years, you will reduce religion to absurdity.
>
> Do not the gods play games with us poor mortals . . . ! (*Inferno*)

These tones reveal the equivocal nature of his surrender. He would like to be obedient; yet he cannot suppress the suspicion that the powers are malevolent humorists who kill men for their sport. Thus, even when Strindberg seems to have repudiated his revolt, he is still rebelling against the authorities he both hates and fears.

On the other hand, his surrender has made him modify the *form* of his revolt. For just as Ibsen, trying to discipline the messianic tendencies of *Brand,* disguises his rebellion in the objective social mode of *Ghosts,* so Strindberg adapts his messianic rebellion, later in his career, to conform with his new desire to submit. The cry of pain one hears in the passage above, in fact, is to become Strindberg's most characteristic tone in such later plays as *Easter, A Dream Play,* and *The Ghost Sonata*—for there his revolt is existential, directed against the meaninglessness and contradictions of human existence. Thus, while Strindberg and Ibsen both begin at the same point of departure, they soon develop in different directions. Ibsen, continuing to believe in the importance of the will, begins to measure his rebellious ideals against the social reality: he seeks a spiritual and moral revolution which will transform the soul of man. Strindberg, coming to believe in a strict determinism (the higher powers), loses faith in his rebellious ideals: he seeks deeper spiritual insights in order to resolve his own painful dilemmas. Ibsen continues to reject God; Strindberg wavers between affirmation and negation, finally giving way to a melancholy fatalism which one never finds in Ibsen. For while Ibsen works through to a Greek tragic *form,* his rebellion remains strong and constant. Strindberg finally works through to a Greek tragic *mood,* his rebellion partially dissipated by his effort to accept and understand.

On the other hand, while Ibsen is the more faithful rebel, Strindberg is the more faithful Romantic, for he will make fewer concessions to the world beyond his imagination. It is here, in the comparative degree of their involvement in the world of others, that the essential difference between the two playwrights is exposed, for Ibsen offers a superficial deference to external reality which Strindberg totally refuses. This is not to say that one is objective and the other subjective —both are essentially subjective writers, insofar as each makes his own internal conflicts the subject of his art. But since Ibsen's resistance to the demands of his unconscious is stronger than Strindberg's, and more disciplined by the real world, he is willing to disguise his spiritual autobiography in the conflicts of semiobjectified characters, while Strindberg remains the unashamed hero of his work, endorsing his psychic, marital, and religious attitudes through the medium of his art. Consequently, while Ibsen will measure the consequences of rebellion on the happiness of others, Strindberg concentrates almost exclusively on the conflicts in the rebel's own soul.

In other words, classicism is a mode totally alien to Strindberg, even when he seems to be exploiting it. For even the techniques of "naturalism" are, for him, a springboard for his unabashed Romanticism. Unlike Ibsen, he is unable to test his subjective responses on the objective world because, also unlike Ibsen, he doesn't much believe in the objective world. Anticipating Pirandello, Strindberg works on the assumption that the world beyond his imagination has no fixed form or truth. It becomes "real" only when observed through the subjective eyes of the beholder, and (here he differs somewhat from Pirandello) especially "real" when the beholder has poetic, clairvoyant, or visionary powers. Strindberg's subjective relativism explains why his art always turns inexorably in on himself and his own responses; in a world of elusive truth, only the self has any real validity. Thus, if Ibsen is primarily concerned with self-realization—or blasting avenues of personal freedom through the cramped quarters of modern society—Strindberg is primarily concerned with *self-expression*—or justifying the superiority of the poet's vision in a world without meaning of coherence. Both are Romantic goals and closely allied. But since Strindberg lacks even Ibsen's grudging respect for external reality, he is by far the more self-involved Romantic, one who worships the "cult of the self" (as he puts it in *Inferno*) as "the supreme and ultimate end of existence." In his personal life, this ego-worship often takes the form of severe psychotic delusions in which Strindberg loses his grip on reality altogether; and it robs his art of such Ibsenist virtues as self-discipline, detachment, and dialectical power. But it provides Strindberg with a Dionysian vitality which carries us along in spurts of ecstasy, lyricism, irrationality, cruelty, and despair—and a dramatic technique which, in his early plays, is almost totally free from the need for balance or moderation, and, in his later ones, has almost totally burst the bonds of restraining rules.

Because of his commitment to a subjective art, it is impossible to analyze Strindberg's work without some reference to his life, especially to that dualism which, like Ibsen's, plagued him throughout his career. In Strindberg's case, this dualism was psychological rather than philosophical, and began at the moment of his birth. The child of a tailor's daughter who had seen domestic service, and a *déclassé* shipping agent who claimed to have noble blood, Strindberg was inclined to regard these circumstances as the source of all his later troubles, interpreting them in a manner which is always psychologically revealing, if not always psychologically accurate. In *The Son of a Servant,* for example, Strindberg expressed his conviction that—since he was conceived against his parents' will (i.e., illegitimately)—he was born without a will (i.e., essentially passive and feminine). And since he identified his father and mother with the highest and lowest classes of society, he concluded that this inheritance accounted for his vacillation between peasant servility and aristocratic arrogance.

On top of this, Strindberg's childhood followed an almost classical Oedipal pattern. He adored his mother with a passion he was later to call (with astonishing frankness) "an incest of the soul," and he hated his father as a powerful and threatening rival. Like Strindberg's feelings throughout his life, however, these early emotions were confused and contradictory. Since his mother had rejected him in favor of his brother Axel, he sometimes detested her as well—feeling at times that she was the dearest creature on earth, at other times that she was depriving him of love and nourishment.[5] And since he generally measured his own weakness by his father's strength, he tempered his hatred of the older man with a kind of cringing fear and respect.

[5] Love and nourishment are always closely related in Strindberg's mind. His striking image of the Vampire Cook in *The Ghost Sonata*—who "boils the nourishment out of the meat and gives fiber and water, while she drinks the stock herself"—probably dervies from his childhood feeling of love-starvation; the Milkmaid of the same play, on the other hand, is (reflecting the other side of Strindberg's am-

The consequences of Strindberg's ambivalence towards his father were later to be realized in his ambivalence towards all male authority, notably in his alternating rebellion against and submission to the higher powers. His ambivalence towards his mother had a different effect, determining the shape of his love life and his general attitudes towards women. Like those Romantics described by Mario Praz in *The Romantic Agony,* Strindberg had split his mother in two—the chaste Madonna and the erotic Belle Dame Sans Merci—and, unconsciously recapitulating his early feelings later in life, he vacillated between an intense worship of the female and an even more intense misogyny. Strindberg was himself aware, in more lucid moments, that his misogyny was "only the reverse side of my fearful attraction towards the other sex" (in his early years he had even been a partisan of free love, companionate marriages, and feminism!). Yet, caught in a tight neurotic web, he was never able to transcend his ambivalence, and alternated between regarding women as evil vampires, sucking out his manhood, and virtuous maternal types who gave him the comfort he so sorely craved.

Sometimes he revealed this ambivalence by dividing women into two distinct classes: (1) the "third sex"—composed of emancipated females—whom he detested for their masculinity, infidelity, competitiveness, and unmaternal attitudes, and (2) older, more motherly women (generally sexless)—such as Mamma Uhl, his mother-in-law, and the Mother Superior of the hospital of St. Louis[6]—whom he adored for their kindness and compassion. More often he tried to combine the two types in one person—and when he succeeded, he usually married her. For he was always attracted to women he could love for their maternal qualities and hate for their masculinity, reacting to them with bewildering changeability.[7] Consider his violent feelings

---

bivalence) a symbol of female generosity and mammary abundance. The miserly Mother in Strindberg's chamber play, *The Pelican* (1907), who starves the household of food and love—thus murdering her husband and weakening her children—is another example of the ungiving, motherly Vampire.

[6] "The nun is affectionate," writes Strindberg in *Inferno,* "treats me like a baby, and calls me *mon enfant,* while I call her *ma mère.* How good it is to speak the word mother which I have not uttered for thirty years." As he writes about the Matron to Frida Uhl, "The mere presence of this *mère* comforts and soothes me. *La douce chaleur du sein maternel,* as Baudelaire calls it (I think it was he), does me good." Elizabeth Sprigge, in her sensitive biography *The Strange Life of August Strindberg,* has called attention to the soothing influence of this gentle woman on the ailing dramatist. Needless to say, I am indebted to Miss Sprigge's scholarship throughout this chapter.

[7] Strindberg writes to a friend about two letters he sent to Siri in the same day: "In one I told her to go to Hell; in the other, to come to Runmarö. Well! What of it? Moods that shift between love and hate are not madness!" All his wives remarked upon these continual alterations in feeling. Harriet Bosse, more sympathetic

towards his first wife, Siri von Essen, as described by Strindberg in *Confessions of a Fool* [*A Madman's Defense,* originally written in French and entitled *Le plaidoyer d'un fou*]. So long as she was married to another man, and their union remained "spiritual," Strindberg worshiped her as a superior being—idealizing her aristocratic bearing, "white skin," and ethereal purity ("frigidity," according to her unromantic first husband, Baron Wrangel). It was Strindberg, too, who encouraged her to go on the stage, but as soon as they were married, he began to accuse her of careerism and competitiveness, not to mention lesbianism, infidelity, drunkenness, coquetry, uncleanliness, bearing him another man's child, doubting his sanity, trying to dominate him, and not keeping the accounts! In his next two marriages—to Frida Uhl, an ambitious journalist, and Harriet Bosse, a lovely young actress almost thirty years his junior—the pattern repeated itself, though with diminishing intensity, as Strindberg gradually realized that his ambivalent feelings stemmed from his own psychotic disorder.

Strindberg's tendency to find a comforting mother and an evil wanton in every women he loved accounts for his curious attitude towards erotic relations. He expects to have his spirit elevated through romantic love, only to find he has been dragged down into the mud:

> In woman I sought an angel, who could lend me wings, and I fell into the arms of an earth-spirit, who suffocated me under mattresses stuffed with feathers of wings! I sought an Ariel and I found a Caliban; when I wanted to rise she dragged me down; and continually reminded me of the fall . . . ([*To*] *Damascus,* Part III).

What he is describing here is the sexual experience; and what he implies is a profound distaste for the sexual act. This distaste—accompanied throughout his life by a pronounced revulsion to all physical functions and secret fears for his virility—provides some clue to Strindberg's vacillating feelings. For his hatred of the flesh was probably the consequence of his nostalgia for the spiritual purity he enjoyed during childhood, when he was permitted to love his mother with a love beyond the body. When he matured, however, and began seeking his mother in the women he married, he had to deal not only with the divided love-hate feelings he inherited from that early relationship, but also with the incest taboo. It was this taboo that caused him to transform the mother-woman into a spider-woman—he had to justify his attraction to her—and when this transformation failed,

---

than the others, put it this way: "I have a feeling that Strindberg revelled in meeting with opposition. One moment his wife had to be an angel. The next the very opposite. He was as changeable as a chameleon" (*Letters of Strindberg to Harriet Bosse,* ed. and trans. by Arvid Paulson, p. 87).

he became impotent as an unconscious defense against his own guilts.[8]
As for his obsession with female domination, Strindberg's desire for a
mother reduced him to a weak and passive dependent, while his intellect rebelled against his childlike state. In short, Strindberg wished
to have the purity and passivity of the child and the masculine aggressiveness of the adult. Desiring to dominate and be dominated,
seeking *eros* and *agape* in the same woman, he was the victim of contradictory needs which left him in perpetual turmoil and confusion.

I must apologize for this bare Freudian treatment of Strindberg's
dualism; but so much of it has been established, or at least suggested,
by Strindberg himself[9] that the analysis is essential, especially since
the roots of Strindberg's art are so clearly sexual and pathological. In
Strindberg's dualism, moreover, we will be able to see the nucleus not
only of his sexual problems, but of his various artistic, scientific, religious, and philosophical attitudes as well. For the struggle in Strindberg's mind between the male and the female, the father and the
mother, the aristocrat and the servant, spirit and matter, aggressiveness and passivity, is the conflict which determines the direction of his
career. If we project Strindberg's dualism onto the whole of his drama,
we shall be able to understand his development from naturalism to
expressionism, from scientific materialism to religion and the supernatural, from a convinced misogynist to a resigned Stoic with compassion for all living things. We shall also understand the changing nature of Strindberg's revolt, for his conversion from messianic prophet
to an existential visionary is directly connected with the resolution of
Strindberg's conflicts after years of horrible suffering.

The mature writings of Strindberg fall into two well-defined peri-
ods, separated by the *Inferno* crisis—a dark night of the soul lasting
five or six years, during which Strindberg wrote no dramatic works at
all. To his first period (1884–1892) belong works like *The Father,
Miss Julie, Creditors, Comrades,* and about nine one-act plays, in
which the recurring subject—treated further in the essays, stories, and

---

[8] Strindberg's uncertainty about his virility is clear throughout his letters; one of
his greatest fears is that he will be considered inadequate as a lover. Writing to
Harriet he remarks: "The day after we wed, you declared that I was not a man.
A week later you were eager to let the world know that you were not yet the wife
of August Strindberg, and that your sisters considered you 'unmarried.' . . . We
did have a child together, didn't we?" (*Letters to Harriet*, pp. 52–58). Strindberg
was also convinced that "where sensual pleasure is sought, there will be no children." In view of his need to keep the sex act pure, it is remarkable that he was
able to make love at all.

[9] Strindberg eventually grew quite lucid about the origins of his feelings towards
women; and though he could never cure himself entirely of his neurosis, he knew
himself to be imprisoned in a cycle of eternal repetition, dating from his childhood.

autobiographical novels written during this period—is the battle between men and women. Almost all of these works are conceived in a
Naturalistic style, which is contradicted in execution by a number of
non-Naturalistic elements—especially the author's undisguised par-
tisanship of the male character and the masculine position. Strindberg's control of the Naturalistic method is further weakened by his
tendency to strip away all extraneous surface details, and sometimes
even to sacrifice character consistency and logical action, for the sake
of his concentration on the sex war.[10] Still, there is no doubt that
Strindberg thinks of himself as a Naturalist during this period—not
only in his approach to playwriting but in his approach to science
and metaphysics as well. Having abandoned the religion of his youth,
he is now a freethinker, with inclinations towards atheism; and having
been converted to Darwinism, he tends to conceive of characters in
terms of the survival of the fittest, natural selection, heredity, and environment. Buckle's relativistic approach to history has taught him
to doubt all absolute truths; and his interest in empirical science has
encouraged him not only to experiment with the chemical qualities
of matter, but even to regard human beings as objects of scientific
curiosity, to be examined without pity or sentiment.

Strindberg's conception of the war between the sexes was undoubtedly influenced primarily by the emotional crisis he was experiencing
with Siri von Essen; but his convictions about sexual relations were
supported by certain philosophical sources as well, which Strindberg
(like the Captain in *The Father*) consulted in order to find support
for his attitudes. It is highly probable, for example, that Strindberg
read Schopenhauer's *Metaphysics of the Love of the Sexes,* which
affirms that sexual attraction is a diabolical invention for the propa-
gation of the race by the "will of the species . . . ready relentlessly
to destroy personal happiness in order to carry out its ends"—and
that the satisfaction of this will leaves the lover with "a detested companion for life." Strindberg's readings in Nietzsche must also have
confirmed him in his sexual attitudes, for the philosopher shared many
of Strindberg's prejudices—not only against Ibsen (whom Nietzsche
called "that typical old maid") but against the emancipated woman
("Thou goest to women?" Zarathustra asks. "Do not forget thy

---

[10] Strindberg's concept of Naturalism is not at all conventional. He rejects the
typical Naturalist play as mere "photography," insisting instead on a special form
of conflict: "This is the misunderstood Naturalism which holds that art merely
consists of drawing a piece of nature in a natural way; it is not the great Naturalism
which seeks out the points where the great battles are fought, which loves to see
what you do not see every day, which delights in the struggle between natural
forces, whether these forces are called love or hate, rebellious or social instincts,
which finds the beautiful or ugly unimportant if only it is great" ("On Modern
Drama and Modern Theatre," 1889).

whip!"). When Strindberg sent *The Father* to Nietzsche, in fact, the German philosopher replied that he was highly pleased to see "my own conception of love—with war as its means and the deathly hate of the sexes as its fundamental law . . . expressed in such a splendid fashion."

In the next few years, a good many more Nietzschean conceptions appeared in Strindberg's work, for he becomes the single most important influence on Strindberg in this period. Under this influence (which lasted until the philosopher went mad, and sent Strindberg a letter signed *Nietzsche Caesar!*), Strindberg continues to develop a rigorously masculine program, which consists in despising weakness, worshiping the superhuman, and regarding life as a war to the death between master and slave, strong and weak, possessed and dispossessed. Strindberg also shares with Nietzsche an overwhelming contempt for Christianity, a religion he declares is fit only for "women, eunuchs, children, and savages." And since he finds Christianity to be a weak and female religion, he begins to reject the softer Christian virtues— like compassion, sympathy, pity, and tenderness—as also suitable only for women.

In their place, Strindberg exalts the hard masculine virtues. The most admirable quality for Strindberg, at this time, is strength— strength of will, strength of intellect, strength of body. Thus, his male characters are often conceived as Nietzschean Supermen, endowed with the courage to live beyond the pale of commonplace bourgeois morality. For Strindberg professes to find a grim pleasure in the tragic quality of human existence and the tough, predatory character of human nature. It is this Nietzschean ecstasy, in fact, that Strindberg opposes to Ibsen's tamer *livsglaede* when, in the Preface to *Miss Julie,* he declares: "I myself find the joy of life in its strong and cruel struggles." In his discipleship to Nietzsche, as in his discipleship to Darwin, Strindberg sometimes vulgarizes, exaggerates, or distorts the master's ideas. Nevertheless, his attraction to Nietzsche is unusually strong—so strong, in fact, that he describes the philosopher's influence on him in the imagery of marriage: "My spirit has received in its uterus a tremendous outpouring of seed from Friedrich Nietzsche, so that I feel as full as a pregnant bitch. He was my husband." [11]

We would not pause to find any significance in such metaphors were it not that Strindberg's life and work also suggest his feminine passivity. For there is abundant evidence that Strindberg's defiant

---

[11] Strindberg is very fond of this image. He uses it again, after reading *Hedda Gabler,* to describe his imagined influence on Ibsen—though now the husband-wife roles are reversed: "See now how my seed has fallen in Ibsen's brain-pan—and germinated. Now he carries my semen and is my uterus. This is *Wille zur Macht* and my desire to set others' brains in molecular motion."

masculinity is more an impersonation than an actuality, designed to conceal the weaker, more womanish aspects of his nature. Strindberg was sometimes perfectly conscious of this—he often expressed the thought that he should have been born a woman—but, at this time at least, he is at great pains to hide it. It is clear, however, from his fears for his virility and his fears of being dominated, that, even when he seems to be blustering most, his masculine identification is highly uncertain. As for the Strindberg hero, he may look like a Nietzschean strong man, but he is quite often in danger of being symbolically castrated. For while the author, in his paranoiac fantasies, will identify with the robust heroes of antiquity, his artistic honesty makes him put these fantasies in perspective: his Hercules is often robbed of his club and set to do women's tasks at the distaff.

Strindberg himself is aware of the ambiguous manliness of his male characters, though not of the reasons for it. In discussing the hero of *The Father* with Lundegard, he writes: "To me personally, he represents a masculinity which people have tried to undervalue, deprive us of, and transfer to a third sex. It is only in front of women that he appears unmanly, because she wants him to, and the laws of the game compel a man to play the part that his lady commands." We may safely question whether "the laws of the game" are responsible for the Captain's passivity; but *something* unmans him, as it unmans almost every male character Strindberg creates in this period. For the typical development of his "Naturalist" hero is from a position of aggressiveness to a position of helplessness: in *The Father*, the Captain ends up in a straitjacket; in *Creditors*, Adolph collapses into an epileptic fit; and even in *Miss Julie*, where the male triumphs, Jean becomes a sniveling coward at the end, shivering at the sound of the Count's bell.[12]

In all these plays, the antagonist is a woman—more accurately, an

---

[12] It should be noted that in two of these plays, the male figure is reduced to impotency by the connivance, direct or indirect, of an older man related to the female antagonist: Julie's father, the Count, in *Miss Julie*; and Tekla's first husband, Gustav, in *Creditors*. Under a Freudian analysis, the older man appears as a father figure, punishing the son, by means of a symbolic emasculation, for his incestuous relations with the mother. This submerged theme—as Denis de Rougemont has noted in *Love in the Western World*—is common to European love literature: its literary source is the Tristan myth, but its psychological source is the family romance. Strindberg's tendency to dramatize the family romance is especially clear in *Creditors*, a play with evokes Strindberg's feelings towards Siri and towards her first husband, Baron Wrangel. As Strindberg half understood ("I loved you both," he writes to Wrangel. "I could never separate you in my thoughts, I always saw you together in my dreams"), Siri and Wrangel are unconsciously identified with his own parents. In *Creditors*, Gustav (Wrangel) revenges himself on Adolph (Strindberg) for stealing away his wife, Tekla (Siri)—father punishes son for his incestuous feelings towards mother. Thus, Adolph's epileptic fit, at the end of that play, is really a symbolic castration.

emancipated woman—an Omphale who will not rest until she has reversed roles with her Hercules, and assumed his position of authority. The conflict of these plays, therefore, is provided by the opposition of male and female, and the issue is not resolved until one of them has conquered. As a member of the "third sex," the typical Strindberg heroine (Laura, Miss Julie, Bertha, Tekla) has a strong masculine streak in her nature too—sometimes even stronger than the man's, for while he ocassionally expresses a childlike desire for tenderness, she remains adamant until she feels herself invulnerable. The paradox of this struggle, therefore, is that while the male is physically, and often intellectually, superior to the woman, he frequently falls victim to her "treacherous weakness"; for, in all plays but *Miss Julie,* the heroine lacks honor and decency, pursuing her ends by subtle, invidious, and generally "unconscious" means. Yet, even when Strindberg permits the woman her victory, he feels compelled to demonstrate her basic inferiority. When she competes with the man in a worldly career, as in *Comrades* and *Creditors,* it is only through his help that she succeeds at all; and the man must be brought to realize, as Strindberg was brought to realize, that the sexes cannot coexist on equal terms.

The Father (1887), though by far the most aggressive work Strindberg ever wrote, is typical of the plays of this period. The work has a contemporary domestic setting, and contains a few hints about the importance of heredity and environment, so Strindberg sent it to Zola as an example of the New Naturalism (Zola admired it, but criticized its obscure social milieu and its incomplete characterization). Yet, it is incredible that *The Father* could ever have been taken for a Naturalistic document. It is more like a feverish and violent nightmare—so irrational, illogical, and one-sided that it seems to have been dredged up, uncensored, from the depths of the author's unconscious.[13] Furthermore, Strindberg's identification with his central character is so explicit that it is sometimes difficult to determine whether the author or the character is speaking; and Laura is such a highly colored portrait of Siri von Essen that the character is almost totally malevolent—and sometimes quite incomprehensible without some understanding of Strindberg's confused attitudes towards his marriage. Strindberg himself was perfectly conscious, at the time he wrote it, of the subjective nature of his play: "I don't know if *The Father* is an invention or if my life has been so," he wrote to Lundegard, "but I feel that at a given moment, not far off, this will be revealed to me, and I shall crash into insanity from agony of conscience or suicide." Strindberg was actually to do neither, though for a long while he was very close to both. But in *The Father,* he was clearly "acting a poem of despera-

---

[13] Carl E. W. L. Dahlström very properly treats *The Father* as a form of hallucination in his book, *Strindberg's Dramatic Expressionism.*

tion," hoping to placate his furies by giving his personal history full dramatic expression.

He was also endeavoring to pay off an old score. For Strindberg partially designed *The Father* as a reply to Ibsen's *A Doll's House,* using Laura as a diabolical contrast to Nora Helmer. One might say that both plays attack conventional sexual attitudes, Ibsen dramatizing the woman's revolt against the tyrannizing male, and Strindberg the male's revolt against the tyrannical woman. But despite the superficial neatness of the parallel, it is not very accurate. For while Strindberg had a personal stake in the "woman question," Ibsen was completely indifferent to it except as a metaphor for individual freedom. Nora's real antagonist is not Torvald, but society itself, insofar as it restricts her desire (shared by most of Ibsen's heroes) for self-realization. The Captain's antagonist, however, is Woman, and he is opposed only to those social conventions which grow from a misunderstanding of the venomous female nature. With the issue reduced to a struggle between the sexes rather than a conflict of ideas, Strindberg's work differs from Ibsen's even in its use of props. In *A Doll's House,* for example, the lamp is an instrument of enlightenment, underscoring significant revelations—but in *The Father,* it is purely an instrument of aggression: the Captain throws it at his wife after a particularly trying interview.

For while *A Doll's House* uses the techniques of the well-made play, hinging on tortuous twists of plot and reversals of character, *The Father* has a positively relentless power which carries it through, without psychological complexity or manipulated action, to a violent and furious conclusion. Compare Ibsen's elaborate stage directions with Strindberg's peremptory notes. The setting of *A Doll's House* is so carefully documented that the Helmer household is as tangible and solid as the real world, but the walls of the Captain's house seem flimsy and penetrable, as if incapable of containing the explosive forces within. Actually, the setting of *The Father* is less a bourgeois household than an African jungle where two wild animals, eyeing each other's jugular, mercilessly claw at each other until one of them falls. It is not to Zola's naturalism that we must turn for precedents, but to works like Kleist's *Penthesilea* and Shakespeare's *Othello*—and to Aeschylean tragedy, for, like Agamemnon and Clytemnestra, the Captain and Laura are monolithic figures hewn out of granite, and stripped of all character details extraneous to their warring natures.[14]

[14] If *The Father* suggests parallels with Aeschylus's *Agamemnon, The Pelican* is very definitely a modern version of *Choephori.* Frederick and Gerda, the two dispossessed children, are Orestes and Electra, swearing vengeance on their mother for the "murder" of their father. The Aegisthus of the piece is Axel, the mother's second husband and coconspirator.

Because of the intensely subjective nature of the play, it is somewhat difficult to separate Strindberg's conscious artistic design from the distortions unconsciously introduced by his sense of personal grievance. On the basis of its bare plot, *The Father* seems to have been conceived as the tragedy of a freethinker. The Captain, a vigorous cavalry officer,[15] who combines a military career with scientific work, has lost his belief in God and the afterlife. Consequently, he must—somewhat like D'Amville in Tourneur's Jacobean play *The Atheist's Tragedy*—seek his immortality almost exclusively through his child Bertha. He therefore attempts to educate her mind and mold her will in strict accordance with his own views, so as to leave a piece of himself on earth after his mortal remains have decayed. This brings him into conflict with his wife. For while the Captain wishes to rear Bertha as a freethinker, preparing her to be a teacher and eventually a wife, Laura wants her to have religious training, and to follow an artistic career. In order to achieve ascendancy, Laura proceeds to destroy her husband. Having learned from the Captain's adjudication of a paternity suit against a subordinate that no man can be sure he is the father of a child, she proceeds to pour the henbane of doubt in his ear about the true paternity of Bertha. His growing jealousy and suspicions, aggravated by his wife's success in frustrating his career, eventually goad him to acts of violence for which he is declared insane. At the end, when he is immobilized and impotent, Laura proclaims her victory and seizes the prize: *"My* child! *My own* child!" (Emphasis mine).

But Strindberg, who had a deeper intention than this in mind, proceeds to universalize the action. When the Captain, writhing in a straitjacket, turns to the audience and cries, "Wake, Hercules, before they take away your club," his words ring with all the activistic force of Marx's call to the workers to shake off their chains. Clearly, *The Father* is designed as a kind of allegory, with the Captain as Everyman and Laura as Everywoman, an object lesson to sanguine husbands, urging them to revolt against their domineering wives. The play, then, is really about a stuggle for power which began long before the dispute over Bertha's education. Considered thus, it is not only the tragedy of a freethinker but the tragedy of a romantic as well, for it is intended to mirror the strife which rages beneath the surface of all modern romantic marriages.

[15] It is interesting that the masculine profession which Strindberg gives his hero belongs to Baron Wrangel, who was also a Captain in the Guards—in Strindberg's one-act play, *The Bond,* the hero is actually a Baron. Strindberg regarded Siri's first husband in much the same manner as he regarded his father—as a figure of superior virility—and often tries to overcome his own weakness by identifying with Wrangel's strength. Even in *Creditors* this partial identification is clear—for if Gustav is the father revenging himself on the son, he is also Strindberg revenging himself on Siri.

In this sphere of action, the Captain is portrayed as a clumsy giant who, having learned too late the true nature of women, is brought to suffer the consequences of his early innocence. When he first married Laura, he had worshiped her as a superior being, attempting like most romantics to find salvation through his love. But, like most romantics, he had failed to reconcile his desire for a mistress with his need for a mother. The two desires were, in fact, irreconcilable, for as Laura tells him: "The mother was your friend, you see, but the woman was your enemy." Yet, it is to the mother in Laura that the Captain turns in his moment of greatest suffering, even though it was the woman in Laura who is the cause of it: "Can't you see I'm helpless as a child? Can't you hear me crying to my mother that I'm hurt? Forget I'm a man, a soldier whose word men—and even beasts—obey. I am nothing but a sick creature in need of pity." If the Captain were willing to remain in a state of childlike dependency, there would be no strife, for Laura can accept him as a child; but since the Captain feels compelled to assert his masculine power, she hates him "as a man." [16] The two faces that Laura shows the Captain lead him to act with alternating tenderness and hostility towards her, an ambivalence reflected in the mood of the play where the energy of battle is occasionally broken by nostalgic interludes, during which the two antagonists pause to reflect, in tones of gentle poetic melancholy, on the mother-child relationship which was their only ground for mutual affection.

It is in these contemplative scenes that the origin of the struggle is revealed. When his romantic expectations of marriage had failed, the Captain—resenting his slavery to a woman he had offered himself to as a slave—began to sublimate through intellectual activity; and his life with Laura turned into "seventeen years of penal servitude," presided over by a ruthless, competitive warder. For Laura, who could respond to her husband only when he came to her as a helpless child, was repelled by his sexual embraces ("The mother became the mistress —horrible"), and determined to avenge herself by dominating the marriage. Though Strindberg only faintly suggests this, it is likely— considering his filial relation to Laura—that the Captain shared her revulsion for physical contact. But his recurring doubts about his manhood made him misconstrue her reaction and become even more aggressively ardent: "I thought you despised my lack of virility, so I tried to win you as a woman by proving myself as a man." This fatal mistake resulted in total warfare between them, to which the dispute over Bertha provides only the catalystic climax.

[16] Considering that the Captain is so willing to act the part of the passive infant, in fact, he seems rather obtruse when, in Act I, he asks, "Why do you women treat a grown man as if he were a child?"

The struggle is the substance of the play, and it turns the entire household into an armed camp. Its outcome, however, is foreordained, since the house is crawling with women, and most of the men in the area are too conventional or too gentlemanly to accept the Captain's interpretation of the female character. As the Captain looks desperately about him for allies, determining who is "in league against me" or "going over to the enemy," the sides divide; and Strindberg's personal stake in this war leads him to divide his characters as well, judging them wholly on the basis of their attitude towards the Captain's position. *The Father* includes, among its *dramatis personae,* an Ibsenist Doctor and Pastor, but they are judged by standards quite different from Ibsen's. Doctor Ostermark, for example, acceptable enough when Strindberg sees him as a humanist, a scientist, and a male, is condemned when he becomes a muddleheaded tool of Laura's; and the Pastor, while occasionally satirized for his religious beliefs, is tolerated because of his masculine sympathy for the Captain.

As for the women, Strindberg marks the deck by identifying all his female characters—those onstage and off—with some form of quackery. And since he associates women, at this time, with religion and superstition, their quackery invariably takes a supernatural form. As the Captain notes:

> The house is full of women, all trying to mold this child of mine. My mother-in-law wants to turn her into a spiritualist; Laura wants her to be an artist; the governess would have her a Methodist, old Margaret a Baptist, and the servant girls a Salvation Army lass.

Bertha herself believes in ghosts, and practices automatic writing upstairs with Laura's mother; and even the Captain's old nurse, Margaret—the most sympathetic woman in the play, since she is the most maternal—is called hard and hateful in her religious convictions. It is Margaret, too, who deals the Captain his death blow by tricking him into the straitjacket (she pretends that she is the mother and he the child, and she is fitting on his woolen tunic). For sweet as she may be, her female nature instinctively aligns her with the Captain's enemies. Since the Captain, like Strindberg at this time, is a rationalist, a materialist, and a misogynist, the lines are drawn between intellectual free-thinking men and irrational, superstitious, and malevolent women. And on this sexual battlefield, almost everybody seems to act in rather mechanical conformity with his or her unconscious alliance.

This sounds dangerously like paranoia; and it is certain that the Captain's persecution complex is one of the major factors in his mental breakdown. But since Strindberg shares his hero's paranoiac distemper, he is clearly undecided about the state of the Captain's mental health. We are as befuddled as the Doctor, for example, as to whether the Captain's acts of violence are to be construed as "an outbreak of temper or insanity." Is he a healthy man driven insane by Laura's poisonous insinuations or are the seeds of madness present in his mind before the play begins? Strindberg hedges. On the one hand, he sees the Captain as a relatively stable man on the verge of an important scientific discovery[17] who, infuriated by the false rumors his wife has spread about his mental condition, the frustrations she has put in his way, and, most of all, the doubts she has sown about the paternity of his child, is goaded into madness ("All steam-boilers explode when the pressure-gauge reaches the limit"). In this view, the Captain's sense of persecution is perfectly understandable since he *is* being persecuted— not only by Laura but by every woman in the house. On the other hand, Strindberg suggests that the Captain's will has been diseased since birth, that he fears for his sanity before the action begins, and that Laura's stratagem merely exacerbates a dangerous existing condition: it is in cases of *instability,* as the Doctor tells Laura, that "ideas can sometimes take hold and grow into an obsession—or even monomania." Thus we have a character who fears for his reason, yet believes his reason to be "unaffected"; who declares himself, by turns, both weak and strong of will; who is subject to persecution mania, yet actually being persecuted. In short, Strindberg, unable to objectify his own difficulties, hesitates between writing a balanced play about a paranoiac character and a paranoiac play about a balanced charater— illogically introducing elements of both.[18] Before ambiguity of this kind, we must simply fold our hands, admitting the futility of trying

[17] The ability to function as a scientist was always a proof of sanity to Strindberg, though it would not make much of an impression on a psyciatrist. In Act I, the Doctor is astonished to think that the Captain's mind might be affected, because "his learned treatise on mineralogy . . . shows a clear and powerful intellect." Strindberg alludes to his scientific experiments again in *Inferno* as proof that he could not be insane.

[18] Strindberg's hesitation is also evident in his conception of Laura's character. Is she consciously evil, an Iago pouring doubt into Othello's ear, a predatory animal who fights with everybody who thwarts her will? Or is she *unconsciously* wicked, the perpetrator, as the Pastor describes it, of "a little innocent murder that the law cannot touch. An unconscious crime." Just as the Captain wavers between his love of the mother and his hatred of the wife, so Strindberg wavers between these two contradictory interpretations of Laura. When there is no more need to lie, Laura tells her husband, "I didn't mean this to happen. I never really thought it out. I must have had some vague desire to get rid of you—you were in my way—and perhaps, if you see some plan in my actions, there was one, but I was unconscious of it." To this, the Captain replies, "Very plausible"—but the plausibility of this explanation is exploded when we remember Laura's other speeches to her husband, her cunning insinuations to the Doctor, and her conscious decision to proceed with her plan right after she has been informed that an insane man loses his family and civil rights.

to extract any logical consistency from this intensely subjective nightmare.

Yet, like a nightmare, *The Father* does possess a kind of internal logic, which makes all its external contradictions seem rather minor; and it maintains this dreamlike logic right up to its shattering climax. For it assumes total warfare between men and women, in which unconscious thoughts are as blameworthy as explicit actions, and every woman in the world is either adulterous or treacherous, and, therefore, the natural enemy of man:

> My mother did not want me to come into the world because my birth would give her pain. She was my enemy. She robbed my embryo of nourishment, so I was born incomplete. My sister was my enemy when she made me knuckle under to her. The first woman I took in my arms was my enemy. She gave me ten years of sickness in return for the love I gave her. When my daughter had to choose between you and me, she became my enemy. And you, you, my wife, have been my mortal enemy, for you have not let go until there is no life left in me.

In the weird logic of the play, the Captain's conclusions are perfectly correct, for just as he was defeated by the evil Laura, so is he finally led into the trap by the maternal Margaret. Caught in a net like Agamemnon, roaring like a wounded warrior, he can shout that "rude strength has fallen before treacherous weakness." But though he remains defiant, it is perfectly clear that it is his own weakness which has betrayed him—for over the straitjacket lies the soft, vanilla-scented shawl of the mother. Even at the last moment, his fatal ambivalence is clear, for after spitting his curses on the whole female sex, he lays his head upon Margaret's lap, declaring: "Oh how sweet it is to sleep upon a woman's breast, be she mother or mistress! But sweetest of all a mother's." And blessing Margaret, he falls into a paralytic swoon. But though the Captain has ceased to struggle, Strindberg's revolt against women continues to the end. For the "blessed" Margaret has betrayed this freethinker once again—falsely claiming that "with his last breath he prayed to God."

Slanderous, prejudiced, one-sided, these are certainly accurate descriptions of the play. Having dramatized the hostility which accompanies all romantic love, and having discovered some of the psychological reasons for it, Strindberg would seem to have invalidated all his insights through his exaggerated misogyny; yet these very exaggerations provide the play with its impact, and the very unfairness with which it is executed provides its momentum. Fourteen years later, in *The Dance of Death,* Strindberg will take up similar characters in a similar situation, treating them with much greater balance, detachment, and cogency; but the tortured, consuming, inflammatory power of this play is something he will never equal again.

Private Tragedy: Strindberg

by Raymond Williams

There is a kind of tragedy which ends with man bare and unaccommodated, exposed to the storm he has himself raised. This exposure in struggle has been a common deadlock of humanism and liberalism. But there is another kind of tragedy, superficially much like this, which in fact begins with bare and unaccommodated man. All primary energy is centered in this isolated creature, who desires and eats and fights alone. Society is at best an arbitrary institution, to prevent this horde of creatures destroying each other. And when these isolated persons meet, in what are called relationships, their exchanges are forms of struggle, inevitably.

Tragedy, in this view, is inherent. It is not only that man is frustrated, by others and by society, in his deepest and primary desires. It is also that these desires include destruction and self-destruction. What is called the death-wish is given the status of a general instinct, and its derivatives, in destructiveness and aggression, are seen as essentially normal. The process of living is then a continual struggle and adjustment of the powerful energies making for satisfaction or death. It is possible to give great emphasis to the state of satisfaction, but within the form of this isolate thinking it is inevitable that satisfaction, however intense, is temporary, and that it involves the subjugation or defeat of another. The desire for death may be less strong, or more deeply disguised, but of course, when achieved, is permanent. Then, within this form, life and death have been transvalued. The storm of living does not have to be raised, by any personal action; it begins when we are born, and our exposure to it is absolute. Death, by contrast, is a kind of achievement, a comparative settlement and peace.

The work of August Strindberg is the most challenging single example, within this range of tragedy. Argued schematically, even in its many orthodox textbooks, such a version of man can seem indifferent

"Private Tragedy: Strindberg." From *Modern Tragedy* by Raymond Williams (Stanford: Stanford University Press, 1966), pp. 106–15. © 1966 by Raymond Williams. Reprinted by permission of Stanford University Press and Chatto and Windus Ltd.

or absurd. But when charged with experience, and with dramatic power, it is often a very different matter. We can see that in many ways the schematic version is remarkably exclusive, of many real kinds of action and feeling. Yet historically the emergence of this version seemed most remarkable for its inclusiveness: bringing many kinds of known action and feeling into a new and powerful light. The tragedy of destructive relationships, when taken into newly described areas of living and persuasively communicated and generalized, had for many the force of a revelation.

Strindberg wrote in his Preface to [*Miss*] *Julie*:

> Personally, I find the joy of life in its tense and cruel struggles, and my enjoyment lies in getting to know something, in getting to learn something.

The center of interest is characteristic: the "tense and cruel struggles" are indeed an epitome. But the attention is modulated, in this early phase of Strindberg's work, by the spirit of inquiry, the desire for knowledge and understanding. Similarly, the inhuman assumptions of Freud were heroically modulated, throughout his life, by the long effort to understand and to heal. The final development of the pattern, when the "tense and cruel struggles" are assumed as a whole truth, and are then merely demonstrated, comes later and in other hands.

When the bourgeois tragedians spoke of private tragedy, they were directing attention towards the family, as an alternative to the state. Society, characteristically, was a lost term. Personal life was a family matter. Already, so early, the possible disintegration of a family, by separate personal desires, was seen as a tragic theme. But the kind of disintegration which was eventually to dominate the bourgeois imagination was much more than this. We have seen how, in liberal tragedy, the fact of inheritance became tainted and terrifying. The world of Strindberg, and of many writers since him, is a stage beyond even this. Within the primary relationships, which are intensely valued, the fact of tainting is taken for granted, and is minor by comparison with the association of love and destruction: an association so deep that it is not, as the liberal writers assumed, the product of a particular history; it is, rather, general and natural, in all relationships. Men and women seek to destroy each other in the act of loving and of creating new life, and the new life is itself always guilty, not so much by inheritance as by the relationships it is inevitably born into. For it is used as weapon and prize in the parents' continuing struggle, and is itself unwanted, not only as itself, in its own right, but continually unwanted, since there is no final place for it where it was born, and yet the loss of this place is an absolute exposure, haunted by the desires of an impossible

return. Thus the creation of life and the condition of life are alike
tragic: a deep and terrible pain which the active desires of loving and
growing only in the end accentuate and confirm: accentuate, because
their joys will be brief; confirm, because by their nature they lead back
into the same struggle and wounding. Love and loss, love and destruction, are two sides of the same coin.

> *Captain.* . . . My father and mother didn't *want* me, and thus I was born
> without a will. So I thought I was completing myself when you and I
> became one, and that is why you got the upper hand. . . .
>
> *Laura.* . . . That is why I loved you as if you were my child. But when-
> ever you showed yourself instead as my lover, you must have seen my
> shame. Your embraces were a delight followed by aches of conscience,
> as if my very blood felt shame. The mother became mistress! That is
> where the mistake lay. The mother, you see, was your friend, but the
> woman was your enemy, and love between the sexes is strife. And don't
> imagine that I gave myself to you. I didn't give, I took—what I
> wanted. . . .

This is the central statement in what Strindberg called "my tragedy,
The Father." The captain is driven into insanity by a wife determined
at any cost to control the child. The man's share in creating the child
was no more than suffered, and now his role is over and he can be
driven out. Yet it is not merely Laura's cruelty, backed by the other
women, which drives the captain to breakdown. It is also the loss of
the will to live, as he discovers what he takes to be the truth about
being a father:

> For me, not believing in a life after death, the child was my idea of im-
> mortality, perhaps the only idea that has any real expression. Take that
> away and you cut off my life.

Yet the taking away comes to be seen as inevitable:

> Have you never felt ridiculous in your role as father? I know nothing
> so ludicrous as to see a father leading his child by the hand along the
> street, or to hear him talking about his children. "My wife's children," he
> should say. . . . My child! A man has no children. It is women who get
> children, and that's why the future is theirs, while we die childless.

In the power of *The Father,* and of *The Dance of Death,* Strindberg
enacts this at once terrible and absurd vision. This combination of
qualities explains the tone of the plays, which are without pity only
because of the simultaneous presence of exasperation and disgust. Suffering is known, and deeply respected, but there is the energy also of
a protest against the impossible and yet the permanent.

It is especially relevant to Strindberg that the vision of destructive relationships is still, at this stage, connected with other energies and faculties. The desire for knowledge, as in the captain's experiments, is real and seemingly absolute, until the generated hatred of the marriage overwhelms it. And, in the speech about the meaning of the child, reference is explicitly made to ideas of will, purpose and immortality. This is part of the tragedy: that these human impulses are cut off by the terror at the roots of life.

Strindberg described himself as a naturalist, and this was much more than a description of method:

> Naturalism is not a dramatic method like that of Becque, a simple photography which includes everything, even the speck of dust on the lens of the camera. That is realism; a method, lately exalted to art, a tiny art which cannot see the wood for the trees. That is the false naturalism, which believes that art consists simply of sketching a piece of nature in a natural manner; but it is not the true naturalism, which seeks out those points in life where the great conflicts occur, which rejoices in seeing what cannot be seen every day.

It is perhaps a pity that subsequent uses of "naturalism" and "realism" have been directly opposite, in each case, to the definitions given by Strindberg. But the essential point is not difficult. For Strindberg, naturalism was primarily an attitude to experience, which determined the substance of his art. Dramatic method followed from the nature of this experience. The principle of selection was quite fairly called "naturalism," in line with the philosophical rather than the critical uses of this term. Strindberg wrote, for example:

> The naturalist has abolished guilt by abolishing God.

In his own early work, this standpoint is evident. It is the main reason why the tragedy is of a new kind. The sentence quoted comes in the middle of an explanation of why [Miss] Julie is tragic:

> She is a victim of the discord which a mother's "crime" has produced in a family; a victim, too, of the delusions of the day, of circumstances, of her own defective constitution—all of which together are the equivalents of the old-fashioned Fate or Universal Law. The naturalist has abolished guilt by abolishing God; but the consequences of an action— punishment, imprisonment or the fear of it—these he cannot abolish, for the simple reason that they remain, whether his verdict be acquittal or not; for an injured fellow-creature is not so complaisant as an outsider, who has not been injured, can well afford to be.

Thus there is no justice and no external law, but there is hurt and revenge, exposure and hatred: a simply human struggle. This is sufficient ground for human beings to destroy each other, and indeed to destroy themselves, as Strindberg goes on to argue, driven by their own ideas and illusions.

Yet still, while the outward connection is made, an alternative standpoint is available. In [*Miss*] *Julie,* particularly, Strindberg connects the destructive passions with a struggle of social classes:

> So the valet, Jean, continues to live, while [Miss] Julie cannot live without honor.

He suggests, even, that Jean is a stronger and higher type, and that we ought to see the struggle in this way:

> There is no such thing as absolute evil; the ruin of one family means the good fortune of another, which is thereby enabled to rise.

This, certainly, is a kind of naturalism, of the type popularized by the false analogy of biological evolution to the struggles of classes and individuals. The "survival of the fittest" was translated as the victory of the stronger type; thus even violent conflict made for general happiness. Strindberg tried hard and brilliantly to retain this conception, though in retrospect it is equivocal:

> [Miss] Julie is a modern character; not that the half-woman, the man-hater, has not existed in all ages, but because she has now been discovered, has stepped to the front and made herself heard. The half-woman is a type that is thrusting itself forward, that sells itself nowadays for power, for titles, for distinctions, for diplomas, as it used to sell itself for money. And it points to degeneration. It is not a good type—for it does not last—but unfortunately it transmits its own misery to another generation; moreover, degenerate men seem unconsciously to make their choice from among them, so that they multiply and produce offspring of indeterminate sex, to whom life is a torture. Fortunately, these women perish, either through lack of harmony with reality, or through the uncontrolled mutiny of their own suppressed instinct, or through the shattering of their hopes of catching up with the men. The type is tragic, offering, as it does, the spectacle of a desperate fight with nature; tragic, too, as a romantic inheritance now being dispersed by naturalism, whose sole desire is happiness; and for happiness strong and good types are required.

The portrait is vigorous, and the analysis is social. But in practice Strindberg could not sustain this alternative view. The class element in the affair of Julie and Jean is important, certainly, but behind it and through it rages a different pattern. It is not only that Jean himself is far from the "strong and good type" of the intellectual commentary. It is that the sex is either indifferent, as with Kristina, or the fever in the blood of Julie, carrying its own violence. Within the particular situation, which has its own importance, the supposedly universal pattern recurs, and it is very much like fate. Between man and woman there is only taking, and in reaction there is hatred. Nowhere, in modern literature, has this rhythm been more powerfully heard. The dance of sexual excitement is again the dance of death.

Strindberg's power as a dramatist is his emphasis on process:

> The psychological process is what chiefly interests the newer generation; our inquisitive souls are not content with seeing a thing happen; they must also know how it happens.

In this sense Strindberg is preeminently the dramatist of a dynamic psychology. He is extraordinarily creative in a purely technical way: in the capacity to find new and dynamic forms through which psychological process can be enacted. The merit of this kind of commitment is in any case its particularity: the convincing detail of an actually destructive relationship. Yet it is true of Strindberg, as of so much psychology in our century, that behind the particularity of detail there is a very firm and even rigid body of generalization and assumption. To show that a particular relationship is destructive can be empirical and dynamic, but the effect is lessened, in any final analysis, when we realize that the relationship follows from an assumed general condition. Nothing whatever has been shown about relationship, and the particularity of detail can be mere embellishment, if the finally governing assumption is a personal isolation in a meaningless world. Relationship is then by definition destructive: not only because isolated beings cannot combine, can only collide and damage each other; but also because the brief experiences of physical union, whether in sexual love or in infancy, are inevitably destructive, breaking or threatening the isolation which is all that is known of individuality:

> We, like the rest of mankind, lived our lives, unconscious as children, filled with fancies, ideals and illusions. And then we woke. Yes, but we woke with our feet on the pillow, and the man who woke us was himself a sleepwalker. . . . It was nothing but a little morning sleep, with wild dreams, and there was no awakening.

This is the feeling of the captain in *The Father*, as his marriage breaks down, but the generalization is characteristic. This world of the sleepwalker, the dreamer, the stranger, becomes, in Strindberg's later work, total. The covering of particular relationships is dropped, and a single consciousness takes over. The human struggle, at this extreme of pain, becomes wholly internal. Other people are simply images within a private agony.

[*To*] *Damascus* is a search for an end to this agony, and it is significant that the search, ultimately, is for death, as the only conceivable end. Characteristically, however, in a world without God, it is

> death without the need to die—mortification of the flesh, of the old self.

It is not only that all experience is seen as destructive, with other people and all past relationships combining into a macabre and cursing pattern. It is also that in this agony the self fragments and is finally alienated. The central character is the Stranger, who is primarily a stranger to himself:

> *Stranger.* It's whispered in the family that I'm a changeling. . . . A child substituted by the elves for the baby that was born. . . . Are these elves the souls of the unhappy, who still await redemption? If so, I am the child of an evil spirit. Once I believed I was near redemption, through a woman. But no mistake could have been greater. My tragedy is I cannot grow old; that's what happens to the children of the elves. . . .
>
> *Lady.* We must see if you can't become a child again.
>
> *Stranger.* We should have to start with the cradle; and this time with the right child.

In this conviction of malign forces which have robbed him of his identity, the Stranger transforms everyone he sees into his own pattern of guilt and aggression. Even his own search for self-knowledge, and his desire to liberate himself and others, are transformed into destructive acts. Every relationship becomes destructive, not so much in its substance as in these inchoate and malignant forces working through it. The Stranger longs for redemption through a woman, but this is only achieved by the transfer of evil:

> The evil in him was too strong; you had to draw it out of him into yourself to free him.

This profoundly sexual image records the destruction of the most living impulse of man. It is paralleled by the destruction of the Stranger's hope of salvation in the new life of a child:

> What is loveliest, brightest? The first, the only, the last that ever gave life meaning. I too once sat in the sunlight on a veranda, in the Spring, beneath the first tree to show new green, and a small crown crowned a head, and a white veil lay like morning mist over a face—that was not that of a human being. Then came darkness.

Far beyond the detail of particular relationships, this powerful imagery reaches to the roots of life and destroys them. And the paradox is that only the most intense love of life, the most burning desire, the clearest perception of beauty, could produce, by reversal, this ultimate terror.

It is not only man the inquirer, man the liberator, who is reduced to blind agony and the desperate wandering search. It is human life as such, spiraling down towards the inhuman and the willed lapse into death. The play ends in the forms of conversion and redemption, but these are without connection and without hope. The phrases of peace cover a simple lapse, when the agony is at last unbearable. This is not a tragedy of man and the universe, or of man and society. It is a tragedy that has got into the bloodstream: the final and lonely tragedy that is beyond relationships and is in the living process itself.

Strindberg's work after [*To*] *Damascus* achieves the kind of stability available after such a recognition. It is the fixed world of collective and overwhelming guilt. As in *Ghost Sonata*:

> *Mummy.* Oh God, if we might die! If we might die!
> *Old Man.* But why do you keep together then?
> *Mummy.* Crime and guilt bind us together. We have broken our bonds and gone apart innumerable times, but we are always drawn together again.

Every attempt to break out, to tell the truth, is met by a revelation of the truth-teller's complicity. The Student, finally, learns that there is no liberaion but death. He sits with the Young Lady under the starlike flowers, but knows that marriage and fulfillment are impossible, in this house of guilt and decay. The girl dies, and again all that can be said is the welcome to death:

> The liberator is coming. Welcome, thou pale and gentle one. Sleep, lovely, unhappy, innocent, creature, whose sufferings are undeserved. . . . Sleep without dreaming. . . . You poor little child, you child of this world of illusion, guilt, suffering and death, this world of eternal change, disappointment and pain. May the Lord of Heaven have mercy on you in your journey.

And the mercy, finally, is in the journey through death. The Lord is the Lord of Heaven, not the Lord of Earth. All created things have been separated from his mercy; only in the lapse back into death can the possibility of mercy reappear. Humanism has quite disappeared, as tragedy has entered the bloodstream. For such a vision of God is the late-medieval view that humanism had challenged: of a God separate from His creatures, who while they live are beyond his reach, and who in the act of living create hurt and evil, their energy turning to fever and the flow of desire turning to self-destruction, until death comes to release them.

It would be difficult to overemphasize the persistence of this pattern in twentieth-century literature. It is a characteristic half-world from which God is absent, or is present only in absence, but in which evil and guilt are close and common, not only in particular relationships but as a kind of life-force: an element that is finally recognized below and beyond individual aspirations and beliefs. While this pattern holds, every actually destructive relationship can be brought, as experience, to its support, and we often fail to notice how interpretation and selection are being consciously and unconsciously guided by the conviction of a general truth. Superficially, this literature is empirical, and it is significantly often autobiographical or founded on reported cases. But the kind of warrant this gives has to be set against the presence in such works of the characteristic absolutes, which are held to be empirical or even scientific in character, and which support a determining general pattern. This is normal in any structure of feeling which is powerfully supported by a particular culture. What is called dogma is the dead tissue, of used and separated beliefs. But the real dogma is in the assimilated pressures, the habitual ways of perceiving and acting, which create an experience and then offer reflection as truth.

Strindberg: The Absence of Irony

by R. J. Kaufmann

I can contemplate nothing but *parts,* and parts are all too little!
My mind feels as if it ached to behold and know something
great, something *one* and indivisible.

—Coleridge

In *The Death of Tragedy* (1961), George Steiner echoes the conventional opinion that Strindberg's work and, by inference, his world view lack any essential unity. "Strindberg's characters are emanations from his own tormented psyche and his harrowed life. Gradually, they lose all connection to a governing center and are like fragments scattered from some great burst of secret energy. In *The [Ghost] Sonata* and *A Dream Play,* the personages seem to collide at random in a kind of empty space. . . . These ghost plays are shadows of drama" (pp. 298–299). Those familiar with the intense effect of *The [Ghost] Sonata* in production (*A Dream Play,* being more intellectualized, is harder to defend) will know that while Steiner is clearly right in stating that the *point de départ* of these emanating images is the deepest level of Strindberg's mind, his subsequent judgments are dubious or wrong. Alrik Gustafson in a brief article (*M.P.* [*Modern Philology*], 1954) flatly states the opposite conviction that: "In spite of all the apparent evidence to the contrary, Strindberg's genius has an essential core, his personality and work reflect an essential unity" (p. 56). His arguments are not given. I believe his opinion not only to be correct, but that Strindberg's work is, in a sense, overunified and suffers from so urgent a need for coherence that he must incessantly trace and guarantee connections in a way characteristic of the obsessed and fearful mind. In this essay, I want to confirm by argument and illustration the unity of his vision and to indicate some of the costs of this unity in

"Strindberg: The Absence of Irony" by R. J. Kaufmann. From *Drama Survey* 3 (1964): 463–76. Copyright © 1964 by the Bolingbroke Society, Inc. Reprinted by permission of John D. Hurrell.

terms of a narrowing of human range and truncation of conventional dramatic possibilities.

The initial critical difficulty is a product of the very thing we are seeking to demonstrate. It can be stated thus: Strindberg's mind is intricately coherent but it is not balanced. His mental and artistic economy depends on his power to accommodate a phobic fertility of terrifying proportions. He and his characters are constantly threatened. His *Inferno, Legends,* and *Confessions of a Fool* [*A Madman's Defense*] are records of the wild and objectively needless heroisms of a mind which finds the same, frightful intentions to rest behind a hundred different routine appearances. It took great courage for Strindberg to live at all. For, not only do other sentient agents, human and supernatural (notably the *Makterna* [the Powers] seek to damage him and his by electrical machines,[1] by sly slegal intervention, and by physical restraints, but, along with other radically romantic minds, Strindberg had a belief in the Omnipotence of Thought, whereby unrealized thoughts can harm others as if they have been enacted. His peculiar playlet, *Simoon* (1890) is a tricky presentation of a "psychic murder," and *Crime and Crime* (1899) gives full-scale expression to this fallacy of the power of acknowledged inner wishes directly to effect the external world, when Maurice (the thinnest sort of *persona* for Strindberg himself) is punished for "causing" the death of his child by briefly abandoning himself and his thoughts to the enticements of worldly success. The Abbé provides at the final curtain one of the few explicit general moral rulings in Strindberg's dramatic canon: "We are responsible for our thoughts, our words and our desires. You murdered in your mind when you wished the life out of your child." What is puzzling about Strindberg is not the disunity or random quality of his thought or art, as Steiner supposes, but his failure to divide his vision critically, so that the normal boundaries between thought and act, interior and exterior reality, past and present, are blurred or denied. Some reasons for this can be indicated, and distinctive features of his personal dramatic style can thereby be accounted for.

Hence, in this essay I want to move through some aspects of Strindberg's romanticism: his attitude towards humor and his peculiar and disturbing form of wit; his addiction to anticlimax; his absorption in the betrayal of innocence; his dedication to suffering; and his ultimate distillation of tolerance. These things can be seen as aspects of a whole, refractions of root obsessions at different levels of generality. Strindberg in various places (e.g., in [*The Son of a Servant*]; in the "Author's

---

[1] See V. Tausk, "On the Origin of the 'Influencing Machine' in Schizophrenia," *The Psychoanalytic Quarterly,* II (1933), pp. 519–56, for the light it throws on one of the typical forms Strindberg's thought took.

Forward" to *Miss Julie*; Preface to *A Dream Play,* etc.) sensitively anticipated much of Freud's more systematic explanation of *dream-work,* through condensation, displacement, and secondary elaboration. Strindberg understood these processes and his critics must "read" this same idiom of multiple awareness and be content to trace and retrace inner connections not always in simple logical order. Furthermore, I try throughout to indicate how the kind of unity that Strindberg seeks is gained at the expense of detachment—his characters are not free to choose, they cannot release their obsessive grip long enough to change, to choose or learn, they lack the illuminating irony and self-humor which is the emotional expression of this missing freedom. His art as a result is often cramped and rhythmically broken.

Take humor and wit. In [*The Son of a Servant*], Strindberg provides an acute and biased comment on humor:

> Humor reflects the double reaction of man to conventional morality. . . .
> Humor speaks with two tongues—one of the satyr, and the other of the
> monk. The humorist lets the maenad loose, but for old unsound reasons
> thinks that he ought to flog her with rods. . . . The greatest modern
> writers have thrown away the rod, and play the hypocrite no longer, but
> speak their minds plainly out.

As always, Strindberg unquestioningly assumes that sincerity is the same as single-mindedness. By Strindberg's reading the function of the comic writer is in Nietzschean fashion to let "the maenads loose," and there his responsibility ends. The doubleness of vision necessary to comic writing, from Aristophanes to Shaw, he sees as hypocritical compromise. The freedom of an irony which says one thing and means another, which lets folly be spoken and then measures it, he will not consider. The active but uncommitted sympathy which animates the busy world of comedy thus is denied to Strindberg, whose concept of judging is indistinguishable from condemnation. There is here as elsewhere a disastrous separation between the intellect and the feelings. Those things are good which cannot be judged or examined, which exist pristinely of themselves. When we judge we despoil and invade the perfection of innocence. This unalterable conviction threads together the quick shifting elements of [*To*] *Damascus* and constitutes a perfectly intelligible link between the Zeuslike Old Man in *The Ghost Sonata* and the play's wraithlike Milkmaid. Strindberg's seemingly most indirect plays are quite direct guilt-fantasies about the rape of innocence necessitated by all forms of masculine assertion. Strindberg could neither avoid these betrayals of innocence nor escape their psychic consequences.

Precociously, the hopeless desire to escape was, characteristically, evident to him, for he knew of his "exile's longing for a lost sunny existence" (*The Son of a Servant*) and, as an ardent reader of Rousseau, he knew in his bloodstream the truth of the latter's sad admission, "human nature does not turn back. Once man has left it, he can never return to the time of innocence and equality." There is a tragedy of knowledge that stems from this Rousseauistic insistence. It is the vexed product of blockage of this wish to return to paradise. The mythos of the golden world, halfway accepted in imagination, provides relief from the pains of over-civilization, and when this relief is longed for but not believed in we approach the tension of tragedy. Superficially considered, Steiner has grounds for his contention that the Rousseauistic and romantic version of crime and punishment displaces the responsibility from the individual and onto society, so that the romantic treatment of evil "leads not to punishment but redemption." He is less satisfying, however, when he goes on to state that "This redemptive mythology may have social and psychological merit, freeing the spirit from the dark forebodings of Calvinism. But one thing is clear: Such a view" being radically optimistic "cannot engender any natural form of tragic drama. The romantic vision of life is non-tragic" (*Death of Tragedy*, 127–128). More carefully examined in terms of its psychological address to evil, romanticism is not opposite to puritanism but a secondary expression of the puritan incapacity to accept the factor of routine corruption in the human soul. Strindberg writes a puritan-cum-romantic drama as intense as tragedy and as it were expanding its authentic area of being. His is a tragedy of formal but unavailing redemption. The romantic is literal-minded; he wishes to possess anything he can imagine—hence ideals are not limits or measures, nor are they guides to action for the romantic as they are to non-romantics who see ideals as things to be aspired after but by definition never achieved. Instead, they are literally demanded and sought as possessions. The romantic is a person who believes that any change is degradation— that is, any change of the things he already admires and loves. At the same time, he wants the rest of the world to be brought up to conformity with those rare islands of truth and beauty which he already "possesses" and which in his austere epistemology alone are known and alone exist. There is a radical tension here, and where there is radical tension drama can be made. The romantic vision had to explore itself, for it obviously is shaped by its own dialectical oppositions. Thus, one can commit the genetic fallacy in the study of romantic literature and confuse the first imaginative phase of romanticism with its whole historical development. For the romantic, Strindberg, change *is* degradation, it is a falling away from the Truth, from Privilege, a loss of essential access to the primal place and source. Much of what he wrote turns on the desire: (1) to lament the evident loss of all good things to Time's predatory action; (2) to invert the order of things so that Time's action is denied; (3) to erect images of Temporal Preserves where this action is prevented or denied; (4) to invest his very words, his images, his symbolic discourse with a vital primacy which makes all else transient by comparison; (5) to register his own life in such a way that the experience of loss is religiously documented, as if by so doing he could be reprieved from death by honesty; and (6) to reinterpret the degenerative cycle as an advance into realms of timeless being where death and change are forbidden. There is no evidence in his canon that he succeeds in this personal quest. The romantic is a religious man, homeless in a treacherous but beautiful sublunary world which he has once felt to be coincident with truth and his own nature.

Furthermore, as a romantic, Strindberg was necessarily opposed to the impositions of the reigning social order, not so much for what these things were in themselves (he is essentially apolitical), but because becoming a citizen of one's historical moment involves surrender of the valid selfhood of the child. Political institutions are the manifest instruments of the changing processes of history as surely as they are its products. They are the agencies of change on the psychological level just as definitely as they are the inhibitors of change on the social and political level. Under this pressure, there is in a man like Strindberg a constant tension between the fierce wish that the past must and shall be ineradicable, so that the "valid" and beautiful first experiences of childhood may be forever preserved untarnished, and the need for forgetfulness, so that the evidence of the active process of self-corruption shall not overwhelm the mind and make for sick remorse and moral failure. Unhappily, of course, the tenacity of memory necessary to hold the "true" moments of past innocence before the mind reinforces fruitless recollection of "sin," "error," and all such deviations from the perfection of technical innocence. Fearing the substitutions of invalid for valid that sublimation requires, Strindberg thus enfeebled his powers of repression and left himself both as a man and as a dramatist incapable of dividing time's unified flow.

This porous relationship to the action of past time has a direct effect on what Strindberg writes about, the way he shapes it, the very style he works in. He never enjoys serenity. Everything important has already happened before his plays begin; the marriage has been consummated; the child has been born; the hatred matured. Original sin is not a concept but a fact for him, as it would be for anyone who restores time to an undivided state. In plays like *Playing with Fire* (1892), where the action calls for a decision arising from the actual encounters presented, the response is for the protagonist thus confronted to flee. The very title suggests the automatic danger of present human involvement.

Most of Strindberg's dramas are petrified *situations,* not *problems* admitting of solution. People find themselves stalled in relationships they can neither control nor abandon. In the primitive sense, they are *fascinated* with each other as Julie and Jean are in *Miss Julie.* Men and women confront each other on an island, literally or figuratively beleaguered, in a state of siege with no extra increment of energy to help them to imagine alternatives. If irony did nothing else it should afford the image of viable alternatives. Yet, these paralyzed situations, unlike the plays of Beckett and Pinter which descend from them, are full of fierce, useless energy. The characters are witty and quick, they think fast, they yoke together images of exotic and domestic things in a ready, plausible fashion. Novalis helpfully remarks that:

> In serene souls there is no wit. Wit testifies of disturbed equilibrium; it is the result of disturbance and, at the same time, the means of restoring the equilibrium. Passion commands the most violent form of wit. . . . The state in which all relationships break up, that of despair or of spiritual death, is the most terrifyingly witty of all.

The precise juncture in human experience which Strindberg repeatedly dramatizes is the point at which passion passes over into despair and spiritual death. And his protagonists have just this kind of desperate alertness until, at last, they can no longer supply the counter-energy to maintain the equilibrium of relationship with another or within their own soul. Laura exhausts the Captain in *The Father.* Jean's body, midsummer heat, and drink break down the precarious equilibrium of Julie's nature amidst spurts of desperate, self-defining wit in which the hidden self is equated with surprising but informative images like the mutilated songbird.

Thus, like many obsessed artists, Strindberg is prescribing through his characters not only to the maladies of the species but to himself. There is little evidence, however, that he absorbed anything very useful to himself from his art. The wisdom of his novels and his plays is clearly bought at the most preposterous prices and is the reward of weariness, not self-knowledge. Few will wish to emulate him or his characters, even in those admissible senses in which tragic art may be spiritually utilized (as by Keats reading *King Lear* or by any of us whose sense of human possibility has been nursed by the *Crito* or *Antigone*). Strindberg's characters see almost everything, but they learn little. More crucially, they suffer terribly, they react to that suffering, and yet they organize no denser view of reality. The Aeschylean maxim, so central to tragic experience, that "we learn by suffering," clearly has little efficiency in Strindberg's world.

This failure to compile an organic body of convinced experience made Strindberg's private existence a manifold and incessant agony. It also throws light on his development of a seminal dramatic art. It is an art rooted in the "mania for sincerity" which Renato Poggioli has skillfully documented in Tolstoy. This mania is complexly rooted and it seems insatiable. The compulsively sincere man wants to avoid being misunderstood, which is to say he wants no strong opinion registered about him or about his actions which contradicts his own. On the other hand, he wants to be understood. This is quite another matter. To be understood demands strong, searching opinions of him and his actions and work or he feels isolated and ignored. Hence, Strindberg and his masculine protagonists constantly force consequences they require but cannot tolerate; they are yearning but defensive, implore truth but resist the honest response. They demand high intelligence in others but are allergic to its expressions. They feel, the moment they learn better through criticism, that the criticism is applicable only to a prior, now-corrected self which they disown. Thus, the criticism is no longer relevant, and if it is not relevant to them it is not truly just. This protective mechanism can be detected in Strindberg and his repertoire of hypersensitive victims again and again.

This mechanism makes for a deep-seated impatience with the indirectness of art and is related to the Romantic malady we earlier mentioned: his *chronic* sense of *anticlimax*. Constantly, he supposes that some person or some experience is going to afford him true insight, true repose, mystic access, or perhaps a final closure with the reality he seeks. His heroes repeatedly cultivate this possibility. But so vigilant is his (and their) critical faculty that he promptly "sees through" manners, pretenses, social charades, and ceremonies, and carries away the limp corpse of this disembowelled hope rather than a healthy sense of moderate participation. One example among countless instances can be quoted just because its unquestioning tone reveals how total was the malady. Strindberg has just experienced "the fulfillment of a youthful dream . . . to have a play of one's own performed in a Paris theater." But it is all ashes, "Now the theater repels me as everything does when one has reached it" (*Inferno*). Yeats' words about Keats' nose being pressed to the glass of a sweets shop apply even more intensely to Strindberg, whose ardor for beauty and panting desire to penetrate the inner secrets of reality had a frantic harshness in addition to the questing, tender Keatsian hope. It is a strain for the most devoted student to read parts of *Swanwhite, A Dream Play,* or the last act of *The [Ghost] Sonata,* so tremulous are the fragile hopes they articulate. This is a malady of the underprivileged who have lived on the unearned imagery of hope.[2] It is the fallacy of excessive predramatization, by which the mind seeks to anticipate the future in detail and hence denies nature anything like organic latitude to express itself in its own way. This is artistically very costly, for what inherently enriches drama is a permissive tolerance of relativity, the sense of the vital otherhood of energy sources beyond the self. One of the meanings of irony is just this ability to let many views seem contextually "right" without editorial interposing of the "true" view. In this needful aspect, the irony of the dramatic writer is very close to "negative capability." Strindberg had a remarkable ventriloqual gift for voicing the thought of others, but the human weight of other minds is not felt from within. It only impinges on the suffering auctorial persona. Hence Strindberg's plays show an increasing narrowness—a rich, deep, wallowing narrowness. His art is finally much like the provincial Upsala which he fled and, fleeing, transfixed with a cruel description: "where men's souls, banished from life and society, grew rotten from overproduction of thought, were corroded by stagnant waters which had no outlet, and took fire like millstones which revolved without having anything to grind" ([*The Son of a Servant*]).

When Strindberg has the gentle Kurt in *The Dance of Death* say, "It can be a duty not to say everything, not to see everything. That's known as tolerance—a thing we all need," we cannot question the authority that rests behind this wonderful assertion, completely true and utterly unutilized in the play and in Strindberg's life. His art has a ghastly candor where the most remote psychic apprehensions of mankind are presented with the patient fidelity of a Dutch genre painter. These scrupulously depicted struggles are with satanic forces nearly Manichaean in their totality—the little Light competes desperately against the mountainous Darkness. But the idiom is naked and businesslike, modern and succinct. The light is indiscriminately full on all objects. Each thing, each speech seems equal only to itself, but somehow it is not. In his art we are made familiar with the unmediated vision of one whose powers of testing reality are minimal and whose powers of self-observation and recording are nearly total. In reading Strindberg the reader's normal process of artistic inference is forestalled—we are certainly acted upon, but do we act? In his art the normal ironic equation is reversed.

Irony is most economically defined as the ability to see one thing or

[2] See for example his characteristic remark after his first personal experience of the beauties of a baronial castle into which he was introduced as a tutor and well treated: "Now he had nothing more to which he could look up. But he himself, on the other hand, was no more below. Perhaps after all, it is better to have something to which one can look up" (*The Son of a Servant*).

one event simultaneously from more than one point of view. The great dramatists teach us to see doubly where we had seen singly. They show us characters who have been cramped by a singleness of vision as the pressure of events moves them towards a redeeming dual vision of themselves and their behavior. In Strindberg, we are forced (in self-preservation or in the interest of social sanity) to see things doubly which *he* sees singly. We must supply protective ironies in the face of his fierce incompleteness. We must grow wiser lest his negations and reductions persuade us to despair. Strindberg is the least ironic of dramatists, though he commands the rest of the dramatist's attack with marvelous instinct. We think of ironic vision as a special mark of modern sophistication, and Strindberg is everywhere in the texture and manner of the latest drama. He is very "modern," yet his art is defective in that very irony which makes drama most itself and no other thing.

Strindberg takes the objects of experience and sets them forth in a direct manner as if we were first seeing what they are. This suggests a deficiency in mystery and interest, yet these depictions of experience are intensely interesting and even mysterious in the impeccable exactitude of their emotional astigmatism. In artistic method Strindberg is more like his younger contemporary, the painter Edouard Vuillard, than he is like Edward Munch, to whom he is more facilely compared. There are obvious continuities in subject and in the imagery of their obsessions between Munch, the painter, and Strindberg, the dramatist. They were equally connoisseurs of isolation and anguish. Most characteristically, however, Strindberg sees people welded into their physical setting so firmly that the decor of each room has a necessary relationship to the occupant—they throw light or darkness on each other. The critic of nineteenth-century writing can no more ignore the detailed map of social and psychological correlatives provided by the accumulation of domestic furnishings on the stage than the historian of art or architecture can. Long before Ionesco or Frisch, Strindberg had intuited a theatrical vocabulary of household objects. It is far too easy for us to associate expressionism in the theater with under-detailed theatrical setting, with Maeterlinckian vagueness, emptiness, and dreamy rangings of archetypes. Stage expressionism is equally capable of utilizing all the protective encrustations of the standard Victorian interior.

The visual experience of Strindberg's best plays is relentlessly domestic and specific in its presentation. Again, like the meticulously claustrophobic canvases of Vuillard, there seems to be a necessary competition for air, light and space between furnishings and people. One of the banes of Strindberg's baneful existence was a visual tenacity which surely has its animistic side. If we collate the extensive stage directions of a late chamber play, *The Ghost Sonata,* for example, with his earliest autobiographical volumes, we note that he brings forward unaltered through the years *objets d'art,* mirrors, window hangings which act as wedges in his jammed memories. He performs feats of contagious cathexis in the theatrical employment of these objects which have been witnesses at the scenes of his early fears, his formative humiliations, and his losses. Vuillard and Strindberg clung to and made artistic strength from the closed, hermetic, claustrophobic pressure of interior existence in the petit bourgeois home. Strindberg can transpose his scene to a tower, a pension room, a crowded café, but always the sense of amassed objects and at least one person too many is felt. Strindberg's world is *de tropistic.* His characters talk desperately to keep the world of otherness far enough away to control it. So potent is *his* awareness of this pressure, that *we* share, primitively, his threatened feelings. Participating as a spectator in Strindberg productions is a harrowing experience—the theater clears with unseemly speed after *The Father* or *The Dance of Death.* His world not only was too much with him, it is too much with us as well. In producing *The Father,* one most telling way to make the set reinforce the play's movement is to contract it in size for each succeeding act. Thus the director makes the set echo an oppressive sense of unmanaged distancing which is another facet of the failure in irony that constitutes my central theme.

Strindberg's plays, his memoirs and his autobiographical novels and stories possess a special tension. It invests his taut sentences. It is hard to convey this critically. Equally, it seems impossible to find appropriate means to represent the artistic consequences of his submetaphorical conviction that life consists of a few "real" experiences endlessly perverted and repeated into a distracting profusion of illusions, each one ruinously separated from the rest and wholly believed in when experienced. What is fascinating in Strindberg's plays is not his proud habit of pouncing on an individual character's rich store of life-lies in order to expose a Count as *really* a lackey, a proud beauty as *really* a mummy, a woman as *really* a black widow spider devouring her mate—for this reductive idiom, whereby all worldly glories are made whited sepulchres is, after all, the weapon of every desert prophet faced by the hateful immensity of the metropolis, as it is of every puritanical adolescent nauseated by the swirling vapors of his own repressed appetites. The most fascinating Strindberg is not this resentful, social outsider cutting pretensions down to size by the exercise of a philosophical snobbery as pernicious as any social snobbery he reprehends. This snobbery is a tedious and vengeful attempt to expel the privileged insider's valued achievements from the category of *the real,* in retaliation for their excluding him from the comity of the self-respecting. But fortunately for his art, what Strindberg manages to do is the opposite of what he theoretically intends—he makes the texture of felt, psychological existence real, absorbingly, hypnotically real. His clinician's power to show us to ourselves in our routine social pathologies is moderated neither by the secure stylization of the satirist nor by the sense we have in reading tragic statement that these depravities are a transient part of our human range, even of our spiritual versatility. In Strindberg's world, what we have always is a sense of the self at the point of maximum exposure, itself and no other thing. Strindberg does not expose the falseness of our pretensions. His attempted ironies at the expense of the hypocritical are adolescent and rhetorical where a Shakespeare, understanding that the deepest hypocrisies are unintentional and almost wholly convincing to their hosts, achieves ironies which are structural and hence tragic. Shakespeare is not himself the gleeful unmasker of his villains—his Macbeths discover themselves. However, Strindberg's way has a marvelous artistic by-product. It can be put thus: he is caused completely to subscribe to the Faustian equation that life is struggle. At the central climax of his early play, *Master Olof,* it looks as if this heroic young religious reformer has triumphed, when he reacts in anguish, "I am too young to have reached the goal so soon. To have nothing more to accomplish! What a terrible thought! No more fighting; that means death!" (Act III). What a man *is* doing *is* his life, and this strifeful being is presented by Strindberg with mortal power. In *The Father,* the Captain struggling with Laura is fighting for his life in more senses than one. These heightened and stylized domestic encounters seem both of the fleeting moment and to have been going on in perpetuity. As if unintentionally he affirms Nietzsche's dictum that "The best parable is a eulogy and justification of all transitoriness."

Strindberg is the least philosophical of dramatists. There is no real thought going on in his plays. True, he busily collects ideas in the rain forests of late nineteenth-century theosophizing, but they are preserved in his plays only as dead, period decorations, pressed flowers in the already crowded Victorian interiors of his scene. And his intellectual tastes are dated, and when he writes a play like, say *Pariah* (1889) or *Debit and Credit* (1893) to document an idea, it is disconcertingly amateurish. He needs to work from the unintellectualized roots of his monomania. Everything relates to everything else in the best Strindberg. It is hard to subordinate, it is hard even to say confidently which is the symbol and which the thing symbolized, so solipsistic is his world and so consistent his distortion of routine experience.

The more purely felt his plays, the more they approach the monologue as a limit—all his greatest plays tend to the condition of *The Stronger*. Similarly, it is rare in a Strindberg play for the protagonist to be excused from the scene, for the action *is* his experience of *being* himself. Part of the tolerance we distill in watching, for example, the conscientious perfidy of Edgar in *The Dance of Death,* or the unquestioning malice of the Judge in *Advent,* comes from realizing just how these people suffer the fate of being what they are, a circumstance Strindberg makes so specifically dreadful that any disapproval from us is superfluous. Thus it is perfectly Strindbergian to be assured in *The Dance of Death* that "it is the indisputable right of every human being to meet with misfortune." Strindberg being terrified, as radical romantics are, by a fear of contingency, of being merely a transient, meaningless accident with no necessary reality, prefers misfortune's painful assurances to metaphysical dislocation. Each Strindbergian character can cry out of his inescapable mishaps, "I know my misery and it is mine alone. I suffer therefore I am!" In this light it is easy to understand Strindberg's excited satisfaction when, at the threshold of maturity, he read a long review of Hartmann's *Philosophy of the Unconscious.* This pessimistic unmasking of life's illusions, and its equation of intelligence with unhappiness, Strindberg found "quite natural," for he was glad that "It was true then, what he had so often dreamt, that everything was nothing. . . . This consciousness had lurked obscurely in him, when as a child . . . he had wept over an unknown grief. . . . That was the secret of his life, that he couldn't admire anything, could not hold anything, could not live for anything, that he was too wide awake to be subject to illusions. Life was a form of suffering" ([*The Son of a Servant*]). Suffering is something he knows how to renew, and hence if life *is* suffering, he can authenticate his life at need. It is not only in such ways that Strindberg anticipates Sartre, for a whole cycle of Strindberg's most characteristic plays from *Comrades* (1886) and *The Father* (1887) through *The Bond* (1892) and *The First Warning* (1893) to *The Dance of Death* (1901) present "No-Exit" situations in which an economical but perverse deity seems to have matched those who are best qualified to torture each other. In Act IV of *Advent,* he goes a step closer to Sartre's specific inspiration and depicts, in afterlife, a mutually repellent set whose "Task it is to torture each other by truth-telling." Could there be a better epigraph for *No Exit?*

Strindberg's plays rest on a devastated vision of an absurd, divinely abandoned world. Strindberg seriously believed that we, here, are the dead caught in the illusion of life, and he actively mourned a sense of a *deus absconditus,* felt Nietzschean deprivation in the God who is dead. This feeling makes for a mocking sense of the littleness, impermanence and, above all, the staginess of left-over human action which is the proper imaginative matrix of the Absurd. From his youth he was consumed by a nostalgia for "the lost paradise which one wishes to recover" ([*The Son of a Servant*]) which darkened into a sense of cosmic exile as he grew older: "In the course of years I have become an atheist, since the unknown powers have left the world to itself without giving a sign of themselves" (*Inferno*). Feeling as he does, Strindberg can have no objective vision of nobility, for he can see nothing in terms of lasting symbolic consequences or of generous self-dedication to humanly meaningful if foredoomed causes. This, too, is a failure in ironic vision. Hence, his dramatic art is one of anticlimax just as his life view, tied as it is to certain romantic axioms about time and value, is one of necessary and constant anticlimax. Things and people *originally have* value and are separated by the process of life from this value. So life is a despoiler of that innocence which is alone valuable. A normal spectrum of values which would counterbalance technical innocence with experience as, say, in Goethe, is not maintained in Strindberg's world, which is a strange, uneasy mixture of the primitive and the sophisticated. Not only was the content of Strindberg's unconscious mind more readily accessible to him than it is to most men, but he was often absorbed into its hectic activity and lived with startling immediacy in a world of contagion, arbitrary collocations of events and meanings, roiling images, and ruinous superstition. It is hard to say with Strindberg where event leaves off and metaphor begins. One feels meanings being gestated and born in his plays, it is almost biologically intimate. It is also why some of his plays are confusing and hard to explain. They mix categories, and Strindberg, normally, lacks any power to create a raisonneur who can subordinate confusion or regulate relationships and readings himself through parable and structure.

Strindberg's plays lack almost wholly the choral, summarizing and reorienting element which from Greek drama onward has been the other half of the turbulent descent into the agon of suffering and risk which we call tragedy. It is not too much to say that Strindberg as a brilliant victim of superstitious reflexes, had no power to coordinate alternate meanings and hence could not create artistic conflict in what we think of as a dramatic fashion. He could depict persecution and advertise consequent suffering, and there is an unmatched monochrome consistency to his representation of fear, decomposition, stalemate, torment, and struggle without outlet. For most men life can be hellish, but it is not lived out in Hell itself. I mean by Hell both literally the *mise-en-scène* of punishment for the guilty dead and a condition reached when nothing meaningful can happen to anyone caught in it. Hell is the condition of moral paralysis—it admits no growth, no disclosures, no recognitions which are not merely confirmatory, and above all, no knowledge which saves, lightens, leads. Hell is, thus, most obviously *not* as life is, "a vale of soul making," and if it is not, it cannot be the setting for tragedy. Tragedy is radically of life. Its roots are there, and tragic is one way life can seem when one is in it.

Strindberg, for all his powers, remarkable and preternaturally acute as they are, lacked above all the power to be in life, to rest there, and to believe in its decorum. Hence he wrote gripping but incomplete plays. They are at once more penetrating and more superficial than other great plays.

The Strindberg Cult

by Victor Svanberg

Strindberg is the personification of everything that is barbaric in the Swedish character.

We work as hard as we can to turn him into a staple of Swedish education. No doubt he is worth knowing, but he is not worth a cult. To teach people to worship him is not to educate them, but to brutalize them. We proudly parade him before the world as the quintessence of Swedish culture. It is hard to think of a better way to parade Swedish unculture.

People of all sorts of minds unite in the Strindberg cult. In the fifty-five volumes of his collected works and in the almost equal number of stages in his chameleonlike development there is something for everyone to admire. The radicals claimed him first. They canonized him for *The Red Room, The New Kingdom,* and *Utopias.* They have been willing to forgive him for his apostasies to the right because of the slight democratic recovery he makes in *Speech to the Swedish Nation. Inferno* and *To Damascus* assure him the love of all pious believers, a redoubled love according to the Bible's words about the angels' joy at the conversion of a sinner. I remember from my own childhood an old orthodox minister who spoke feelingly about this Saul-turned-Paul. Elderly uncles find patriotic edification in *Gustav Vasa,* just as my grandfather did in *Engelbrekt* and his Dalecarlians. Because Strindberg's peasant hero who shakes the royal hand in the apotheosis scene at the end is half-drunk and wholly unkempt, the patriotic spectator can leave the theater confident that his sentiments are built on sound and liberal realism.

But the Strindberg congregation also numbers simpler folks in its pews. A bachelor can delight in *Married* without having to hide what he is reading. Of course it is not pornography; it is certified great literature. Without embarrassment, newly engaged couples can indulge their taste for sweets in *Swanwhite,* for everybody knows that Strindberg never wrote pap. Every little henpecked husband can see himself raised to tragic grandeur in *The Father* and can happily daydream about throwing a lamp at his own shrew.

Women's cult of Strindberg, beginning with the flowers they sent him during the *Married* trial, is an amusing chapter in itself. At the time, perhaps, it could be explained as female compassion for someone pitiful. Today, presumably, it is a matter of a rage for equality: to admire what men admire. Another and much simpler way of accounting for the applause with which women greeted *Miss Julie* and *The Dance of Death* is to assume that every woman is a masochist at heart—a statement which I, for one, believe applies only to a vanishing breed of women. I venture to offer a third and rather more complicated explanation. Women approve of the marital squabbles in Strindberg because the squabbles enable them to triumph over this alleged titan in his lifelong, desperate, and forever futile attempts to settle his accounts with the weaker sex. We have to look long and hard for better proof of woman's triumph over man than Strindberg's misogyny.

Then there are the fools, both genuine and fake. They can be grateful to Strindberg for a goodly part of their current dignity and rights and freedoms. Today we forgive a fool anything. It doesn't matter how malicious you are. Just publish your malice as *The Confessions of a Fool [A Madman's Defense]*, and you are sure to get sympathy.

But even quite normal and humble people can derive comfort and pick up callousness from Strindberg. One example will have to be enough. It is a very human trait, and in a way a rather attractive one, to feel uncomfortable when we have to depend on help from others. It is noble—evidence of proper pride—to dislike the thought that others are making sacrifices for our sake. But Strindberg provides the debtor of delicate sensibility with a remedy somewhat less than delicate. He and his characters are experts in the art of rationalizing ingratitude. The method is very simple: one looks for secret motives of egotism in the helper. It is an unfailing method for those who, like Strindberg, take it for granted that selfishness is the sole motive for human behavior. Whoever did Strindberg a friendly turn could count on being treated as his enemy. Just as love in his lexicon was synonymous with hate, so was friendship synonymous with treachery. And just as his marital infernos have led many a humble husband and wife to enact a hellish phase in their own marriage, so his poisoned concept of friendship distorted a number of unselfish acts into manifestations of a vampire psyche. "When I stripped you naked, you died!" was Strindberg's funeral oration on Geijerstam.[1] That is the triumph of a barbarian. If you flay your friends with a flint knife, they die, but you haven't thereby proved your victim's guilt. The flayer is more disgusting than his victim, however many black banners the former waves in the air. To go on in metaphor: the fact that the human body contains rather unappetizing guts doesn't mean that nakedness is ugly. Or, nonmetaphorically: even if we grant there is an element of egotism in every friendship, friendship can nevertheless be beautiful and the friend worthy of gratitude and confidence. Strindberg can teach you all there is to know about every human frailty, but he cannot teach you that respect for human frailty which we call humanity.

Here someone will object: "Sir! You are a moralist! I'll admit that Strindberg's ideas are badly conceived and thought out and that not all his actions are attractive. And I'll admit that these same defects cling to his imaginary characters. But don't ask too much of a poet! A poet may be great despite, yes, *because of* his intellectual and moral shortcomings. And isn't Strindberg's art alive precisely because of its inconsistencies; isn't his power impressive precisely because it is brutal?"

That is how the most fashionable of contemporary Strindberg cultists talk.

I answer: "Sir! You are an esthete. You are infatuated with foulness refined. Go to Baudelaire if you want, but leave Strindberg out of it! Let us save for some other occasion the difficult question whether stupidity really can be beautiful and whether a poem can be enjoyed without regard to its subject and its ideas. In Strindberg, at any rate, such distinctions cannot be made. For if nothing else is certain about him, this is: he had no desire to be an esthete. He wanted to tell the truth, and it is as truthteller he must be judged."

During his life Strindberg was the target for many attacks. Almost all of them came from the right. My attack on what is admired in Strindberg today comes from the left. He used to be attacked for his radicalism. What I miss in him is genuine, uncompromising radicalism.

The best of Strindberg is his social satire and his psychology in the 1880s, but there are weaknesses even in his works from that period,

---

[1] [Gustaf af Geijerstam (1858–1909), novelist and editor. He was widely recognized as the original of "Little Zachris," the despicable central character in Strindberg's novel *Black Banners* (1904; published 1907). The cruel injustice of this portrait of an old and loyal friend has hurt Strindberg's reputation ever since.]

weaknesses which he partly shares with his contemporaries the naturalists and partly suffers more from than they because his naturalism
remained external and fortuitous.

The achievement of naturalism was a road-building effort which
no modern would want undone, but no more can he want to remain
where the naturalists stopped. What the naturalists taught us is that
man is a creature of nature and that culture is powerless to shackle
human nature even when it tries. That is the reason why most of
traditional culture does not even get a hearing in court today.

But nature can and must be ennobled. That is our task: to build
a culture that does not violate but develops nature. The naturalists,
however, had small taste for such a culture and Strindberg none
at all. Like his French predecessors he gave a personal interpretation
of the concepts of naturalism, and, more than theirs, his interpretation emphasized the antievolutionary bias of the theory.

The notion that man is first and last a zoological specimen can be
used in more ways than one. Zola's heroes and heroines inherited
their maker's robust appetite for life. Similarly, Maupassant's characters are all erotomaniacs like himself. The manifestation of instinc-
tual life that Strindberg made his specialty was hatred. That explains why his naturalistic truthtelling was not just lopsided and cor-
rosive, for so is every new gospel, but thoroughly false and thoroughly
negative as well. When his naturalistic coideologists stressed and accepted self-assertiveness, they demolished the older—Christian—value
structures, but they put new ones in their place. Zola and Maupassant,
Jacobsen and Bjørnson, exposed much that is gross and disgusting
in naturalistic expressions of life, but life itself is always with them
a positive force. Sex, the delights of the palate, the eye's pleasure in
colors and shapes, the joys of ownership, the exercise of power—these
may not be life's highest values, but they are primary prerequisites
for any healthy culture. The kind of self-assertion we call hatred, on
the other hand, is inconquerably brutal and hopelessly negative.
Strindberg's hatred derives from nothing, presents no case, claims to
have no reasons; it is a primitive and irrational urge to harm others
because the self has no other way of asserting itself. Love can breed
hate, but in Strindberg the causal relationship is reversed. When *he*
analyzes the nature of love, he finds hate at the root. Male and female
seem to him like two hostile races, two rival species. He convinced
himself that his view was only a modification of theories of evolution
and natural selection. That is nonsense.

As we all know, the Darwinian struggle for existence implies that
individuals within the same species fight among themselves for power,
food, and sex. In this struggle the strongest and most adaptable speci-

mens survive and go on to breed a tougher race. This is what we mean by "survival of the fittest." Sexuality is part of this pattern of selectivity because the male courts the physically most attractive female and the female favors the strongest male. There is nothing in this that justifies Strindberg's insane notion that the sexual act itself, in animals and in man, is a battle. Darwinism is implicitly optimistic and life-affirming. When Levertin says of Strindberg that in hating woman he hated all life, he speaks in its spirit.

So far from being an isolated case, this misconception of a basic tenet in naturalism is typical of Strindberg. Actually, he came fairly late to naturalism, and it never influenced him very profoundly. When it ceased being fashionable elsewhere in Europe he discarded it, the way a woman stops wearing an unfashionable dress, and put on a prophet's garb, à la Peladan. All he absorbed from the naturalistic *Weltanschauung* was what reinforced his own personality, and that personality had already been shaped by other forces.

To account for Strindberg historically cannot be done in a few pages and is not my intention here. My intention is to assess his actual significance. But in order to understand both the scope and the limitation of his influence on others, it is necessary to state, however briefly, the most important of the impressions that determined his development.

One of Strindberg's strongest experiences in childhood and youth was of a religious nature. He grew up in an atmosphere of sectarian fanaticism, and its spirit never left him. Whatever creed he later professed he professed fanatically. However often he changed his beliefs, his beliefs were always absolute. He regarded his opponents, whether Christian or atheist, with the kind of jealous rage that wants to burn heretics at the stake. It was not *his* merit that the time for such fires was past. It never occurred to him that someone with a different opinion from his own could be either wise or honorable. Every enemy to him was either a fool or a knave. Generosity was missing from his decalogue of virtues. The self-righteousness, the pharisaism, of the religious zealot marked his way through life.

In his contempt for his own human environment and for mankind in general, Strindberg is an heir to the early Christian ascetics, like Tertullian. *The Red Room, By the Open Sea,* and *Black Banners* are all equally misanthropic. For a short time only European winds blew away his life-denials: in his Rousseauistic phase in the mid-80s he dared to believe in the goodness of nature and wrote his most wholesome books: *Utopias* and the first part of *Married*. In the long run, however, naturalism turned his thinking in an opposite direction. Strindberg drew from it new arguments for his nihilism, and it left

with him a residue of cynicism after it had blown across his mind
and he had returned to bigoted belief. After the *Inferno* crisis his
view of life is a wonderful hybrid of pseudoscientific and semi-Chris-
tian inhumanity, as any reader of *The Blue Books* must know.

One cannot say he was ever a true Christian. For all its other-
worldliness, there is in Christianity a strain of generous tolerance,
mainly in the New Testament doctrine of redemption, but Strindberg
had no eye for its gentler appeals. The god of his old age was Jehovah,
who visits the iniquities of the fathers on the children. When this
monomaniac misogynist finally found a meaning in marriage, as in
Advent, it was only that husband and wife are meant to torture one
another for their sins. Rather than hailing him as the founder of a new
religion, as some Germans have done, we should credit Strindberg
with nothing more than a new sacrament of hatred. I fail to find
in his piety anything new, any sign of progressive thought or feeling—just a heap of atavisms. As a matter of fact, we must go back
beyond the Jews to find in the history of religion anything equivalent
to his temperament. What is the second half of his life's work but one
vast human sacrifice, with bodies dangling in the sacred grove?

We are told that if Strindberg butchered others, he first of all
butchered himself. That, I think, is a bad excuse. No one should be
denied the right to torture himself if he so chooses, even to kill himself. But self-torture does not bestow the right to cut and flay others.
Besides, it is a question whether Strindberg really crucified himself
in a spirit of genuine humility. At a closer look, his penitences turn
out to be pleas on behalf of his wounded innocence. In his ledger
he reckons vices and virtues backwards and ends the account when
the balance is in his favor. If not sooner he usually finds that point
in his childhood, when he slunk around "afraid of the dark, afraid
of a beating, afraid of displeasing everybody." Next to the god of
the pious fanatics, the bourgeois father was the great, unredeemably
destructive experience of Strindberg's childhood. From a sociological
point of view, the Strindberg personality is a product of the stuffy,
petty prison of the middle-class home.

Patriarchy, that immemorial institution, was perhaps never more
intolerable than during its final stages: the bourgeois family. A Roman
pater familias ruled a great variety of subjects: wife, children, sons'
wives, slaves, sometimes clients. His power was fearful, but his tyranny
was made tolerable by its sheer extent. An aristocratic head of a mano-
rial household in the 1600s also moved in a wide world, which helped
to distribute the pressure. His wife was his consort and helpmate in the
management of the ample household when he was at home and his
vicar when he was away at court or in the field. His children, often

a dozen or more, constituted a small republic by themselves in the middle of the monarchy. But a tradesman in a Stockholm apartment in the 1800s had not many subjects. With few servants and relieved of household concerns, he concentrated his curses and his authority on a not unlimited number of children. His absences from home were not refreshing journeys but the daily shuffle to office or shop, from which he returned to unload the day's accumulation of frustration and rage in the bosom of his family. From cash registers and account books he acquired the habit of pedantically counting assets and liabilities in small coin.

The type has survived into this century. The older ones among us have met him, intimately or at a distance. His is the regime of, "Boy, you better have change for the busfare I gave you."

Add to this that a tradesman in an era of economic laissez-faire—as distinct from the land-owning patriarch of earlier times—could easily be ruined and that bankruptcy meant even fewer pennies at home, and we have a complete picture of the environment in which the maid-servant's son grew up. It branded him with the mark of the slave more deeply than he ever realized himself. One might have expected that he who had suffered so grievously under family tyranny and rebelled against it so vigorously would have wanted a different kind of order in his own home. But not at all! One is rather inclined to say that he set out to retaliate in kind and succeeded. As often happens, the liberated victim of oppression became an oppressor himself. As a husband Strindberg was an old-fashioned domestic tyrant. It is both tragic and comic to observe how circumstances which one might have thought favorable to an enlightened modern marriage instead called up all his most primitive instincts.

The playwright marries an actress, interested in his art and with artistic ambitions of her own. But all he wants from her is that she cook his meals, mend his socks, and wait on him hand and foot. He doesn't realize that the demands he makes on his wife inflict a worse spiritual suffering on her than anything his mother, the maidservant, ever had to go through. His desk is not in an office, like his father's. It fills a home. He is a bohemian making a philistine's demands on his family, a spendthrift requiring others to save money. Untidy himself, he is infuriated with disorder. A bundle of raw nerves, he can't stand nerves in others. Worse yet, because of his vocation, he crisscrosses Europe with his wife and children. His home shrinks further to the size of a hotel room. Not only cannot his wife pursue her own career, she cannot even be what he wants her to be: a wife. She is reduced to the woman who takes care of his room. And when she tries to kill the time *he* spends at his desk and seeks to fill *her* idle hours with amusements, he gets jealous like a Turk—jealous of the male guests in the hotel and sometimes of the women, too.

In trying to sketch the tragicomedy of Strindberg's life as it appears in his own and his daughter's autobiographies, I have also tried to sketch the core of his significant descriptions of life: his countless analyses of love and marriage. They are not, as has been claimed, universal. They express the feelings of an age of transition, when men thought they treated women as their equals but actually used them as slaves. In other areas of life, too, Strindberg is the victim of a split between old and new. Demanding rights for the individual and dethroning authority, he respected no other personality than his own and submitted to its authority. For some time it has commanded the obedience of many others.

Let us make it quite clear what Strindberg was: an interim kind of person with hard, old-fashioned fists and weak, modern nerves. A sick man to feel sorry for. A period to be done with.

The Character and the Soul

by Maurice Gravier

The German expressionistic drama did not immediately find its final form. Rather, we think of it as the paradoxical and often excessive product of a long literary development analogous to concurrent developments in psychological science and in the graphic arts. As early as 1901, Wedekind heralded the new art in *King Nicolo.* Kokoschka had his first dramatic sketches performed in Vienna in 1907. With the plays by Sorge, Hasenclever, and Kornfeld just before World War I, the first wave of expressionistic *Sturm und Drang* breaks over Germany. The most representative works of expressionism appear on stage after the collapse of 1918, and it is only toward 1920 that an effort is being made to formulate a theory of expressionistic drama, to abstract its very idea.

But if we look for the origin of that idea, we find that it did not suddenly leap into being in the 1900s; nor was it born in Germany. Clearly, it first grew to maturity in the mind of the Swedish playwright August Strindberg, and its germs are in his preface to *Miss Julie*— commonly considered one of the most striking manifestos of naturalism in the theater.

Miss Julie, the heroine of the play, yields to the advances of her foppish valet on midsummer night. Unable to resist her lover's suggestion, she commits suicide after her fall. How do we explain, how do we "motivate" (to use the term from traditional psychology that Strindberg himself used in the Preface) such an unexpected lapse followed by such complete despair? Strindberg flatters himself on having looked for a number of explanations instead of being satisfied with one simple and manifestly inadequate motive; he considers psychology and physiology, he invokes the laws of heredity and conditioning, and he allows for the power of suggestion. For Miss Julie is a weak character. Strindberg takes pride in having made his characters "somewhat 'characterless' ":

"The Character and the Soul" ("*Le caractère et l'âme*"). From *Strindberg et le théâtre moderne* by Maurice Gravier (Lyon and Paris: I.A.C. [Editions], 1949), pp. 99–110. Copyright © 1949 by I.A.C. (Editions). Translated by Otto Reinert.

The word "character" has in the course of time acquired several meanings. It was originally used, most likely, to denote the basic, dominant trait of the soul complex and was used interchangeably with "temperament." Later, it became the middle-class term for the human automaton, so that a person whose nature had stagnated and who had adjusted once and for all to a certain life role—who had, in a word, stopped growing—was called a character, while someone still developing, the skillful navigator on the river of life, who trims his sails, tacking and veering with the changing gusts of wind, was said to be lacking in character. The expression was pejorative, of course, because such a person is hard to catch, hold fast, and register. This middle-class concept of the immobility of the soul was transferred to the stage, where the bourgeois has always ruled. A stage character became a gentleman who was fixed and finished, who invariably turned up drunk or gay or sad, and who, to be a character, needed only some bodily defect, a club foot, a wooden leg, a red nose, or to repeat over and over some simple phrase like "That's capital!" or "Barkis is willin'." This simple view of people survives in the great Molière. Harpagon is nothing but miserly, though he might well be not only miserly but also an expert businessman, a good father, a good committeeman. And, what is worse, his "flaw" is highly profitable to his daughter and his son-in-law who are his heirs and who therefore ought not to blame him, even if they do have to wait a while before they can go to bed together. That is why I don't believe in simple stage characters.

Even if we assume that characters who are all of a piece ever really existed, they have become unacceptable in a transitional age like ours, an age of hysterical revolutions, in which innovations turn old traditions upside down and new ideas, spread by the press, assault the teachings of the past even in the humblest minds.

My souls (characters) are conglomerates of past and present stages of culture, of bits from books and newspapers, pieces of humanity, torn shreds of holiday clothes that have become rags, exactly as the soul itself is a patchwork thing.

With these words Strindberg's pickaxe smashes the structure of the classical theater (for isn't it just hypocrisy on his part to call it bourgeois?). If we can no longer count on the stability of human character, how can we hope to validate the explanations provided by traditional psychology? At a quick glance, perhaps, it may seem to be merely a question of turning our attention to the problems presented by a volatile consciousness, refined or decadent (Miss Julie is a *fin de siècle* figure) and to analyze it from without with an independence of method and with a degree of daring not possible before. Strindberg will not remain content with the simple or even simpleminded representations of human character current till then. He presumes to greater truthfulness, to getting closer to nature by capturing its caprices, contradictions, and paradoxes. Apparently, he does not go beyond the limits of naturalism. And yet, for the term "character," he prefers "soul." New perspectives are opening up.

The fundamental error of the classical theater, according to Strindberg, is its commitment to consistent characterization, for man is self-consistent only when he places his consciousness under constraint, when he hardens and drains himself of his vital substance and strips himself of his spontaneity. This truth, which he discovered in contemplating Miss Julie and her valet Jean, was one that Strindberg kept on professing throughout the rest of his career. Man never stops developing or contradicting himself, and the only true picture of man is one that reveals the multitude of inconsistencies and contradictions in his soul. Near the end of his life, in the *Open Letter to the Intimate Theater* and in *The Blue Books,* Strindberg praised Shakespeare for having understood so well how to render the accidents and the wayward variety of the psyche.

> People often confuse character with the typical or the eccentric and demand what they call consistent portrayals. But there are inconsistent characters, weak and characterless characters, incoherent, disintegrated, capricious characters.

> Let me illustrate this by referring to the most recent of my *Blue Books,* where I show how Shakespeare succeeded in describing human nature in all its phases, in contrast to Molière, who literally gives us nothing but types, without life and limb (the Miser, the Hypocrite, the Misanthrope, etc.).

However, not even Shakespeare, for all his genius, is up to the task when he creates characters *supposed* to be inconsistent, fragmented, self-fragmentizing, and incomprehensible. Considering the number of images a film camera must record in order to show a simple movement of an arm, one must grant the poet the right to use ellipses and shortcuts and distorting approximations.

Leafing through Strindberg's chamber plays, we find a number of speeches that illustrate these remarks. For example, in *Storm,* Gerda asks her ex-husband, the "Gentleman" who has not seen her for a long time, whether she has not aged. He answers:

> I don't know. They say that after three years not an atom in the human body remains the same. After five years everything is new, and that's why you who are standing there is someone else than the person who used to be suffering here. I can hardly bring myself to call you by your first name—so much of a stranger do you seem to me. I imagine I would feel the same way about my own daughter!

In *The Burned House,* the Stranger asks the Stonecutter about the character of a woman he has known. The Stonecutter is astonished; what does "character" mean, is there a question of occupation? (On old Swedish census forms, "character" sometimes denoted title or profession.) The Stranger replies that he means "temperament" or "personality," a bias of the mind. The Stonecutter says:

> I see. But one's temperament isn't always the same. With me, it depends on the person I'm talking to. With a friendly sort, I am friendly. With someone wicked, I turn into a ferocious beast.

A little later he sadly adds:

> No, sir! You just can't figure people out!

Some time later, the Stranger meets the Lady, who has never met him before but whose brother-in-law he turns out to be. She had heard of him, however. He asks her if she thinks he resembles his descriptions. She has to admit that he doesn't and adds:

> Well, people are always being unfair to one another. They paint each other, but the pictures are all distorted, each according to the painter's own image of himself.

The Stranger elaborates on her point:

> They do as directors in the theater do and give each other parts to play. Some of them accept their parts; others won't because they prefer to improvise.

Here is a nuance of meaning missing from the Preface to *Miss Julie*. These paradoxical and contradictory appearances of men are not really very important, for they are forever changing. There can be no enduring pleasure or profit in the representation of images in such incessant flux. It is all just surface and false illusion. The individual human being, an unstable composite, hardly deserves to have his ephemeral traits fixed forever. Must we cry, then, paraphrasing Pascal, "What vanity is theater!"? Not at all, for behind the deceptive curtain of superficial psychology there is a deeper reality. Behind men, is there not Man? True, we still need to learn how to transcend the limits of individuality. Here, too, the chamber plays give us invaluable clues. In *The Pelican,* the Son is talking with his sister Gerda. He thinks that as long as people behave like somnambulists they do well to follow common morality. Gerda agrees with him and gives herself as an example.

> They told me I was not nice when I called that bad which was bad.
> . . . Then I learned to keep my mouth shut . . . and then I was liked for my good manners. Then I learned to say what I did not mean, and then I was ready to enter life.

When her brother insists on talking about important matters, she stops him. Later he promises to be silent. She pleads with him to speak and pursues her thought to its conclusion:

> No, I'd rather have you talk, only not about that! For when you are silent I can hear your thoughts. . . . When people are together, they talk—talk endlessly, but only in order to conceal their thoughts, to forget, to make themselves deaf. . . . They like to hear news, all right, but only about others. They hide what concerns themselves.

In such passages Strindberg pulls down the pillar on which the classical theater and traditional psychology rest. Until then, it had seemed as if the long psychological debates that furnish the tragic substance in Corneille and Racine, Goethe and Schiller, contributed to our understanding of the human soul, its heroism and its passions. Not so, Strindberg implies. Among his fellow men man talks only to deceive or to be deceived, or else to break a silence that frightens him. He hides from others the real motives for his actions, and if he lets himself be swept along on the tide of daily living he will ignore those motives himself, for he is a sleepwalker.

Man must be set free from this desperate state of self-hypnosis. The theater has the obligation to put us in touch with a truth more profound than that which finds expression in the full clarity of our consciousness. The new dramatic author has awakened to a life closer to the core of being and will awaken his audience to this new awareness. Instead of describing and imitating "characters," superficial labor without significance, his business is to express the profound movements of the soul. This is the very principle of expressionistic theater. Since, moreover, the author cannot know any other consciousness than his own, the new theater will necessarily be autobiographical and confessional. The poet mistrusts logic and its artifices, and the drama he writes will seem inarticulate and even arbitrary to the layman. Since so-called conscious life conceals the more substantial truth and is only a form of sleepwalking, we can reach the realm of the subconscious only by the royal highway of the dream.

In some expressionistic plays, for example Werfel's, the influence of Freud is harmoniously joined with that of Strindberg. Slowly understood and appreciated, Strindberg and Freud gained the allegiance of the German literary world at the same time. This may seem surprising, for Strindberg may not have known Freud, and Freud owes nothing to Strindberg. But both were nourished on the same reading, and they had the same French teachers: Charcot, Bernheim de Nancy, Ribot, Toulouse, Janet. Strindberg followed closely the contemporary trends in scientific psychology. Anxious to appear as an independent science, psychology broke with philosophy and with what it considered the too summary methods of introspection and analysis in literary criticism, immersing itself instead in comparisons and measurements. Fechner and Wundt devoted, without much success, their efforts to psychophysiology. Somewhat later, experiments with hypnotic suggestions and hallucinations were expected to yield the secrets of the mind. Psychopathology was going to illuminate the problems that had remained insoluble as long as one was limited to studying only the sane. Diseases of the personality would reveal the functions of the cerebral machine. And, thanks to psychoanalysis and the study of dreams, the new "depth psychology" had reliable methods at its disposal. By the kind and the number of problems and discussions it raised, it entered areas of thought formerly reserved for metaphysics, giving birth to a kind of metapsychology.

As Hermann Hesse remarks:

> The obscure awareness of psychic phenomena and situations is reflected in the construction of a suprasensory reality, which science in turn transforms into the psychology of the subconscious. One might venture to analyze the myth of paradise and the fall, of good and evil, in this manner and turn metaphysics into metapsychology.

Freud liked to analyze the great myths of mankind, but, scientist and physician as he was, he was always cautious when he left the domain of the individual consciousness and approached the problems raised by the supraindividual unconsciousness. But Jung, the Zürich psychiatrist and Freud's ex-disciple, had fewer such scruples. He was quite willing to search the collective unconsciousness for archetypes and confidently predicted that our culture would move toward a new religious fervor, a "second religiosity," to use Oswald Spengler's expression.

> The rational order of any culture necessarily gives birth to its antithesis—that is, the deliberate destruction of the culture. . . . The irrational element neither can nor should be eliminated. We need the gods, and the gods cannot die. . . . What I mean is that there is always an impulse or a complex of conceptualization that tends to comprise a maximum of psychic energy and which, by means of it, subjugates the self.

Thus, the triumph of metapsychology is the result of a movement that marks a return to the past and to attitudes which the previous age had considered absurd. Its agent is a new zeal, which prostrates itself before old idols. In Strindberg's development, too, there is a kind of new floodtide, analogous at every point to the one just described. Strindberg abandoned first the vagaries of traditional psychology and was anxious to prove himself abreast of the latest developments in scientific psychology. He tried to push farther than anyone else the strict requirements of the naturalistic method and to encompass from without figures as compound, complex, and fugitive as the degenerate aristocrat Miss Julie and her servant Jean. But he found that the more refined his analysis, the more it merely listed and made distinctions among the forces that moved the surface mind and that after he had painstakingly laid bare his characters' tormented past, he was as far as ever from their core, the inner self he wanted to reach and touch. He gave up the effort—and at that point his conversion takes place. The Inferno crisis intervened and set him on other paths, but the preface to *Miss Julie* suggests that as early as 1888 Strindberg had gone beyond the stage of orthodox or—as they would have put it in Berlin at that time—"consistent" naturalism.

Henceforth, the solitary Strindberg knew that the clue to the soul's enigma must be sought within himself. The central characters in his later plays are most often only fragments or mirror images of himself, and these self-reflections are surrounded only by mechanical beings, somnambulists capable only of automatic gestures. They are our neighbors, whose secrets we do not know and who, unawakened to the deep life of the soul, remain self-unaware. Strindberg is obsessed with dreams, and, like Freud and Jung, he is sure that dreams, despite their apparently childish and trifling form, take us to the very center of the self and disclose the intimate and secret depths of the consciousness. And, again like Freud and Jung, he sees a connection in dream motifs between the vast and powerful interpretations of classical myths and those of Buddhism and the Judaeo-Christian imagination. Religion attracts him with its promise of forgiveness, and his restless and lacerated consciousness turns intermittently to it, hoping to find there, finally, a formula for peace and resignation.

Thus, the excesses of rationalism carried modern culture to the edge of the irrational. Naturalism pushed to its logical limit left Strindberg on the very brink of the abyss. Disillusioned and compelled to revise every article in his philosophical creed and every norm in his esthetic, he set out—we now can see—on a new and daring road and took the modern theater with him. This is not to say that Strindberg invented expressionism, the art of expressing oneself (*Ausdruckskunst*), either as concept or as term. He probably never even heard the word used, for it was coined by the painters to describe a new trend in the graphic arts. The painters had tired of being passive vis à vis their subjects. Dissatisfied with mere imitation, with receiving *impressions* from without, they now wanted their soul's *expression* to burst forth from their inmost depths. Since they no longer aimed at verisimilitude, it is unfair to accuse them of creating an arbitrary art. No longer did they want to reproduce objects but to render in a harmony of colors and lines their own inner harmony or to make the discords of their souls perceptible in the graphic play of contrasts. Obviously, this analogy between pictorial and literary expressionism is quite crude. But the two movements share a common origin. Wearied of their long submission to the tyranny of external impressions, both painter and writer turn their sight inward. The desire of the artist's soul is not for receiving but for giving. The writer and the painter stop recording sense impressions and begin to express the secret life of their psyche. And since psychology, painting, literature, and dramatic art all moved in the same direction between 1900 and 1920, we can only conclude that all these spiritual manifestations were carried by one of those shock waves that strike the European mind every fifty years or so. Strindberg had very early—one might almost say, too early—discovered the new road to follow. And having played for some years the role of misunderstood innovator in the German world, he was to become, long after his death, a leading figure in the new movement.

Just like Strindberg, the theorists of expressionism build their dramatic structures on the antithesis of "character" and "soul," between classical psychology and depth psychology. Thus, Paul Kornfeld's manifesto is entitled, "On Spiritual and Psychological Man" (*"Über den beseelten und psychologischen Menschen"*).

Goll, in his preface to his farce *The Immortals,* casts a nostalgic eye on classical Greece and her tragedy of unfathomable, Pythian depths moved by superhuman passions. He regrets that modern drama has settled for more modest, merely human, dimensions:

> Postclassical drama has regarded man as an end in itself: the soul divided against itself, psychology, discussion of problems, reasoning. Our concern is with *one* reality, *one* kingdom, and all scales have consequently been reduced. There is always a question of *one* man, never of *Man.*

Kornfeld fights psychology, the whole traditional concept of character, and all those who fail to realize that character is nothing and soul everything:

> If man is the center of the world, it is not because of his gifts but because he is the mirror and the shadow of the Eternal and because he is, though born into this world, the steward of the divine. His soul is a vessel for wisdom and love, for consciousness, for goodness and knowledge, for piety and for knowledge of good and evil. It is the source of infinite rage and infinite peace. Human character contains multitudes: subterfuge and cunning, benevolence and humanity, arrogance and revulsion.

It contains multitudes: our virtues and our vices and the feelings they arouse. . . . In order truly to know Man, we must recognize the divine or, properly speaking, the nonhuman in others, in the byways and mazes of their character. The same is true of self-knowledge: instead of examining and analyzing the complexities of what is only too worldly in ourselves, we must acknowledge what is other-worldly, that is, to experience it in the most sublime sense of the word, and not meanly spy on ourselves. For we refuse to be mired in the vileness of human character, we refuse to be lost in the spasmodic chaos of our faults. We want to feel that sometimes, in our most sainted moments, the clay that holds us breaks open and lets out a holier ray.

Let us leave to daily life to care about character. Let us in our best moments be nothing but soul. For the soul has celestial longings, while character is only of the earth.

Of human essence psychology teaches nothing but anatomy.

Man, according to Kornfeld, is a victim of his double nature, prisoner of his flesh and its worldly lusts and of accidents of character and intellect, wholly attuned to the practical life, while his soul, God's child, longs for God. And it is his fate to suffer from this inner discord, to sicken for a harmony of being that he can never recapture in his earthly existence. The function of art is to lead man to where he can set himself free from his arbitrary destiny, from his flaws and his desires, and fulfil himself once again as "God's pure creation, pristine man, nothing but soul" (*"reine Schöpfung Gottes, Urmenschen, Nurbeseelte"*). The spectator who finds such an art strange and alien proves only his own corruption; steeped in his worldly appetites, he has lost his cosmic sense and forgotten what it means truly to be human. The new art will turn away from psychology, "this discipline which, if we are to believe its name, is the science of the soul, but which actually is nothing more than the debased science of character and of the causal connections that unite man's functions and his instincts." The new art seeks

> to remind mankind that it is made up of human beings and to remind the individual that he has a soul, his only center and his very being, and that everything else is deadweight that drags him down or a net that entangles his soul during its sojourn on earth.

In the same vein, Goll wants the dramatist to cross the borders of the narrow realm in which he has been shut up until now. Drama should show man doing battle with that which surpasses him, the cosmic, the supracosmic, the suprasensory.

> To begin with, all external forms must be shattered—the rational temper, conventions, morality, everything in life that is only form. As

far as possible, both men and things must be shown naked, and, for maximum effect, everything should be magnified.

The new drama breaks with realism. The actor who is to die on stage shouldn't first go to the hospital and observe how his fellow be- ings die and then on stage, more or less skillfully, mimic their final convulsions. From now on, says Kornfeld, it must be a matter of mak- ing the audience realize that someone *is dying*, not to show *how* he dies. Dramatic art should stop trying to be photography, stop living on illusion. The actor will deliberately turn his back on reality and become only "the embodiment of an idea, a feeling, a destiny." Goll would like actors once again to wear masks, for behind his mask the actor will no longer be tempted by realism, and realism will once and for all be banished.

We should no longer try to make our theatrical settings "real." They can suggest the transcendental only by recognizing the reality behind reality. Pure realism has been a stumbling-block for all literature.

Thus, what the theorists of expressionism wanted above everything else was a drama that would no longer depict the individual in all his physiological and psychological particulars and with all the marks of society upon him. They wanted to go beyond individual men in order to get at Man. Let us move through and beyond the accidents of reality, they said, and seek timeless truth. Instead of giving proper names to dramatic characters, let us call them "the Gentleman," "the Father," "the Stranger," "the Son," and "the Stonecutter." That was Goethe's way: he, too, declared war on realism, tried to know Man, and trans- cended the particular in order to reach the universal. The expression- ists, souls turned toward metaphysics and metapsychology, are engaged in a quest for the common substratum in all humanity. They want to probe to the very roots of existence; they thirst for the absolute. Their language borrows its seriousness, its certitude, its inflexible authority. from religion. It is as if they have come down from Mount Sinai bring- ing with them the tablets of a new law.

But the more we study them, the more clearly do we see that it is above all from Strindberg and perhaps *only* from Strindberg that they have their main ideas and particularly the basic distinction between soul and character. It is certainly in his spirit that they tell their fol- lowers to reject classical psychology and to mistrust the orderly rea- soning of stage characters too much in love with logic. It is by his example that they recommend the pursuit of the mystical, the commu- nication of "things behind things," the trust in structures that may ap- pear arbitrary and which certainly distance us from lifelike reality but bring us closer to truth. It is partly from Strindberg's dramaturgy that they have drawn the wisdom in which they instruct the actors. The latter are to be inspired visionaries rather than accurate and meticulous exhibiters of everyday reality.

The manifestos written by the theorists of expressionism do not carry he resonance of Strindberg's reflections on the esthetic of drama. Kornfeld's and Goll's language is sometimes offensive in its childish, declamatory excess. But they force themselves to sound that way. Theirs is the fanaticism of recent converts. And if they overelaborate and exaggerate it is because their gospel is not their own but someone else's. Earlier, in the age of naturalism, the German playwrights and theorists borrowed isolated elements from Strindberg—characters, themes, and situations. Now they seize the core of his "mystical" theater: the antithesis of *soul* and *character*. But the idea has not ripened in *their* minds; they have not experienced the difficulties that Strindberg went through when he wrote *Miss Julie,* and, more important, they have not been through the Inferno crisis. Competently (and, on the whole, with complete sincerity) they apply the formulas bequeathed to them. But too often their gestures and their words have about them the air of something acquired second-hand. By all the evidence, German expressionism is only the expressionism of a second generation, for the daring genius who first promoted expressionism was Strindberg.

Strindberg and the Theater of Tomorrow

by Pär Lagerkvist

Thus finally to Strindberg.

There could have been reason to mention him before, and with reference to some of the statements in the foregoing one could not help making the comment: but still this cannot be said about Strindberg. Or: yet all of this is found in Strindberg.

And it is a fact that he has meant the renewal of the modern drama, and thereby also, the gradual renewal of the theatre. It is from him and through him that naturalism received the critical blow even if, moreover, it is also Strindberg who gave naturalism its most intense dramatic works. If one wishes to understand the direction in which the modern theatre is actually striving and the line of development it will probably follow, it is certainly wise to turn to him first of all.

We can only discuss his form here since this little essay is, on the whole, concerned with it alone. Not because this point of view is the most fruitful but because in this particular connection it has its importance.

Strindberg's distinctly new creative work in the drama, where he is, more than in any other area, an *imaginative writer,* begins first after he had gone through the religious crisis out of which he emerges, on the whole, freer of alien influences, entirely absorbed in himself, enclosed in his own suffering and his own shattered, agonizing world. It is as if

"Strindberg and the Theater of Tomorrow" (Editor's title). From *Modern Theatre: Seven Plays and an Essay* by Pär Lagerkvist, translated by Thomas R. Buckman (Lincoln: University of Nebraska Press, 1966). Copyright © 1966 by The University of Nebraska Press. Reprinted by permission of the publisher and translator. This selection originally appeared as part of "Modern Theatre: Points of View and Attack" in *The Tulane Drama Review* 6 (November 1961): 20–26.

This selection is excerpted from an essay, written in 1918, in which Lagerkvist calls for a new, imaginative, theatricalist drama and stagecraft, inspired by medieval theatre and Shakespeare, to take the place of Ibsenite naturalism. Earlier in his essay, Lagerkvist has argued that in neglecting spectacle for dialogue and "plasticity for mimicry," in being exclusively concerned with social problems and psychological analysis, and in pursuing faithful but artificial stage verisimilitude, naturalism is dull, desiccating, and unresponsive to the spiritual realities and needs of modern man.

confronted by the need of finding expression for these new, complex conditions of the soul where nothing is at rest, where all is unquiet, anguish, a never ceasing vacillation, where feeling is replaced by feeling, faith by doubt, when existence itself and the external world seemed to him to crumble, to dissolve; as if he then no longer found the old form sufficient, but must press forward, seeking a new one in which all this could be reflected, one which was restlessly changing and complex as the conditions of the soul which it should make intelligible.

From his letters, one sees that he himself is conscious of this, and at the age of fifty, with an immense production behind him, is anxious and doubtful about the result. Thus he writes to Geijerstam from Lund when he sends him *Advent:*

> Here is the Mystery in the spirit of Swedenborg! Never have I been so uncertain as now if I have succeeded or missed the mark. Have no idea whether it is good or worthless. Tell me frankly!—Approbatur, Cum laude, Non sine, or the like. One word only! But no judgments of friendship. A criticism, Sire!

Hereafter, the drama—and the direct, intimate confession—is his true expression. And it is conceivable that it was to be the drama because it, in all respects, is his most personal form, his finest tool.

Strindberg himself characterizes *Advent* as "a mysterium." And not only here but also in *To Damascus* there is a mood of the Middle Ages, of Catholicism, and of severe and naïve religiosity which afterward always remains. I do not know if Strindberg specifically had the medieval drama in mind when he created this motif of the passion play to which he returns time and time again. But in the freedom with which the dramatic theme is handled, in the seeming looseness and the apparently fortuitous juxtaposition of the scenes which one feels in reading but which on the stage is not noticed, and in the immediacy and richness of the narration there is much of the medieval drama. But still, quite naturally, everything is entirely new.

As there are in Strindberg's historical dramas evidences of Shakespeare (for whom, toward the end of the century Strindberg shows renewed interest, and says that he has then really discovered for the first time), likewise in the dramas which are his most remarkable and most ruthlessly personal, there are vestiges of the Middle Ages. And his interest in Shakespeare can, of course, explain his movement toward the medieval view, since Shakespearian drama in its complexity, luxuriance and liveliness still retains so much from that period. Now, certainly, he had in all respects a keen interest in drama and a need to seek new dramatic forms, new and richer means of expression.

In regard to form, he succeeded completely for the first time in making a reality of all that he was profoundly seeking, in the chamber plays; in these extraordinary dramas which open a whole new world to our eyes, as rich in human experience as they are in poetry.

Here, everything is directed to one purpose—the liberation of a single mood, a single feeling whose intensity unceasingly grows and grows. Everything irrelevant is excluded even if rather important to the continuity or to the faithfulness of representation. Everything which occurs is meaningful and of equal weight. No minor roles, but all having an equal right to a place in the drama, and all equally necessary in order that the play will become what it is intended to be. And actually no "persons" in the usual, accepted meaning, no analysis, no psychological apparatus, no drawing of "characters." And yet, no abstractions, but images of man when he is evil, when he is good, when in sorrow, and when joyful.

Simplification. And, nevertheless, richness. Richness too in the form itself, because of the fact that everything plays its part, nothing is lifeless, all is inspired and put into the drama as a living part of it; and because the theme is always shifting, and is clipped off, to be pursued on another plane. Confusion, but a confusion with meaning and order.

Here, naturalism is entirely cast aside; its straight line abandoned and instead a much richer form is created implying an incomparably broader range of expression, a multiplicity of new possibilities.

In the presence of these dramas no one can fail to see how insufficient the naturalistic form is, and how narrow its limits. For no one can doubt that Strindberg, if he had been forced to develop the themes in *The [Ghost] Sonata, The Pelican,* and *The Black Glove* in one fixed realistic plane, never could have wrung from them that fullness of moving humanity which has made them stand as the most profound and remarkable imaginative writing that he produced. Nor, can anyone doubt that it was just through the new mode of expression which he created that Strindberg was able to speak so directly and openly to us, to touch hidden strings in our consciousness which we, perhaps, had sensed but whose sound we had never before heard.

One may merely add that Strindberg is not a great dramatic writer because he found this new form.

But, that this form allowed him to show the full magnitude of his greatness.

Strindberg's drama such as it gradually became signifies in all respects revolt and renewal. And one cannot imagine that it will have anything else but a revolutionary effect on modern drama because it so completely destroys the old foundations, creates new ones instead, and so clearly shows a way which leads forward.

Ibsen, who was long the modern writer *par préférence* because he exhaustively plodded through all of the social, sexual, and mental-hygienic ideas and ideals which happened to come up for discussion, merely weighs us down with his perfectly consummated and fixed form, impossible of further development; and besides, only fills, in an admirable way, an unoccupied place which otherwise would have been empty. Strindberg, on the other hand, opens a perspective forward which is stimulating and exciting and allows us a premonition of what lies deepest within us, not because he informs us about what we think or ought to think—for how often do we really share Strindberg's opinions?—but just because in him we find the very disquiet, uncertainty and faltering pulse of our own day.

A new form has never been created more beautifully, or more completely as a result of inner personal compulsion.

And yet, as the form finally appears to us, it is never purely and simply the fruit of personality; innumerable other factors have also had their influence: everything which lives and moves about the writer, all he has seen and experienced, all of the life and time which was granted to him. The *form* never becomes entirely his personal property, but that of his time and perhaps posterity's as well.

Had Strindberg lived some hundred years ago the result would never have been this form, but another. It developed as it did because it was natural, obvious and necessary that it do so.

If we take a similar turn we shall do so not only because it is right but also unavoidable, provided we wish to go forward and not backward. And the rightness of it is all the greater for there being nothing to gain without a new quest; nothing finished, clarified and benignly arranged which only requires that we adopt and use it. Whoever would simply appropriate Strindberg's scenic devices would not profit much by the attempt. Everything must naturally be derived from his own feeling and need. For Strindberg himself this form was fully realized; for his contemporaries and for posterity it is still something which is coming into being.

But the quest is open to anyone if the motivation is instinct and not secret agreement with oneself.

In that sense, however, it seems there is no seeking to be found. What has been taken by force is something that, in a much higher degree remains Strindberg's inviolable personal property. It is that genuine Strindbergian atmosphere in a drama, the storm and eruption—the violent outburst of a morbid and raging genius. This is what they have hurried to take possession of. In Germany—with a shriek as from jubilant dervishes—and even, if much more modestly and decorously, in Sweden.

What else can the result of this be but a Strindberg in an inferior edition? And where do they intend to go with this thunderbolt in their

baggage? So fateful when it flashes and flames against a world, so tame
when it merely seems to threaten the author.

Whenever this has happened it has been partly because more attention was given to Strindberg's earlier naturalistic production than to
his later work which raises a front against naturalism. Thus, he became
easier to place, could be put into a familiar pattern and utilized without so much trouble.

But, however strong and passionate Strindberg's earlier dramas are,
the emphasis still does not lie there. His later plays, from the point of
view of humanity, are richer, finer, more profound and fervent. And
as imaginative writing, far more powerful, and liberating in a quite
different way. For here, in spite of everything, the light has finally
broken through. Here one can breathe and live, and believe also in the
good.

But it has been Strindberg's fate—and probably will continue to be
for a long time yet—that he is valued first and foremost for his bad
qualities, both as a writer and a man. All of his repellent and morbid
features were seized upon; these have been regarded as the most interesting. For this best suited modern literature.

Perhaps, however, Strindberg can be viewed more reasonably without therefore losing any of his magnificence or interest. Perhaps one
may love the beauty and the value in his work, and understand, but
not love, its inferior qualities.

It would then be easier to see entirely without prejudice where he is
greatest as an imaginative writer and where he falls short.

The sweeping renewal of the modern drama which Strindberg represents in his later development cannot be explained away. It is a revolt
against the old, not a development from it. And it is this, his last
achievement, that makes it impossible to circumvent him even if one
has entirely different purposes and goals.

Ibsen can be circumvented; as a milepost with a Roman numeral on
it. But Strindberg is in the middle of the road and one is allowed to
pass, only provided that one has first understood him and what he
actually has signified.

Naturally I do not mean that Strindberg should quite simply be
taken as a tutor in the art of dramatic writing. Indeed one cannot be
taught in that way, not even if it merely is a question of form. And
one "ought" in this case to do nothing other than that which is compelling, otherwise the whole endeavor will be floating in mid-air.

The inner compulsion must be there no matter how it can have
originated. That inner compulsion which alone gives imaginative writing meaning and vitality. That compulsion which in youth seems less
threatening, and, perhaps, even is lacking, which explains why most of
what a young literature creates is of rather little value. This greatest

wonder of life: that everything becomes more circumscribed, shrinks about us until there is finally only one way. No longer a choice, nor an external chance. But the compulsion from within.

If the struggle for a new form does not also mean the struggle for a deeper personal view then for heaven's sake it should be avoided. And if one does not need to understand Strindberg's importance one ought to leave him alone.

All that I have wanted to affirm is that Strindberg's newly created dramatic form, despite all its subjectivity, nonetheless corresponds to an artistic instinct in our age.

So much about the drama.

But the modern theatre? Has something similar happened here? Has the art of acting and the art of play production generally, abandoned its old platform, looked for new forms of expression, proposed other goals than before?

Many attempts which have been and are being made to find newer and freer forms, indicate that there has been dissatisfaction with naturalism. From different points of departure and with different concepts in mind concerning what is essential on the stage, attempts have been made to create anew from the older forms or in spite of them.

Foremost may be mentioned the intimate theater which arose from the drama of Strindberg and whose founding Strindberg himself brought about through his remarkable preface to *Miss Julie*.

"First and last a small stage and a small auditorium," is the demand he makes. And afterward he always holds fast to it, throughout his entire development. His own theater comes into existence chiefly to put this idea into practical effect. And here it acquires its most interesting form through the introduction of the so-called "drapery stage." This is the most extreme consequence, and it is better and more sensible than stopping half way.

But if this way is, on the whole, the right one, is another question. Many of his plays—like much of naturalistic drama in general—could be played to advantage on such a stage. But many, and among them the most important ones, could only lose by it.

The fact cannot be avoided that a small stage implies, first and foremost, reduced possibilities. Such a stage is confined within a small space from beginning to end. When an effect built upon contrasts is necessary it is helpless and can do nothing. It has no possibility of expression through proportions, distance, and antitheses.

Therefore, as long as the drama makes only small demands on décor or is only loosely and temporarily attached to its outer framework, all may be set in order. It is merely necessary to retrench all along the line, to make a virtue of bareness. But, where the external, as in Strindberg's later dramas, is intimately associated with the internal, where it participates, and intervenes; and where the fantastic in the concept and figuration also demands a fantastic scenic form, it will not do at all.

The tendency is negative throughout, goes back to the most primitive forms of theater, such as, for example, the theater of India of which the intimate theater with its drapery stage is a conscious or unconscious copy. (Strindberg also gives sometimes quite the same stage directions as those found in the Indian drama: that a person shall pretend to open a door, etc.) But while the Indian theater was satisfied with this because it had to be, in our day it can only seem artificial, and one cannot believe that the theater would ever seriously choose this path of self-sacrifice and meagerness, even if it were so bidden by Strindberg.

The merit, surely, lies in the fact that in a time of confusion in such matters this theater really implies a definite style. But in this there lurks a danger for the actor which weighs even heavier, and which has already been felt—the danger that instead of enriching his acting skill, and liberating his imagination, he is led to *stylize* his presentation which kills his individuality. Stylization is the antithesis of all art and in our day it is the spectre which threatens everywhere. One need only think of a "stylized" landscape painting hung as a background to give "atmosphere"—as happened in Strindberg's theatre, and which he insisted upon in, to choose an example, the last scene of *The Ghost Sonata* —in order to understand what the end would be.

On this point and for that matter in his whole attitude toward the theater, in his suspicion of it and his wish to see it changed quite simply into an awe-inspiring pulpit for the playwright, Strindberg is no more than the exponent of his own generation's taste and ought not to be regarded as anything else. It would be unfortunate if his instructions were taken *ad notam*. Unfortunate both for the effect of his own dramas and for later development.

Undeniably, the building of a tradition has to some small degree already begun, so that we have a certain *manner* of playing Strindberg just as we have long had a definite Ibsen tradition. And what is almost even worse, we have acquired—from Germany—a taste for playing his fantastic dramas within a frame of turbid *jugendstil*, pretentious, empty, meaningless.

All of which shows how little *the theater* has understood how it should utilize the new elements in *drama* which appeared with Strindberg, and that it will probably be Strindberg's fate not only as a man and as an imaginative writer, but also in his capacity as the greatest dramatist of our age, to be swallowed whole without an attempt to distinguish the better from the worse, the meaningful from the less meaningful.

Strindberg, the One and the Many

by Eric Bentley

Ibsen and Strindberg were born in Norway and Sweden respectively, but their mode of life, their style, and their "message" made them European figures almost from the start. (This is in itself—if we think how much Racine, say, is confined to France or Schiller to Germany—a remarkable fact.) And that they are not Europeans of one generation only, Europeans of the turn of the century, is demonstrated by the revival of interest in them, particularly in Strindberg, in recent years. It was not merely the centenary that did it (though it is remarkable how potent an arbitrary symbol like a date can be). One notes in France in particular a sort of reenactment of the Strindberg revival that in Germany occurred a generation ago.

The German Strindberg movement was a rebellion against the high-toned middle-class drama of the preceding generations, definitely including Ibsen. Wedekind was a spokesman for the movement when he described Ibsen's characters as domestic animals and called for beasts of prey in their stead. In his essay on acting, he shows himself aware that those who have acted the parts of domestic animals can scarcely present the beasts of prey too: in other words, that a new sort of acting was required, a wilder, far less naturalistic sort.

The Dionysiac vision, the Dionysiac theater came perhaps to seem dated in the period between the two wars, even if this seeming was but part of the false sense of security and progress of those years. Yet it was in this period that the French actor Antonin Artaud called for a "theater of cruelty"—a Dionysiac theater. Since 1945 Artaud has been the most quoted of all theatrical innovators. As a direct result of a general trend in Artaud's direction, Strindberg was also talked of and revived. In the past year I have seen three Strindberg productions in Paris: *To Damascus,* with Sacha Pitoëff in the main role at the Vieux-Colombier; *The Ghost Sonata,* with Roger Blin, at the Gaîté-Montparnasse; and *The Dance of Death,* with Jean Vilar (who also directed), at the Studio des Champs-Élysées.

The last of these was a valuable occasion, since I learned from it that Strindberg's naturalistic tragedies can only be adequately rendered by actors of the kind Wedekind called for, actors who can project great emotional intensity, and project it *without interferences.* This might seem to be the traditional habit of actors, yet in recent times we have grown used to seeing the passions interfered with by the decencies. Our actors are like little boys too brave to cry: their emotion peeps through the mask of their heroic impassivity. Ibsen is the playwright who has made most skillful use of such emotion half-hiding behind such a mask. An Ibsenite actor has to present a man at war with himself. A Strindbergian actor is at war with someone else, often his wife. His emotions come right out of him with no interference whatsoever and fly like bullets at the enemy. It is quite a different pattern, and calls for quite a different sort of performance, a Dionysiac performance. After trying out their choicest domestic animals in *The Father,* London and New York will presumably stop trying to join Strindberg to the genteel tradition.

Jean Vilar's *Dance of Death* proves that Strindberg's naturalistic plays are still effective theater, and it demonstrates how they are to be made effective, but beyond that? Certain doubts I have always had about Strindberg have been reinforced rather than dispelled by seeing more of him in the theater. We cannot be so crass as to dismiss plays like *The Dance of Death* and *The Father* as museum pieces; but there is something in them, certainly, that encourages us to do so. They are not alive in all their parts; or their parts do not come together as a whole; or—? Well, something is wrong which cannot be put right, as some have tried to put it right, by accepting Strindberg's disorder as that of his age. The artist's task is not to portray vagueness vaguely, disorder disorderedly. On the contrary! He cannot show chaos to others if he himself is lost in it.

Sometimes, Strindberg is content to give us raw chunks of life. As we see *The Dance of Death* we think "How real how real how real" and then? We are reminded of our own marital quarrels; Strindberg gets his finger on the sore and leaves it there. *The Dance of Death* is in two long parts. If, as is usually the case, only the first is performed, we have the impression of incompleteness. We have received a two-hour sample of marital misery, remarkable for its intensity and concentration, yet shocking in its monotony, its monomania. We have heard a single note endlessly extended, a prolonged shriek. Who would return to have the same note sounded, the same sore rubbed during the Second Part?

Sometimes, to be sure, Strindberg imposes a pattern upon the chunks of life. *Imposes* a pattern. Willfully: that is, by will-power, and by will-power somewhat petulantly, self-assertively, perversely exerted. If one sees *The Father* shortly after, say, *Rosmersholm,* one is surprised to find the disordered Swede achieving more clarity of outline, a more readily discernible formal pattern, than the famously calculating, wire-pulling Norwegian. In this instance Ibsen is struggling with life's chaos and is not completely the victor: his material will not quite yield an order. Strindberg decides not to wait on his material to yield anything: he has an order ready-made in his pocket. There is consequently something wooden and inorganic about the play, "well put together" as it is. The victory of the wife does not quite grow out of the human resources of the story; it receives an extra push from the author's philosophy; and technically, it has to be put through by the desperate expedient of mesmerism. Here Strindberg is not artistically *exploiting* Grand Guignol, which might be possible; he is *succumbing* to it—which means he is here not seriously dramatic enough, not seriously human enough. The macabre can be good when it is successfully serious (that is, when it points to horror that is real and important) or when it is successfully flippant (that is, when it asks to be *enjoyed,* as in melodrama). But when it wants to be taken seriously and is arbitrary and unreal—! Strindberg brings Eugene O'Neill in his wake.

What of the "other Strindberg," the Strindberg of the dream plays? I must confess that the Paris productions of two of these did not enable me to judge what there is in them. These productions were *avant-garde* in the worst sense. High ideals went hand in hand with artistic nullity and technical incompetence. (There are people who, in their indignant rejection of commercialism, power, and success, make virtues out of poverty, weakness, and failure.) Reading casually through a play like *To Damascus,* one has an impression of a mildly interesting, mildly boring jumble—I almost wrote "jungle." It is mysterious, but is it profound? Is anything about it profound, that is, besides the mystery? A prospective producer has to give the play more than a casual reading in order to decide whether to set it aside as pretentious religious *kitsch* worthy of Franz Werfel or Dorothy Sayers or whether production might not dispel the clouds and bring something to light.

What the text is to a casual reader the Paris production was to every spectator, casual or otherwise. What seems vague to the reader was left vague. The director had not applied himself to his primary problem—which, when there is anything worth clarification, is to clarify. When the images presented to our eyes are uninteresting in themselves and insignificant in relation to the play, when the tempo of the dialogue and the movements is left to be as it may, slow or fast, jerky or smooth in any sequence that chance may produce, a director has done his utmost to kill both play and audience.

Like a film, a play has a visual track and a sound track; the internal and mutual relations of the two are the director's charge. Faults in the sound track can always be attributed, rightly or wrongly, to insufficient rehearsal. Faults in the visual track can with more confidence be attributed to bad planning and bad workmanship. It goes without saying that directors of Strindberg's dream plays used the kind of lighting—we might call it cliché chiaroscuro—against which I have several times written. (Whatever is shadowy and unclear is art.) Now, whatever may be said of the appropriateness of the Appia-Mielziner lighting to some plays, to Strindberg's it is appropriate only in corresponding very closely to the dubious side of his mentality. Strindberg would no doubt have approved of it. But to my mind he resembles Wagner in that he needs to be freed from his own ideas of décor, which are bound up with the provincial pictorial art of his time. What could the sudden appearance of Böcklin's *Isle of the Dead* do for *The Ghost Sonata* (Strindberg recommends projecting it on the back wall) except to deliver the *coup de grâce*?

The assumption that whatever is shadowy and unclear in art is a product of the general revolt against realism in modern French theater. (Reality is not art, therefore unreality *is*.) In his dream plays Strindberg was himself in revolt against realism, yet he could not escape from what seems to be a law: that realism is a decisive element even in works not generally regarded as realistic, a point that has been proved with high reasonableness and enviable erudition by Erich Auerbach in one of the important scholarly books of recent years, *Mimesis*. Strindberg's ghosts, like Ibsen's, irrupt into a society that believes itself quite unghostly. That is the point. That is why you need on stage solid tokens of that would-be solid society: the house with all its Victorian furniture is a presence of the utmost importance. An ironical presence—because while its solidity makes it the symbol of bourgeois unghostliness, it is itself something of a ghost—the past living on in the present. The irony is completely missed if, as in the Paris production of *The Ghost Sonata,* the corporeal reality of the house is brought into question and instead of an actual room we see various ghostly properties veiled in the kind of lighting—or unlighting—referred to above.

On the further successes and failures of the French "theater of cruelty," I speak elsewhere.[1] Suffice it here that its revival of Strindberg has met with only moderate success. Despite the renewed cur-

---

[1] [See Bentley, *In Search of Theater,* Pt. II, Chap. 7, and Pt. V, Chap. 1.]

rency of his name, Strindberg remains a stumbling-block to producers, as much in France as in America. What about Germany? It has been a matter of some interest to observe what would be the fate of those moderns who made such a reputation there twenty or thirty years ago, suffered a partial or total eclipse under Hitler, and are now again in the running. Up to the present the evidence seems to be that the years have treated the expressionist very roughly indeed. Wedekind rather less so, Sternheim not roughly at all. Strindberg, as suits his nature, remains an ambiguous figure. In France he can still come forward as *avant-garde* in the worst sense; in Salzburg he can come forward as in the worst sense conservative. I saw *Easter* there— not at the summer festival but before the local citizenry in the Stadt-theater. The impression given was one of religious *kitsch*. Mention religion and your audience of solid citizens will put up with non-sense to an infinite extent. It is hard for a playwright to induce awe by any honest means, but by mentioning Jesus Christ he can do it in half a second. Such is the unearned awe of religious *kitsch*. Not all Christian theology, it seemed, nor even Haydn's music, which Strind-berg orders his musicians to play, could save this play from bathos.

In Berlin I saw *Comrades* and reported [2] that what once seemed a savage account of family relations made pleasant entertainment in a city that had recently suffered violence so much worse than any Strindberg dreamed of. When the roof is blown off your house, you can look back with nostalgic amusement to the squabbles you used to have beneath it. Some people condemned *Comrades* as untimely, fatally "dated." My impression was, rather, that it benefited greatly from a change of air. The comedy in the play was disengaged. The incubus of the Unhappy-Genius-and-his-encounter-with-the-Woman-Question receded. There are many Strindbergs. Two of them—the Strindberg of the family-quarrel plays and the Strindberg of the re-ligious dream plays—have been more famous than the others. Will they continue to be so? From my reading, I have often thought what a lot there is to be said for the history plays, which are seldom seen anywhere but in Sweden. From my recent theater-going I should recommend the comic Strindberg (*Comrades*) and, even more cor-dially, the folk poet. For by all odds the most beautiful and satisfying Strindberg production I have ever seen is that of *The Bridal Crown* in Vienna.

When I first read Strindberg, I wanted unconditionally to see him staged. I would now be interested in seeing a Strindberg production only if a number of very exacting conditions were met. Strindberg is

---

[2] [See Bentley, *In Search of Theater*, Pt. I, Chap. 5.]

difficult. He is difficult in that he is great, and he is difficult in that he is not supremely great but in part a victim of a confused and confusing age. This means that a director has to approach him with the respect that is due to genius, has to be loyal to him, modestly subject to his will, and yet at the same time has to deal with his faults, thus assuming, undeniably, an attitude of superiority. It is not the duty of a director to reproduce a playwright's faults. Direction is not scholarship. Its task is not to show Strindberg's faults, but to make the best of him. In principle, a director has the right to adapt any work except a masterpiece. (In practice, one hesitates to make this admission because so few directors are worthy of the responsibility. Even if a play is imperfect, does Director X have the talent or the taste to perfect it? One must fight the present-day tendency of everybody to think he knows better than everybody else.)

The Bridal Crown is not a play that can be put across "as it stands." It demands a director who will comprehend it as poetry, stagecraft, and philosophy. Since there are unstageable things in it, it demands adaptation too. One scene calls for a fight between people sailing in two separate boats. Another takes place on the ice, which divides and later joins together again. Experience with *Peer Gynt* indicates that to the degree that you try to present the spectacle indicated in such texts you overwhelm the drama; you turn it into a Night Out. In even writing these stage directions—which are no stage directions— the poet has jumped the banks of his medium; the director must bring him back within them. Berthold Viertel, the director, took the liberty of streamlining the latter part of his script, a process justified also by the tenuous human content. For *The Bridal Crown* is another play in which Strindberg uses Jesus as the *deus ex machina*. The device, used without irony, is too facile. Such "solution by religion" could carry conviction (at least to Christians) if believing and repenting and atoning were shown as *processes* involving conflict, as they can be in a novel. But when they are thrown at the audience as *faits accomplis*, as they tend to be in a play, they are invalid.

The Bridal Crown is the story of a girl who kills her illegitimate child in order that she may pretend to be a virgin bride. Although Strindberg imposes a doctrinaire ending, his presentation of the situation itself is brilliant and original. It consists in a very precisely measured mingling of realistic and fantastic elements. The realities are touched with fantasy, the fantasies are rooted in reality. Hence the director's second great problem. Let him push the play, or let it slide too far in one direction or the other, and it will lose its precarious balance, its fine tensions, its poetic and ironical juxtapositions. A naturalist drama is here, a *Rosa Bernd;* a symbolist drama too *à la* Maeterlinck; but they are Scylla and Charybdis for the director.

Berthold Viertel showed himself the ideal director of the play. His streamlining was discreet, his balancing of realism and fantasy as nice as could be imagined. The production had everything that the Paris production of the fantasies lacked; every image was carefully adjusted, the lights were used to illuminate, not to conceal, the timing was exact and meaningful down to the smallest sigh and smile. The mistiness in which the text might tempt the director to leave the play had been cleared up. If a supernatural Waterman has to sing from the water in the mill-race, he appears quite simply and we see him and he sings. No fuss. No hocus-pocus. Once properly staged, the figures of Strindberg's fancy have an admirable concreteness. As to the figures who are more grimly and realistically conceived, they too are seen with a peculiar luminosity of vision. The girl's family and the boy's are at odds. We see them in their family councils. In Viertel's production each man was a portrait, and the group was more than the sum of each. This is all a matter of work and attention to detail, if you wish. Blessed are those who work and give attention to detail!

Whenever a piece of theater has been particularly delightful, producing the exhilaration that the theater-goer is always seeking and seldom finding, one is hard put to explain to anyone who wasn't there why the evening was superior to all the others. Criticism cannot hope to recreate the object of criticism and should not try. But it can try to disengage some of its special qualities. The special quality of Viertel's mind and art is genuine sensibility. It is curious that while certain Viennese critics discussed him as a Left-wing director with social intentions, what Viertel's work preeminently shows is the quality Left-wing directors have scorned or ignored: finer feeling, personal feeling. Elia Kazan is much more in the tradition of the Left in this respect: he has a sense of the kind of feeling people are *supposed* to feel, the kind that is "dramatic," the kind that is "socially significant," of all the kinds of feeling (the two or three) that go to make up Broadway wit and Hollywood moralism. These are all surrogates for *human* feeling. The revolutionary act is to go back and find the real thing, unhurriedly, without fanfare.

There has been a lot of talk of Stanislavsky of late among people who are worlds away from him temperamentally, humanly. Viertel's fresh, direct, and delicate humanity, his patient thoroughness in preparing his productions, his realism, which can render all the transitions between sweet and bitter, are closer to the Russian master in spirit than anything else I have come across.

In *The Bridal Crown* Viertel was assisted by a crowd of gifted people and outstandingly by his leading actress, Käthe Gold, and his stage designer—one of the two or three best designers in Europe today—Teo Otto. I would not say that Miss Gold departed from the text, but she used some hints in it for all they were worth. The girl in a folk play is easily seen as insipid and merely pathetic, and pathos is an emotion that is intolerable unmixed. Miss Gold followed out Strindberg's intimations that Kersti is a sturdy peasant, mettlesome and proud, and she put all her amazing technique—her mastery of swift movement, sudden turns, change of tone—at the service of the idea.

Otto found settings that were perfectly in harmony with Viertel's reading of the play. He too must have found it hard to think freshly about material so steeped in unfortunate associations—naturalist or symbolic. I can imagine a *Bridal Crown* ruined by "grim reality" on the one hand or on the other by the cute and by now commercialized fantasy of children's books, Christmas cards, and Disney films. Otto used the handsome realism that he had formerly applied to plays by Brecht and other moderns—that is, not a piece-by-piece reproduction of real rooms and houses, but a selection from reality, and a selection that, so far as it goes, is solid and real and, so far as is plausible and feasible, beautiful.[3] Thus in *The Bridal Crown* we see the timber of the Swedish interiors, the flowers on the windowsill, the northern sunlight. Where the real thing—such as a waterfall—cannot be offered without fuss, the substitute—a sheaf of luminous cords pulled tight like bowstrings—does the job and looks well into the bargain. Otto's designs remind us that folk and fairy plays echo a people's zest in living and joy in nature and are not, even by anticipation, propaganda for Holy Year.

It may be that I preferred *The Bridal Crown* to other Strindberg plays in Europe last year because it was so much better produced. But this may not be the only reason. I have stated some misgivings about the "European Strindberg" of the problem plays. May not the "European Strindberg" be in the end a more provincial figure than the Swedish Strindberg? The paradox would be by no means unprecedented. A man's imagination is not more likely to be fed by general problems rather abstractly considered or even by his unhappy marriages than it is by his home, his people, and his people's history—their sins, their pleasures, and their myths. Some recent critics of *The Father* declared themselves tired of Strindberg's obsession with one point. I am tired of the critics' obsession with one Strindberg.

[3] [See also Bentley, *In Search of Theater*, Pt. II, Chap. 3; and plate 6.]

PART THREE

Some Major Plays

Miss Julie

by Martin Lamm

. . . The French translation of *The Father* had brought [Strindberg] in touch with Zola. Zola received a copy of the play in manuscript and praised it in a letter [to Strindberg] that was used as preface to the French edition. Following its publication, the manager of the Théâtre Libre—the theater started by André Antoine with Zola's blessing—accepted *The Father* for production. As a result, Strindberg now dreamed of completing the naturalistic reform of drama. During the summer of 1888, while living in Denmark, where he had moved in November of the previous year, Strindberg wrote *Miss Julie* and *Creditors* for the Théâtre Libre. On August 10 he sent the manuscript of *Miss Julie* to his Swedish publisher Bonnier. In his covering letter he said, "With the enclosed I presume to offer you the first naturalistic tragedy in Swedish, and I beg you not to refuse it thoughtlessly lest you regret it later. For, as the Germans say, 'Ceci datera'—this play will be recorded in the annals."

This time Strindberg's dreams of greatness were to come true, and his pride in *Miss Julie* was not misplaced. The play is one of the easily counted Swedish works that mark an epoch in world literary history. As time passes, we see more and more clearly that it is the masterpiece of naturalistic drama. . . .

Zola's theories of drama, found in the prefaces to his own plays and, later, in a number of volumes of collected articles and theater reviews (the most important of which is "Le naturalisme au théâtre," 1880), may be regarded as direct applications to drama of his program for the experimental novel. And most of Zola's own plays are dramatizations of his novels. With his ponderous talent for epic, Zola really lacked every gift of the dramatist, and his discourses on drama often witness to a striking lack of understanding both of the requirements of the stage and of the significance of drama as art. Nevertheless, it

"Miss Julie" by Martin Lamm. From *Strindbergs dramer* (Stockholm: Albert Bonniers Förlag, 1924), vol. 1, pp. 301–30. Copyright © 1924 by Martin Lamm. Translated and abridged by Otto Reinert. Used by permission of Albert Bonniers Förlag AB.

could be argued that his concept of drama has been of greater importance to the development of modern drama than his concept of the novel has been to the development of the modern novel. This is partly because the drama of his time was in much greater need of change than the novel and partly because the physical stage so easily lends itself to naturalistic illusionism. With increasing thoroughness, Zola's followers carried out his idea that the stage is a room and the proscenium arch an imagined fourth wall, until in time it was superseded by new fashions. . . .

With his extremely simple view of art, Zola thought of plays as having exactly the same function as novels: that is, to further scientific inquiry through physiopsychological experiments that could contribute to the establishment of "natural laws," by which he primarily meant the laws of heredity and environment. To serve this end drama must obviously abstain from every form of tendentiousness and propaganda, just as physical science must consider all the evidence and not only that which will support a preconceived hypothesis. Drama, moreover, should dispense with what Zola called "fable," by which he meant ingenious intrigue, and instead present a raw slice of reality and allow people on stage to appear and behave exactly as they would in real life. . . .

[But Zola also] accepted the unities of French neoclassicism, because they could further the stage illusion of reality. . . . His successors in the Théâtre Libre group went even further than he in actual practice: in the name of verisimilitude they observed all the three unities. To get around the difficulties imposed by the demand that the action on stage occupy no more time than the same action would in real life, they eliminated curtain falls within the play, and one-act plays became the common form of the drama of pronounced naturalism. In *Miss Julie* and *Creditors* Strindberg has already begun to move in the same direction. In his next plays he goes even further. On the model of the Théâtre Libre he compresses his action to a single, brief, powerful scene of the kind known in France as a *quart-d'heure*. Obviously, the degree of dramatic concentration necessitated by observing the unities is not easily reconciled with the demand for smooth naturalness in action and dialogue, and the drawbacks of the technique are apparent in Strindberg's later plays.

In choice of subject, *Miss Julie* perfectly answers to Zola's intentions. Strindberg says in his Preface that he took the story from real life, "as it was told me some years ago, when it made a great impression on me." . . . It is the kind of sensational story we might read in a tabloid. A couple of external events accelerate the action: the entry of the dancing peasants forces Miss Julie and Jean to hide in his room, and the Count's return, signalled by the bell, precipitates Julie's suicide. But we may well feel that both seduction and suicide would have taken place without these accidental events.

In other parts of the play we discern remnants of Ibsenite plot-making. In the opening scene Kristin cooks a mess of food for Julie's bitch Diana and tells Jean about Julie's annoyance with Diana for sneaking out for a mesalliance with the gatekeeper's pug. Clearly, we have here something like a symbolic prelude to the main action about Miss Julie's own sexual misstep. When Kristin learns about the latter, she reminds her mistress that she had been proud enough to want to have Diana shot. The episode with the greenfinch near the end is another illustration of Ibsen's method of symbolically anticipating realistic action. Julie wants to take the bird with her when she elopes, to keep it from falling into the hands of strangers. When Jean kills it, she goes into a state of virtual shock. She feels only disgust for her lover: "Kill me too! Kill me! You who can butcher an innocent creature without so much as a quiver!" The little episode has some resemblance to Ibsen's use of the wild duck motif, and Geijerstam may be said to have had a point when he observed in a letter to Strindberg that it would have been much simpler to open the window and let the bird fly.

But aside from these rudimentary remnants of symbolism à la Ibsen, the plot of the play is exceedingly simple and strictly observes the three unities. Since there are no act divisions, represented time and actual theater time coincide exactly. The cast is reduced to three people. When Strindberg wrote in a letter he sent to Seligmann[1] with the manuscript of *Creditors* that in *Miss Julie* he had made "a compromise with romanticism and stage decor," he probably had in mind his excessive emphasis in the stage directions and in the Preface on the kitchen furnishings, the peasant ballet, and the light from the rising sun flooding the kitchen in the final scene. Almost certainly, he got the idea for the last from the curtain scene in Ibsen's *Ghosts,* where also the bright sunshine outside contrasts sharply with the desperate mood inside. In his first reference to *Creditors,* in a letter to Bonnier of August 21, 1888, Strindberg says that his new play is "even better than *Miss Julie,* with three characters, one table, two chairs, and no sunrise."

In naturalistic simplification this represents a step beyond *Miss Julie.* Strindberg's commitment to French neoclassicism is both more delib-

[1] [Seligmann was the Swedish publisher who accepted *Miss Julie* after Bonnier had refused it. However, he made his acceptance conditional on certain changes being made in the text. Strindberg agreed but apparently failed to look closely at the proposed changes, for when he saw the printed version he objected to the publisher's "stupid and impudent collaborations." But he never got around to restoring the original text, and as a result standard editions and stage productions of *Miss Julie* still include Seligmann's "improvements."]

erate and more absolute than Zola's. In his article on modern drama
["On Modern Drama and Modern Theater," 1889] Strindberg praises
Racine's and Corneille's psychological analyses in contrast to the excess of external action and the chaos of characters in romantic drama.
He says of Molière that with him "French drama reached a point at
which all theatrical paraphernalia had been dropped and the changing life of the soul had become the main thing to such an extent that
the splendid vivisection of Tartuffe takes place on a bare floor with two
stools." As early as a year before he wrote *Miss Julie* he noted this
correspondence between the psychological drama of neoclassicism and
the theatrical program of naturalism. He finds fault with Zola's later
plays for not attempting this grand simplicity but stressing instead ex-
ternals and composite effects.

Thus, *Miss Julie*—as Strindberg never tires of assuring us in the
Preface—deals with a "case," and an unusual one at that. Strindberg
intends his case to prove a natural law: . . . Darwin's thesis about the
survival of the fittest. So far, this is orthodox Zolaism, but Strindberg
allows much more room for psychological motivation than does Zola.
He says in the Preface that he does not want to proceed on the basis
of "physiology alone"—an approach which the story to some extent
invites. This is noteworthy, because it suggests that Strindberg had
already come under the influence of the reaction against Zola's exclusively physiological concept of human behavior which had begun to
find expression in France by the mid-1880s and to which Strindberg
soon was to declare himself a sworn adherent. His remarks in the
Preface on characterization and psychological motivation in *Miss Julie*
show him to be a disciple of the founder of modern psychology, Ribot,
whose pronouncements in *Les maladies de la personnalité* appear,
slightly changed, in the Preface and which have, needless to say, influenced the play itself.

Ribot objects to "metaphysical psychology," which conceives of the
human personality as resting on some "basic" trait. In contrast, "naturalistic psychology" assumes that the human psyche is an unpredictable
complex and not at all analogous to an automaton.

Strindberg reflects this view when he says [in the Preface to *Miss
Julie*] that the word "character" originally denoted "the dominant and
basic trait in the soul complex," but then became the middle-class term
for the human automaton. He announces his disbelief in "simple stage
characters" of the kind he finds in older drama, even in Molière, and
whose psychic life can be expressed in a single word, like "jealous,"
"stupid," or "brutal"—characters who are "fixed and finished" from
the moment they enter and who demonstrate their individuality

through some bodily defect or mannerism or through the incessant repetition of some catch phrase. . . .

Influenced by Georg Brandes's analyses of Shakespeare, Strindberg, as early as in *Master Olof* [1872], had turned away from the usual method of characterization that stresses only that side of the character that is necessary to the plot, and had already acquired a sense for telling little details. In *Miss Julie* he is still inspired by the same distaste for schematizing the psychological action in a formula, but now he goes much further. He wants not just to disclose all the small traits locked in mutual battle in the human soul but also to account for their presence in terms of the influence of heredity, environment, and "the age." For him, just as for Taine, human personalities are products of natural laws.

The task Strindberg set himself is obviously impossible, and one might have expected the characters in *Miss Julie* to be less like ordinary human beings than like Doctors of Psychology forever analyzing their own and other people's psyches.

One major reason why that is not the case is obviously that Strindberg failed to be as strictly scientific as he intended. Another reason is that this way of describing people was exactly suited to his own temperament. He never had been and was never to become a spontaneous creator of character in the grand manner. This was because he had no intuitive sense of "the basic trait" or "ruling passion" in human character and lacked the ability to perform the imaginative psychological synthesis that is required for that kind of character-making. Substantial, integrated people are conspicuously absent from his world. What he did possess, and that to an exceptionally high degree, was the analyst's skill in distinguishing among different aspects of an individual personality and the ability to observe revealing little details of behavior, to describe human beings as changing and developing, and to render their mutual relationships. He was particularly successful with those disharmonious, fractured natures whom he identified with his own. He needed models as starting points, but he succeeded best when he was not too closely tied—as he often was—to the particulars of personality and circumstance in his models, but was free to use them only as points of departure for shaping the psychological action imaginatively.

This was exactly the case with *Miss Julie*. Scholars have pointed out the details in the play that show that Strindberg based the contrast between the plebeian Jean and the Count's daughter on the difference in social background between himself, "the Maidservant's Son," and his aristocratic wife. . . . His first description of the Baroness [Siri von

Essen] in *A Madman's Defense* strikingly anticipates Miss Julie of the opening scenes: "now charming and kind, now unapproachable; alternately frank and vivacious and reserved, cold, and distant." Through just such sudden changes in mood Julie both excites and controls Jean. Similarly, Strindberg modeled Jean on himself. His violently brutal cynicisms seem much more like Strindberg's own than like the language of a count's valet, who certainly would have learned to purge and restrain his speech. Jean's fussiness with food, which Kristin complains about, was a fault that Strindberg himself admitted to.

. . . [But] there is no question here, as there is in *Comrades* and *Creditors,* of direct autobiography or faithful portraits of real-life models. The situation in the play has no counterpart in his own life, and the speeches are not borrowed from his and Siri's unhappy marital dialogues. The drama has gained a great deal in artistic value because of Strindberg's objectivity. He has felt free vis-à-vis his models, it has been easier for him to be fair in dividing sympathy between them, and he has not felt constrained by the scrupulous verisimilitude which actually ruins the illusionistic effect of several of his other naturalistic plays.

Miss Julie is in all essentials a fictitious figure and as such one of Strindberg's most compelling. He has done what he set out to do: to depict a "characterless character" without simplification but also without losing a sense of its whole. . . .

Jean is a very rich and vital character, rendered with a superb sense of grotesque humor, but as we listen to his speeches we don't have the same feeling [as with Julie] of confronting a psychological problem. Social climbing is his chief characteristic, and it is difficult to take his lyrical and elegiac effusions as anything more than conscious or unconscious dissembling. . . .

Kristin, of course, is nothing but a type, but she is a splendid type, who in her sullenness, her occupationally determined world of feeling, her pitiless piety and churchiness, and her innate respect for class distinctions as insuperable illustrates a whole side of the Swedish national character. . . .

Given the limited cast and the stripped plot of *Miss Julie,* Strindberg had to resort to artifice in order to be able to suggest something of the etiology of souls. The introductory scene between Jean and Kristin throws brilliant light on Julie's and Jean's characters before they appear together on stage—Jean revealing his natural vulgarity and his taste for extravagant upper-class manners while he and his fiancée gossip about the "crazy" Miss Julie and all her ways. But in order to give us the conditioning past Strindberg has to let Jean tell Julie the story of his childhood in the first part of the play and, after the seduction to some extent has levelled their class differences, to let Julie feel compelled to tell him hers. . . . Although Jean warns her not to reveal her secrets, she starts telling him about her upbringing and about her parents' eccentricities and the relationship between them. It must be admitted that the reader wishes she had taken Jean's advice, for these confidences are so improbably clear-sighted that they seem to be addressed to the audience rather than to her partner. They are Strindberg's concession to the naturalist's ideal: the "scientific attitude" that explains human behavior in terms of heredity and environment. But they are also part of the purpose announced in the Preface of making the motivation complex and the viewpoint multiple. . . .

[Strindberg's] reasoning suffers from the same logical fallacy that vitiates Zola's program for the "experimental" novel—viz., the tacit assumption that the fictional world is ruled by the same laws that rule in real life. The spectator cannot possibly keep the whole chain of causality in mind during a performance, even if he arrived at the theater having just read everything Strindberg has written about the causes for Julie's actions. Causality is something else in literature than in life.

This does not mean that Strindberg's loyalty to naturalistic theory has flawed his play. Quite the opposite: it has served to rid it of the excessively rigid motivational patterns that characterized drama before Strindberg, particularly Ibsen's. If the spectator has no obligation to reckon with motives that are not suggested or are not even discernible in the play, neither does he, on the other hand, need to get a logical motivation for everything that *does* happen. Shakespeare's kind of drama gives the playwright much more freedom of plot and characterization than Ibsen's. In extending the causal chain beyond what can be apprehended by an audience, Strindberg has happily achieved a result quite opposite to the one he intended.

Miss Julie is acting under the influence of the various factors that Strindberg considers relevant. Her acts are impulsive, so that often a later action cancels an earlier one. Torn between his selfish plans and the intermittent blaze of his passion for Julie, Jean, too, acts without a steady purpose. There is room left for pure chance, which Strindberg, interestingly enough, lists among the determinants of a dramatic action.

The degree of novelty in Strindberg's method is best measured by the objections which contemporary critics, used to Ibsen's dramaturgy, made to the deficient motivation in *Miss Julie*. They particularly found Julie's suicide improbable because her "fall" has not yet irretrievably compromised her and because she cannot possibly know already that it will have consequences. In the Preface Strindberg says that Miss Julie would have killed herself even if her father had not held her accountable for her lapse, because she has an inborn sense of honor and cannot live without self-respect. But the play itself rather leaves us with the impression that her suicide is not the result of clear deliberation but of a moment of fortuitous hysteria. . . .

The instability of characters who are acting under a multiplicity of motives turns the extremely simple action into something rich and suspenseful, leaving room for unexpected resolutions. And Strindberg's dialogue adds further nuances. Here, too, he had good reasons for regarding himself as an innovator, even if his new manner in dialogue also takes a turn different from what he had intended. He tells us in the Preface that he has deviated somewhat from conventional dramatic dialogue,

> inasmuch as I have not made my characters ask silly questions in order to elicit witty replies. I have avoided the symmetrical and mathematical manner of the artificial French dialogue and allowed the brains to work spontaneously, without rules, as they do in actual life, where no topic is ever fully exhausted because one turning brain offers the other a random cog to catch. That is why my dialogue rambles, providing itself with a subject in an early scene for elaboration later, picking it up, repeating it, expanding it, adding to it, just like a motif in a musical composition.

I have already suggested that Strindberg's dialogue is actually not so "artlessly improvised" as he claims. On the contrary, it often drives the flashing exchanges to sharp crescendoes. Strindberg was too much of an artist and too impatient to adapt to his uses the extemporaneous chatter of everyday conversation that Zola prescribed and which playwrights like Granville-Barker and Chekhov carried to extremes. But Zola's attacks on the older style of French dialogue taught Strindberg how to conceal the dialectical skeleton in stage conversations. There are very few superfluous speeches in *Miss Julie,* and the random aimlessness of the dialogue is more apparent than real. But it is true that Strindberg's dialogue works much more often through suggestiveness than does that of his predecessors. The characters often talk about one thing, intoxicating themselves on their own phrases, while it is clear to us that their thoughts are on something else. Much more than Ibsen's, Strindberg's dialogue reveals the unconscious and unpremeditated levels of the mind.

. . . [For example,] throughout [the last scene] the audience is quite aware of the discrepancy between word and thought in both speakers —more aware than the speakers themselves. While Jean lulls himself with dreams of the future, he is also thinking of how to get rid of Miss Julie without losing his job. Julie begs him to tell her he loves her, hardly because *she* loves *him*, but because she needs to believe that what she surrendered to was love and not to a moment of sudden desire for a man she neither loves nor respects. That is why the spectator is hardly surprised when after a score of speeches the two begin to trade coarse insults. . . .

We have here all the new features that Strindberg wanted in dramatic dialogue: minds are working without "rules," and the speaker is therefore only half conscious of the contrast between what he says and what he thinks. The same topics recur, often in the same words, but with new psychological import. There is a deliberate technique behind this way of carrying on dialogue, but the design is masterly and charged with drama.

Structurally, *Miss Julie* divides into two distinct parts, linked by the interlude with the dancing peasants—a rather feeble substitute for a curtain fall. In productions abroad there is usually an intermission at this point, but both parts are crescendoes rising to catastrophe: the first to the seduction, the second to the suicide.

The first part is remarkably brief, just half the length of the second. This may seem surprising, for one would have thought that the playwright needed more time to establish the likelihood of Julie's fall. Actually, of course, it is clear that Strindberg is trying to create the impression that it is the result of surprise and accident, and the fast pace is therefore a necessity. Strindberg gains his effect by eliminating all passages of exposition in the strict sense. Jean's opening words, "Miss Julie's crazy again tonight, absolutely crazy," takes us to the heart of the situation, which is then quickly explained by Kristin's and Jean's gossip about Julie in an exchange which also reveals Jean's real nature. In the first part of the play, Jean is really the more attractive of the two main characters. He responds with proper restraint to Julie's advances and warns her again and again not to commit any indiscretion. And Julie is not yet a very likeable character. She is provokingly seductive, at the same time arrogant and cheap. There is a quality of unwholesome eroticism about her, and we keep recalling what Jean has said about her mother: that she wore dirty cuffs but had to have cufflinks with coronets on them.

But in the second part of the play our sympathies shift and Miss Julie becomes clearly the main character. This part seems to me to be artistically far superior to the earlier part. Julie's flux of feeling is described with poignant pathos—from her complete numbness of soul after the seduction to her fearful discovery that the man she has given herself to is mean and petty. Her lingering sensual desires pull her in one direction; her growing disgust with Jean—a disgust that manifests itself in frenzied outbursts of hatred of all men—in another. Strindberg, obviously, intends her disgust to make a polemical point, but it is not really psychologically implausible. . . .

. . . There are both magnificent poetic fantasy and implacable naturalistic causality in the final scene of *Miss Julie*, and, unlike some of Strindberg's other play endings, it makes no concessions to sentimentality. It is obviously because of Strindberg's close allegiance to the naturalistic program that *Miss Julie*, unlike his previous play, *The Father*, and his next, *Creditors*, lacks a moral thesis. "The naturalist has abolished God with guilt" are Strindberg's own words in the Preface, and the play has few traces of his usual misogyny. It is apparent only in his attempt to attribute Julie's tragedy to her upbringing as a man-woman. His play is meant to prove a general law of nature, just like Zola's novel cycle about the Rougon-Macquart family. A modern reader is likely to find the meaning of *Miss Julie* in the demonstration that basic differences in upbringing and social position cannot be reconciled, even temporarily, and Strindberg himself seems to have had this theme in mind. He says in the Preface that love in any higher sense is impossible between two persons so different. But he also wanted his play to be an example of the adaptation to social conditions of Darwin's doctrine concerning the survival of the fittest and the destruction of the weak in the struggle for existence. Miss Julie, the descendant of a decadent noble family, goes under, while Jean, with healthy proletarian blood in his veins and a robust appetite for life, is a "race-builder," the progenitor of a new social species. He is the winner of the contest, says Strindberg, and will probably end his days as hotel owner. And even if he may never realize his dream of becoming a Romanian count, his son will probably go to the university and end up as a county executive. This is what Strindberg in the Preface refers to as the problem of "rising and falling" and which, in a rather simple-minded way, he suggests in the scene where Julie and Jean tell one another their recurrent dreams: hers, that she has climbed a pillar and wants to get down; his, that he is lying under a tall tree and wants to climb to the top.

In the Preface Strindberg tries to convince himself that he watches this development with pleasure. The fall of one family marks the rising fortunes of another, and this is a good thing. "When we have become as strong as the original French revolutionaries it will do us good to see the forest cleared of old, rotting trees that have stood too long in the way of others with equal right to a time in the sun—as much good as watching the death of someone incurably ill."

If our response to the ending of the play is rather less joyous than this, it is because Strindberg, his professed objectivity notwithstanding, has conceived of Miss Julie's destiny tragically. She is the refined aristocrat who succumbs in the struggle with the coarse proletarian Jean. For the fact of the matter was that Strindberg's Darwinism had already for some time clashed with his growing antidemocratic sentiments and his cult of the superman.

Strindberg was always anxious to assert that the latter was a fully developed attitude in him before he had even heard of Nietzsche, and he seems to be right. He first picked up the superman idea when he met [Verner von] Heidenstam in Switzerland in May, 1886. From the account of their talk in the great hall at Brunegg, which Strindberg wrote a few months later and which he included in the conclusion to "The Author" [the fourth and final section of Son of a Servant], it is plain that Heidenstam, the aristocratic individualist, tried to convince Strindberg that the latter was neither a socialist nor lower-class. "As an established writer you are upper-class compared to me, an unknown. You belong to a new aristocracy of mind, which is on its way to a new House of Lords; I belong to the dying aristocracy of brawn, for we are dying, half killed by the aristocracy of wealth, which is already being challenged by the newest aristocracy, that of labor." It is clear that Heidenstam's words were vividly in Strindberg's mind when he wrote in the Preface to Miss Julie that his heroine is "a remnant of the old warrior aristocracy, which is now going down and giving place to a new aristocracy of nerve and brain." Since Strindberg as early as the 1870s had begun to move in the direction of an antidemocratic ideology, the germ which Heidenstam's words planted in his mind grew fast. Its growth was hastened by his visit to Germany, where militarism ruled; it was nurtured by his steadily growing hatred of "the pygmies," among whom be counted both socialists and women; and it came to full fruition and received its stamp of authority when in the summer of 1888 Georg Brandes put Nietzsche in his hands. He had probably read Nietzsche by the time he wrote Miss Julie. He mentions him in a letter to Heidenstam dated May 17, 1888, and in the Preface he acknowledges that Miss Julie was written under Nietzsche's influence.

But it must be said that the Preface is no clearer than his earlier comments on this issue. We might have expected Jean to be a powerful superman vis-à-vis the decadent Miss Julie, but both the Preface and particularly the play itself leave a different impression. Miss Julie is the exceptional individual, an aristocrat with sensitive nerves and delicate feelings, who strays among lower-class people who don't understand her and who besmirch her ideals with their rough and dirty hands, gloat over her defeat, and torture her to death. It is possible that Strindberg, when he began work on his play, felt more akin to Jean, the rising "race-builder," than to Julie. But as the play progressed he was drawn more and more to Julie, whose aristocratic hypersensitivity was so much like his own, and less and less to Jean, who represented the new aristocracy of robust nerves that was to succeed hers. The last step in this development is marked by *By the Open Sea* [1890], where Strindberg creates a superman in his own image. The hero of the novel, the fishing inspector Borg, is a genius, but he is a superman only by virtue of his gigantic intellect; physically he is small and frail, and psychologically he is a tense and excitable decadent with some of Strindberg's own susceptibility to changing emotions. His tragedy is his failure to maintain his superiority over the rabble without having the exquisite machinery of his mind picked to pieces by the crude population of fishermen among whom he lives. His fate is a little like Miss Julie's, and when in the last scene of the novel he sets sail for the open sea in a full storm he is sailing toward death just as surely as Miss Julie's walk from the kitchen to the barn with the razor in her hand is a walk toward death. Strindberg's otherwise often brutal superman cult is here softened by his conviction that the superman is a dying species and that the pygmies will inherit the earth.

Strindberg and the Danse Macabre

by Walter Johnson

While Strindberg remained as fascinated as ever by his own time after his Inferno years of 1894 to 1897, he became more intensely interested than ever before in the late Middle Ages as well. That two-fold interest helped lead to many developments, among them his creation of new dramatic techniques through (1) the extension of his superb realistic-naturalistic technical practices of the pre-Inferno period, (2) the transformation of medieval dramatic ideas and devices into techniques that became highly Strindbergian, and (3) the addition of modern technical elements that were essentially his own. All three matters, taken together, are frequently and loosely spoken of as expressionistic by most scholars and critics.

Strindberg's intensified post-Inferno interest in the Middle Ages stemmed both from his renewed interest in history and his so-called conversion. The latter led to increased attention to Biblical morality and religious faith and to a concern with the medieval mystery and morality plays throughout the post-Inferno years. It is significant that all the major historical plays except *Master Olof* were written after 1897; all of them are concerned in more ways than one with morality. It is equally significant that all his other post-Inferno plays are in technique or thought or both related in varying degrees to the medieval drama.

The three Damascus plays, for example, are to an appreciable extent, adaptations of the techniques of such morality plays as *Everyman*. *Advent* and *Easter,* to cite two more examples, are highly reminiscent of both the morality and mystery plays. Parallels to the medieval stress on life as a pilgrimage appear again and again in the post-Inferno plays, historical and nonhistorical. In all these plays there are, moreover, parallels to the Biblically inspired medieval concern with human nature, the relationship between the individual and what Strindberg calls the Eternal One, and the moral problems implicit in both. There is in addition to all this sort of thing Strindberg's amazing psychological insight into the tragic tensions within modern man and his uncanny ability to bring those tensions into tangible expression for the stage.

The companion plays, *The Dance of Death I* and *The Dance of Death II* (1901), received a name that is ultimately medieval in its implications, and they have in them such elements as an emphasis on death, the vampire motive, and the repetition of the pattern of life generation after generation, which were of decided concern to the Middle Ages. Yet the two plays are as modern and contemporary as any plays could be. Strindberg had the genius for taking what he needed by way of inspiration and detail and transforming what he received into something peculiarly his own and always subtly different from anything he had done before. What he did in *The Dance of Death* plays illustrates all this.

The story that Strindberg tells in *The Dance of Death I* is the story of a modern marital hell created by a frustrated army captain stationed on an island called Little Hell and by his equally frustrated ex-actress wife. The story he tells in *The Dance of Death II* is of the same captain, now retired and for the first time really free to go to work as a vampire. What the late Middle Ages had for Strindberg by way of inspiration and detail for the dramatization of these stories can easily be demonstrated.

Medieval Europeans had good reasons for being aware of death as something ugly, horrible, and gruesome. Plague, war, disease, disaster, and want provided constant visible evidence that the priests were quite right in insisting that not only was Death taking neighbors, friends, and relatives but might at any moment take the individual himself. Both the morality and the mystery plays were used, moreover, by the church to warn medieval people about their frequently frantic attempts to conceal the macabre realities from themselves by escaping into worldly pleasures.

Recorded on thousands of paintings (murals, frescoes, oils, and water colors), engravings, and woodcuts and in many sculptures, poems, sermons, and plays was the so-called Dance of Death or *danse macabre*. On or in these medieval works of art are stressed such macabre matters as the omnipotence of death, its usually unexpected and undesired coming to everyone, its disregard for both rank and position, and the ugly and horrifying details of dying. Death, generally represented as a skeletonlike personified figure in many of these works of art, is presented as ready to lead everyman, everywoman, and everychild into a rough equivalent of the long dance, which ends for each individual in his final collapse as he holds the hand of Death. The medieval dances of death that survive place the emphasis squarely on the grotesque and the horrible; they apparently were deliberately designed to serve as warnings to everyone that he had better prepare for the next life by changing his way of living through acceptance of the moral code of the church and through trying to live up to it. The church understandably enough took advantage of the medieval fear of death and the agony of dying by emphasizing, too, the transitory nature of human life and the terrifying consequences of sin—judgment day and eternal punishments in Hell. The priests did not mince words about the frailties of human nature and the presentation of both Purgatory and Hell as anything but figurative.

In the last of the Damascus plays, Strindberg promised never again to relate the story of his own suffering as he had been doing in surprisingly faithful fashion from the beginning of his literary career through the Damascus trilogy. He did not promise, however, not to direct his attention to other people's suffering or to the evil in other people's lives. In fact, with his newly reacquired faith in the moral nature of the universe, his suspicion that this life may be something like a dream state and not the *real* life, and his intensified interest in both good and evil, Strindberg naturally enough turned his attention to a family situation well known to him, found in it resemblances to the medieval dance of death, and composed in the companion plays two of the most effective dramas the modern theater possesses.

Strindberg's interpretation of the marriage is not primarily an objective case study in dramatic form; it is, instead, a deliberately distorted transformation of the source material to intensify the marital misery so that it will serve, figuratively, as a modern dance of death.

To understand what is at the core of the particular marital hell, one needs to recall that during the last fifteen years of his life Strindberg's plays deal to an appreciable degree with the problem of evil, its nature, its origins and causes, and its results. Perhaps no passage in all these plays throws more light on Strindberg's thinking about human nature and its potentials for evil than Indra's daughter's speech in *A Dream Play* (1901):

> All these are my children! Each one by himself is good, but they have only to get together to start quarreling and turn into demons.

That both Edgar and Alice in *The Dance of Death* have had potentials for personal and social good Strindberg suggests in abundant detail, but he makes it clear that they have become demons, whose inherent selfishness and egotism have never had real chances to be curbed or effectively controlled in an unhappy environment. Their whole marriage has been the nominal union of two constantly selfish and egotistic human animals. In their struggle for the freedom of their individual egos, they have become a devious vampire and a frustrated middle-aged coquette, whose only bond is an animallike sexual attraction for each other, whose tactics are those of the jungle, and whose days are, to paraphrase the title of a Strindbergian disciple's play stemming not a little from these companion plays, a "long day's journey into night." In that journey, neither one has been willing to accept the smallest degree of personal responsibility: instead they blind themselves through rationalizing. Nor does Strindberg feel that Edgar and Alice are exceptional:

> *Alice.* Is he a human being?
>
> *Kurt.* When you asked that question first, I answered no. Now I believe him to be the commonest kind of human being—the kind that possesses the earth. Perhaps, we, too, are of the same kind—making use of other people and of favorable opportunities?

Strindberg applies what he says about evil universally, and, through what Kurt suggests, provides a remedy—submission, resignation, and humanity, all of them in striking agreement with the implications of the medieval dances of death. For the worldly life that Edgar and Alice lead is, figuratively speaking, a dance which usually turns their thoughts from death and the true sadness of their days. It is significant that so many theater critics down through the years have found Edgar's solo dancing of a Hungarian dance to the accompaniment of Alice's playing of Halvorsen's *Entry of the Boyars* one of the high points in the stage productions of the first *Dance of Death.* The lively, enthusiastic dance performed in grotesque contrast to the deadly and boring environment serves as an effective parallel to the medieval dance in which the living try to escape from thoughts of their own mortality. Just as the medieval dance ends in certain death, the captain's dance ends with his own collapse.

In a much broader and figurative sense, the twenty-five years have been a dance of death. The story Strindberg has to tell by way of illustration of his major theme in *Dance of Death I* may be said to be a repetition of basic steps which promise to lead to something that will break the ghastly pattern, but each time the promise fails and the pattern begins again. The lives of these two have tended to turn their thoughts from both death and the sad reality of their days.

Yet they never quite succeed in rationalizing away either thoughts of death or awareness of the sadness of the reality completely. Against the dismal and symbolic background of their prisonlike home, these two have lived in "the most unreasoning hatred, without cause, without purpose . . . ," seemingly "without end." Except on rare occasions, they have tortured each other so effectively and thoroughly that Kurt can say with well-motivated justification:

But tell me: what is going on in this house? What's happening here? There's a smell as of poisonous wallpaper, and one feels sick the moment one comes in. I'd prefer to get away from here, had I not promised Alice to stay. There are dead bodies beneath the floor, and the place is so filled with hatred that one can hardly breathe.

That the two are undergoing tortures similar to those depicted in a Swedenborgian hell—and, for that matter, any kind of hell—is clear to anyone who will read the play with a little care. That they are aware of the nature of their reality even though they usually try to conceal it from themselves is clear enough. As Edgar says, "But all life is horrible." But, only when Edgar has been struck down by his heart attack, can he even approach the idea of assuming his partial responsibility for having created this living death:

Life seemed so peculiar—so contrary, so malignant—ever since my childhood—and people seemed so bad that I grew bad, too.

Strindberg's presentation of the reality of one marital hell is a macabre interpretation of tortured human beings, tortured not only by each other and others but by themselves.

In the midst of the nightmare that their life together is, they rarely succeed in eliminating thoughts of death. Alice is keenly aware of it, not as something that will strike her personally but as a two-fold thing: (1) her own release from the prison of her marriage to Edgar and (2) a weapon by means of which to torture Edgar. She is, for example, delighted by the signs of Edgar's aging—his failing eyesight, his increasing inability to enjoy his tobacco and whiskey, his illness. Edgar, on the other hand, tries to conceal as long as he can the significance of all these matters by insisting to Alice that he has never been seriously ill, that he will live for twenty years more, and that he will die like an old soldier—suddenly, painlessly. Yet his very insistence and occasional involuntary admissions reveal that he fears death and that he does not really believe that when it is over there is "Nothing left but what can be put on a wheelbarrow and spread on the garden beds." Strindberg traces with great but unobtrusive care Edgar's concern with death: the outward statements, the inner anguish, the heightened fears when it looks as if he is going to die, his grasping for straws then, and his renewed pretense when he recovers a little. There is, for Edgar, no resignation, no humility, no submission. He has become one of the living dead, figuratively, just as his marriage has been a living death.

But the first *Dance of Death* ends in a fashion decidedly parallel to another aspect of the medieval dance of death. Just as the *danse macabre* combines the gruesome and the grotesque with grim humor, Strindberg's first play ends with the grimly humorous scene of the two principals in the marital hell planning the celebration of their silver wedding:

> *Captain.* . . . Think how dull life is nowadays! In the old days a person struck, now one only shakes a fist!—I'm almost certain we'll celebrate our silver wedding in three months . . . with Kurt giving you away! . . . And the doctor and Gerda present . . . The ordnance officer will make the speech and the sergeant major lead the cheering! If I know the colonel, he'll invite himself! Yes, go ahead and laugh! Do you remember Adolf's silver wedding? . . . His wife had to wear her wedding ring on her right hand because the groom in a tender moment had chopped off the left ring finger with a knife. (*Alice holds her handkerchief to her mouth to keep from laughing.*) Are you crying?—No, I think you're laughing! Yes, we weep in part, and laugh in part! Which is more proper . . . don't ask me! . . . I read the other day in a paper that a man who had been divorced seven times, consequently married seven times . . . finally ran away when he was ninety-eight years old to remarry his first wife! That's love! . . . If life is serious or only a joke, I can't tell! When it's a joke, it can be most painful, and when it's serious, it's really pleasantest and calmest. . . . But when a person finally tries to be serious, someone comes along to play a joke on one! For example, Kurt! . . . Do you want a silver wedding? (*Alice silent*) say yes!—They'll laugh at us, but what difference does that make? We'll laugh, too, or be serious . . . whichever seems best!
>
> *Alice.* All right!
>
> *Captain (seriously).* We'll celebrate our silver wedding then! . . . (*Gets up*) Cross out, and go on!—So, let's go on!

II

The companion play takes place in a setting directly opposite to that of the first play. Instead of a home that is a prison, figuratively and literally, the setting is that of the beautiful quarters that Kurt has arranged for himself. They are cheerful, beautifully furnished, designed for pleasant living. The man who has provided himself with this home has achieved to a remarkable degree the submission, resignation, and humanity needed for living in a world where other people, too, have their being. It is a promising setting, threatened, however, by the implications of Strindberg's well-motivated reversal of themes.

In the first *Dance of Death*, the dominant theme is that of the marital hell, but one other important theme—Edgar as vampire—is introduced and appreciably developed. A third important theme—the repetition of a pattern of life in one generation after the other—is suggested.

In the second *Dance of Death*, the importance of the themes is reversed. The dominant theme is that of Edgar as the vampire, that of the repetition of patterns in following generations is developed, and the marital hell is reduced to a secondary theme. All three are important, however, and Strindberg again treats them in counterpoint to each other.

It is the vampire theme, however, that in the second *Dance of Death* primarily supplies the macabre elements. In the first play Strindberg makes clear what he means by vampire:

> *Kurt*. . . . for just now when he felt his life slipping away, he clung to mine, began to settle my affairs as if he wanted to creep into me and live my life.
>
> *Alice*. That's his vampire nature exactly . . . to seize hold of other people's lives, to suck interest out of other people's lives, to arrange and direct for others, when his own life has become absolutely without interest for him. And remember, Kurt, don't ever let him get hold of your family affairs, don't ever let him meet your friends, for he'll take them away from you and make them his own. . . . He's a magician at doing that! . . . If he meets your children, you'd soon see them on intimate terms with him, he'd advise them and bring them up according to his own whims, and above all against your wishes.

The Edgar who in the first play was in constant danger of discharge has now been retired and on the basis of a pension that cannot be revoked, he is free to go to work as his egotism directs. The tragic mortal afraid both of life and death in *The Dance of Death I* has become one of the exceptionally active living dead in *The Dance of Death II*. It is to his activities in the destruction or selfish use and manipulation of the genuinely alive that the second play is primarily devoted. Edgar thrives and flourishes through the theft of ideas, things, and people. The illustrations are many; the point is clear: even those who have resigned themselves to earthly life and have accepted the ideal of humane living are in constant danger of losing in the uneven struggle with the vampires. The implications are macabre indeed.

Note, for example, the development of the secondary theme of the repetition of the pattern of life in a following generation. Edgar's daughter, Judith, lovely to look at, endowed with potentialities for becoming not only her father's image but also for becoming a woman who can love as well as hate, is a major pawn by which Edgar manipulates and uses the whole community—the aging colonel would like to marry her, and Edgar as the prospective father-in-law of the person in somewhat remote control of Little Hell can use the colonel's name most conveniently and effectively to gain his ends. It is egotistic Judith, humanized by love, that gives the vampire the death blow, however.

When he is dealt that blow, Edgar in his self-deception says, with ironic intention, "Forgive them for they know not what they do."

In Strindbergian terms, everything repeats itself, even the good repeats itself. In his development of the relationship between Judith and Allan, Strindberg has not only indicated clearly the possibilities for evil, but has shown just as clearly the possibilities for good in human beings in association with each other.

In the second play's continuing but somewhat subdued battle between husband and wife appears the use of a technique that Strindberg himself mentions in an unpublished note:

> What if all [the characters] should talk in asides? And in so doing blurt out their real thoughts, which they have to conceal in the masquerade of life, have to conceal for the sake of bread and butter and social acceptance, because of wife and children.

It is true, of course, that Edgar and Alice usually say what they believe will benefit themselves selfishly, but it is also true that they frequently do say exactly what they think about each other, relatives, acquaintances, and neighbors. It is one of the remarkable facts about Strindberg's dialogue that it frequently becomes the blunt expression of inner thought, and not the measured conventional exchange of primarily controlled ideas or patter.

In spite of the fact that Strindberg supplied unsurpassed psychological motivations for this macabre tragedy and detailed analysis of character which penetrates even to the unconscious and the subconscious, the major emphasis is not placed on either the dramatic motivation or the construction of plot but on the intensity of the atmosphere of horror and comfortless isolation. Concentrating on one point—symbolized by the dance of death, Strindberg presents a nightmare in which life becomes an evil dream. The plays suggest that actual death may be something great and even majestic in its release from the horror of a living death on Little Hell.

However distressing the companion plays may have been for the easily identified primary models for Edgar, Alice, and Judith at the time the plays first appeared and were presented, they are, dramatically and theatrically, among the very best plays in modern drama. As far as I have been able to discover, the only production of them that has ever completely failed was a production in mutilated form on Broadway. Two Americans back in 1948 apparently rewrote the plays, condensed them into one, changed the setting to Hawaii, converted the characters into Americans, and called the play *The Last Dance*. It closed after seven nights. The plays as Strindberg wrote them can hardly fail to grip and to fascinate readers or theater audiences.

Shakespearean Elements in Historical Plays of Strindberg

by Birgitta Steene

The distinction that Clifford Leech has drawn between a history play as either "drama of document" or "drama of ritual" is a little confusing.[1] For when a drama is primarily a documentation of past events, then it has really moved out of the realm of drama and is merely history masquerading in pseudoartistic guise—as were the early English chronicle plays. Nor is the term "drama of ritual" a very happy one, implying as it does a tautology—drama of drama—since ritual and symbolic action, embodied by actors on a stage, is the very essence of all true drama and not something restricted to the good history play. What peculiar qualities give a drama its definite identity as "history"? Why should not Shakespeare's *Hamlet* or Strindberg's *The Outlaw* * be included among their authors' history plays? Is *Richard II* a "history" or a tragedy? What particular tendency in *Gustav Vasa* makes it seem less "history" than *The Saga of the Folkungs*, and *Erik XIV* hardly a history at all?

A remote setting and a treatment, in part, of historical rather than fictional characters are not enough to warrant a play the name of "history." Nor does a playwright's use of a particular historical source produce necessarily a history play. *Macbeth* is based on chronicle matter and *Lear* on a folk tale, but both are tragedies. Strindberg went to factual accounts for *Gustav II Adolf* but to popular legend for *The Saga of the Folkungs,* and yet both of them are in at least some respects "histories."

I suggest that, in order to justify the name of "history," a drama must

[1] See Irving Ribner, *The English History Play in the Age of Shakespeare* (Princeton, 1957), p. 101.

* [In the original article, the titles of Strindberg's works appear in Swedish. They have been translated throughout by the editor.]

fulfill four basic requirements: (1) it must have a definite politico-historical background and deal with a specified period in the past; (2) it must have epic scope both in plot and structure, which means for one thing that it needs a panoramic stage; (3) its conception of character should be horizontal rather than vertical—the protagonist should have width rather than depth, be a public figure rather than a private man; (4) it must embody the author's coherent historical purpose to give form and unity to a drama that would otherwise be mere confusion.

For such a drama to move outside the rather narrow orbit of local history, it must also express—like all serious art—the playwright's moral attitude towards his subject matter, an attitude which, if he is successful, will run parallel with but also transcend his historical purpose. Unlike the protagonist in tragedy, however, the personality of the protagonist in a "history" cannot be relied upon to convey this attitude; for an ideal "history" hero is more often than not unconsciously immoral. It is the peculiar distinction between tragedy and "history" that, in the former, the protagonist has a moral conscience—he doubts and questions his own values; in the latter, he has the function of the epic hero, a man of outward deed, in whom there is little discrepancy between thought and action—a man whose motto is expediency and commodity rather than truth and goodness, a man who seldom asks what is right or wrong but always "what works"? The "history" hero is the forerunner of the American pragmatist.

Shakespeare and Strindberg illustrate two solutions to the dilemma of the serious writer of historical drama who wants to express a moral purpose and yet support or demonstrate objectively a norm of political behavior which often uses unscrupulous and dishonest means. In Shakespeare, England or Respublica emerges as the true hero;[2] what the individual kings cannot represent is instead conveyed by an allegorical hero. In Strindberg's *The Saga of the Folkungs,* on the other hand, where the whole morality pattern is compressed into a single play, the history hero is an abstraction—an ideal concept of a king—expressed through indirection by criticism of the ruler.[3] And the king himself transcends his personal role as weak monarch to become a symbolic victim, sent by God to cleanse the crown and the country. Shakespeare's method leads to an epic morality pattern; Strindberg's leads to religious ritual.

Both Shakespeare and Strindberg saw history as a "mirror" of the

---

[2] E. M. W. Tillyard, *Shakespeare's History Plays* (New York, 1946), pp. 320–21.

[3] Strindberg makes it clear that this criticism is to be taken as objective judgment by letting the humble characters of the chorus express it very emphatically. Cf. also pp.[130–31], below.

present, which explains in part the abundance of anachronisms in their historical production. There was a time when critics accused Shakespeare of ignorance, and when Strindberg could not get his *Kristina* produced because it was too unhistorical. The interesting thing, however, is that, as historical dramatists, both writers were actually very conscientious students. We can safely assume that Shakespeare read his Holinshed and Hall, that he more than glanced at the *Mirror of Magistrates,* that he was not as ignorant of Machiavelli as Tillyard wants to make him, that he paid some attention to *Gorboduc, Tamburlaine,* and *Edward III* and worked his way through *The Troublesome Reign of King John.* And if Strindberg scornfully brushed aside the standard "high school" history books of his day—he was not such a traditionalist as Shakespeare—he made all the more thorough a study of Fryxell, Bäckström, and Afzelius *Sagohävder [Chronicles],* those gossipy versions of Sweden's royal past. The more scandalous the stories the more delighted he was, first because they could be put to good dramatic use but second and not least because this was a life he recognized, a true picture of human beings as he saw them.

Like all good dramatists, both Shakespeare and Strindberg used their sources as seemed most relevant to their artistic purposes. They altered old events, telescoped historical time, and changed biographical facts when this was demanded by dramatic expediency—although reluctantly at times. It took Strindberg seven years to overcome his scruples about recasting the unwieldy material for *Earl Birger* of *Bjälbo;* and Shakespeare asks pardon for historical omissions in the prologue to *Henry V,* Act V:

> Vouchsafe to those that have not read the story,
> That I may prompt them: and of such as have,
> I humbly pray them to admit the excuse
> Of time, of numbers and due course of things,
> Which cannot in their huge and proper life
> Be here presented.

> (Lines 1–6)

But they commonly depart boldly from their sources, often in order to reinforce a theme. Thus, the introduction of Knut Porse in *The Saga of the Folkungs*—the historical Porse had been dead for over twenty years—gives a new dimension to the love-and-intrigue theme. And Shakespeare's Henry V shows a mercy to the citizens of Harfleur that the historical Henry never did, a change that reinforces the main theme of the play, the emergence of the ideal king.

However, such manipulations to make Henry fit Shakespeare's adopted purpose as Elizabethan historian differ strikingly from

Strindberg's usual portrayal of royal characters. While Shakespeare presented glorified representatives of Tudor myth and the Elizabethan concept of de facto kingship, Strindberg rejected contemporary, unrealistic attitudes towards Swedish rulers of the past. In most of the plays following *The Saga of the Folkungs* his main objective seems to have been to portray his historical figures "realistically." Having decided that most of the Swedish kings had already apotheosized themselves, he did not hesitate to change Charles XII from the young warrior and hero king of popular belief to "the great criminal, the berserk fighter, the idol of rascals," to present Kristina as a compound of unsuccessful *femme fatale* and emancipated man-hating half-woman, and to let Erik XIV undergo a metamorphosis from romanticized lute-playing poet to a neurotic son of the *fin-de-siècle*. This tendency to a "realistic" rather than an "historical" (i.e., flat and largely unintimate) portrayal of characters was, as we shall see later, one reason for Strindberg's failure to realize fully his grand historical plan.

As in the case of Shakespeare, Strindberg's view of history was part of his *Weltanschauung*. After his "inferno crisis" in 1894 he rejected his earlier atheistic position and, via Swedenborg, Linnæus et al., came to accept a semimystical view of life controlled by "powers" or supernatural agents, in their nature and function not too different from ambiguous and fickle Fortune of the early Middle Ages—both capricious and providential, seemingly irrational, but ultimately instruments of a divine and purposeful will. Strindberg now rejected Buckle's evolutionary interpretation of history; history was no longer materialistic progress but the working out from generation to generation of a retributive justice. He planned to illustrate this in a series of history plays on themes ranging from Saint Erik to Gustav IV Adolf, unified through the concept of a providential will—with kings as figureheads, the struggle for the throne as the main theme, and the whole nation as the epic setting.

The conception behind Strindberg's plan was no doubt influenced by a cyclic reading of Shakespeare's histories as these plays appear in Hagberg's Swedish translation of 1847. But his historical design was even more grandiose and extensive than Shakespeare's. The cycle was to have covered almost 700 years; it is hardly surprising that it was never completed. The scope of his task and the expansion of his subject matter over so many royal families no doubt contributed to its collapse. His providential scheme was not always, as in Shakespeare, directly related to specified political motives. He was politically much more objective than Shakespeare and his plays therefore lacked unity of political interest. It is significant that the only part of his historical cycle with a scope and a completeness comparable to Shakespeare's is that which deals with the House of the Folkungs, where the controlling theme of retribution is partly fused with—and not as so often later superimposed on—the political action.

Not only did Strindberg's grand cyclic scheme collapse; even within the plays that were written we notice a peculiar process of disintegration. Strindberg's somewhat archaic providential reading of the past was incompatible with his innate tendency towards skepticism. His view of life was consistent and stable enough at the time he wrote the first history play within the cycle, *The Saga of the Folkungs*; gradually, however, he moved toward a less uniform and philosophical approach to his historical material. At the same time his interest shifted from thematic development to analysis of character. It may very well be about this time that he wrote: "Even in a historical drama, *the purely human* is of major interest, and history the background; soul's inner struggles awaken more sympathy than the combat of soldiers or the storming of walls; . . ." [4]

The quotation, from his essay on the historical drama, has often been held to point to one of the basic analogies between Strindberg's and Shakespeare's history plays.[5] But a study of three of Strindberg's major historical dramas—*The Saga of the Folkungs, Gustav Vasa,* and *Erik XIV*—will, I think, show that what they share most with Shakespeare's histories is something far more fundamental than a "realistic conception of character," that in fact Strindberg's growing emphasis on the king as an individual, "the purely personal," paralleled as it was by his partial renunciation of an attitude towards history which was also Shakespeare's, actually led him away from his master. As he steered away from Shakespeare, the scope of his individual plays narrowed down to a living-room perspective, so that many of his historical dramas convey, not a uniform and homogeneous view of the past, but "partial perspectives of the modern theater." [6]

Strindberg once remarked, "The bloody war of the Folkung . . . is very much like the Wars of the Roses in England." [7] And his own *The Saga of the Folkungs* is in many ways the most Shakespearean of his historical dramas. In some of its major motifs it is, as Miss Bulman has pointed out (p. 140), a rough counterpart to Shakespeare's *Henry VI* trilogy: the quarrel of the nobles in both plays; the theme of Ingeborg and Porse paralleled by that of Margaret of Anjou and Suffolk; the threat of the Danish War balanced by the Cade rebellion.

---

[4] [*Open Letters to the Intimate Theater,* translations and introductions by Walter Johnson (Seattle: University of Washington Press, 1966), p. 266.] Italics mine.

[5] See Joan Bulman, *Strindberg and Shakespeare* (London, 1933), p. 171.

[6] Francis Fergusson, *The Idea of a Theater* (Garden City, N.Y., 1953), pp. 156–58.

[7] [*Open Letters,* p. 240.]

The Saga of the Folkungs has some of the diversity and epic scope of *Henry VI,* but it is less episodic in its structure. In spite of its bold use of three parallel minor actions, the three contrasting love stories— the naturalistic (and "Strindbergian") love-hatred of Porse and Inge- borg, the intoxicating passion of Algotson and Blanche that fades away with death, and the idyllic Ferdinand-Miranda love of Erik and Beatrix —the play is clearly conceived and firmly controlled. The main theme of *satisfactio vicaria,* i.e., Magnus' expiation of an ancestral crime, is expressed not only in Magnus' personal destiny but in the very move- ment of the play—the strong ritualistic elements in the plague scene, the choral singing, Birgitta's and the Maniac's prophecies. Even the bloodletting of Porse in the opening scene can be regarded as a mock ritual and an anticipation of his "sacrificial" speech after the deposition of Magnus:

> Thirty years ago, on the day of Saint Simon and Saint Jude, Prince Mag- nus, the legally elected and chosen King of the realm, was beheaded on the Island of the Holy Spirit. He was admittedly innocent but was sen- tenced to death because of his father, King Birger. So there has been blood guilt on the Swedish crown since then; for that reason, say our spiritual ancestors, misfortune and years of disaster have come as punish- ment upon Magnus. The crown has now been cleansed, the judgment of God has been fulfilled, and the blood guilt atoned for (IV, i).

The plague scene (Act IV) deserves some attention. Strindberg took it from Boccaccio, but his use of it indicates his "Shakespearean" ability to make a source an integral part of his own structure. The scene has a tremendous impact when presented on the stage, and not merely that of visual effect or of pageantry. It has in one sense the same function as the son-who-has-killed-father—father-who-has-killed-son scene in *3 Henry VI* (II, v): to depict vividly the horrors of internal chaos and dissension. In Shakespeare the scene is brief, pathetic, and highly arti- ficial. Strindberg's episode is more realistic than stylized but neverthe- less suggests a ritual pattern and sets the essential tone of the play. His use of the plague scene actually transcends anything the early Shake- speare could do and reminds us more of the mature Shakespeare, who knew not only how to bring ritual elements into his plays but also how to make them dramatically effective. The plague scene is the dramatiza- tion of a physically and spiritually diseased society.

The analogy between *The Saga of the Folkungs* and *Henry VI* ex- tends to the portraits of the kings as rulers. Strindberg's Magnus is, like Henry VI, a pious "weakling," fit for a monastic life but totally in- capable of ruling a kingdom. Magnus' title to the crown is as deeply flawed as Henry's. Both rule in times so tumultuous that only a force-ful ruler could preserve the crown against attack. Because of Magnus' and Henry's weakness, the great nobles seize a chance to strike at the throne and become more eager to fight one another than the common enemy abroad. In the end, the weakness of the royal figureheads and the internal discords bring about the loss of most of the two countries' foreign possessions.

Both Henry and Magnus are criticized by other characters for their lack of initiative. Queen Margaret points out that

> Great lords, wise men ne'er sit and wail their loss
> But cheerly seek how to redress their harms.
>
> (*3 H. VI*, iv, 1–2)

And in *The Saga of the Folkungs* Ingeborg reprimands Magnus, "Yes, complain now, that's what you can do! But act, never!" (I, ii). And later on to Porse, "My son has himself caused his fall . . . a ruler must be able to do the impossible" (III, i).

Thus in both plays it is a serious shortcoming in a king ever to yield to despair; such behavior is incompatible with royal duty and respon-sibility. There is, however, one important difference. The total effect of *The Saga of the Folkungs* conveys something more than a political issue about the demands of kingship. Magnus is defeated, not only be-cause he is weak, but because God has chosen him as a *satisfactio vicaria;* through Magnus the crime of the Folkungs is finally expiated. This explains Magnus' passive role, which has often been criticized. Like Richmond in *Richard III,* Magnus' character has to be underdeveloped, because his function is instrumental rather than active. On the symbolic level we do not have a king deposed by his rebellious people; rather we have a martyr of God, used by his creator to fulfill the retributive purpose for which he was created. But Magnus' function is not only to expiate a private ancestral sin; he transcends his role as the last of the Folkungs, and through his sacrifice his own society is purged of its evil. Ingeborg and Porse are banished, Birgitta is penitent.

Together with certain aspects of his next historical play, *Gustav Vasa,* Strindberg's *The Saga of the Folkungs* offers the closest analogy to Shakespeare's histories. The first important point of comparison is the method of painting history on a broad canvas. The effect is a vivid and animated picture of a bustling world where the grotesque mingles with the pathetic, and where a whole age comes to life on the stage. Strind-berg's conscious adaptation of Shakespeare's "free composition" allows him maximum variety—widely spaced character grouping and wide

changes of scene, parallel actions, and multiple plots.[8] At the same time
we have a feeling of control, and this—perhaps the very essence of the
play—is achieved by constant reference to a unifying theme, in *The
Saga of the Folkungs* to that of *satisfactio vicaria*. Furthermore, the
historical background—the Wars of the Roses and the war of the
Folkungs—gives us a similar picture of two countries torn by rebellion
and disorder at home, and by fighting and loss of their conquests
abroad. Finally, Strindberg's providential world view enables him to
see history and its political actions as Shakespeare ultimately saw them
—as a purposeful pattern of divine justice and not merely as a capricious sequence of events.

But, in Shakespeare, the suggestion of the political action as part of
a ritual pattern, an expiation for the initial crime of deposing and
murdering Richard II, is a pattern which emerges clearly only from a
reading of all of the histories. In *The Saga of the Folkungs* on the
other hand, the ritual action *is* the play. By the telescoping of this aspect of the providential pattern of Shakespeare's histories into a single
play, *The Saga of the Folkungs* leaves in part the world of social and
political affairs to move into a realm of religious ritual and incantation.
Through the fate of Magnus the drama comes to ignore the question
of the relation between public and private virtues in a king (the theme
of *Henry VI*). Strindberg's drama is a "history" in its panoramic scope,
in its setting and in its literal action; but on an allegorical level—
through its basic religious pattern—it also passes beyond the local history play.

In Strindberg's next play, *Gustav Vasa,* the Shakespearean technique
of presenting history in a vast perspective is already on the wane, and
I find it hard to agree with those critics who regard this drama as the
climax of Shakespearean construction in Strindberg (Bulman, p. 145).
True, its character grouping is roughly based on the two *Henry IV*
plays, with Erik and Göran corresponding to Prince Hal and Falstaff,
and Prince Johan to Prince John and Hotspur (the king wishes Johan
to be his successor). The analogy, however, is so superficial that a reader
who did not happen to know that Strindberg was particularly fond of
Henry IV might never notice the relationship. More important perhaps
is the juxtaposition of high political affairs with familiar pictures of
low life. As in *Henry IV* the vision of reality is expanded to include
court and tavern, king and country folk—but this is actually a Shakespearean carry-over from *The Saga of the Folkungs.*

---

[8] ". . . I was determined to study his [Shakespeare's] method of contructing a
drama. It was at that time that I noticed his structure was both formless and at
the same time strictly pedantically formal." [*Open Letters,* p. 58.] Cf. Bulman, p.
109, and Martin Lamm, *Strindbergs dramer* (Stockholm, 1926), II, 102.

Another Shakespearean feature is the interruption of the main action in Act II—the rebellion against the king—to introduce two parallel actions: Jacob and Herman Israel, a variation of the father-son relationship, and Prince Erik and his boon companion Göran, who are hardly an integral part of the play but are perhaps brought in to furnish a link to the already planned sequel, *Erik XIV*.

In spite of the rapid movement of *Gustav Vasa* and the frequent shiftings of scene, the final impression is not that of the panoramic spectacle of *The Saga of the Folkungs*. The different impact of *Gustav Vasa* is due partly to a toning down of the providential view and partly to Strindberg's changing concept of the king from a public symbol to a three-dimensional individual—a change which takes place within the play itself. The controlling idea from *The Saga of the Folkungs*—the sacrificial role of the king—figured in the first draft of the play but was later discarded. Yet there are numerous remnants of this original conception in the final version. The opening scene is a more obvious staging of a ritual than in *The Saga of the Folkungs*: the choral rhythm of the speech between Måns Nilson and his wife, the beating of the drums off stage, and the culmination of the ceremony when the bloody coats from the blood bath are brought in. Another possible vestige of a sacrificial plan is the beggar scene of Act IV, which seems like the reenactment of the old ritual of the Fisher King—the disguised ruler descending among his people.

This drama, as is true of most of Strindberg's historical plays that followed it, takes its title from the ruler, an indication of an altered purpose in his composition; he is no longer writing a religious "saga," but the life of a king. In that sense the play is closer to the construction of Shakespeare's individual histories than is *The Saga of the Folkungs*.

In its changing concept of the king, *Gustav Vasa* has its parallel in Shakespeare. The drama in a way moves from a *Henry V* to a *Richard II*, i.e., from an identification of the king with his public office to an indication of moral self-probing, a questioning in the protagonist himself of his role as king and as private man. The change takes place in the second half of the play. Up to that point, Gustav, though far from a religious symbol as was Magnus, has nevertheless been regarded by his people and his family as an ominous "duplicate" of the Eternal One, a concept which the king himself accepts. But, as the drama proceeds, the king changes from a threatening, and for two acts invisible, public symbol to a private man. This metamorphosis is paralleled by a narrowing of the panoramic scope of the play as we move from the country into Stockholm, from Dalarna into the king's parlor. Gustav is still preoccupied with political problems and the threat of rebellion, but the focus is now almost entirely on his personal conflict. Although

Strindberg makes an open and rather undramatic use of his providential philosophy, he restricts it to serve as personal motivation for Gustav.
The result is that the earlier portrait of the king as a forceful ruler of
his country now changes into a Swedish replica of Richard II, who sub-
stitutes action for a dependence upon divine protection.

The analogy between Gustav and Richard goes further than that,
however, for there is in both an attempt at self-exploration, a questioning of their own moral standards, and a dishonest dismissal of the problem through a histrionic dramatization of themselves. It is primarily
this changing perspective of the king from an overpowering public
symbol to a potentially tragic hero that accounts for the hybrid quality
of the drama. *Gustav Vasa* is Strindberg's *Richard II*—partly "history,"
partly tragedy.

Many critics see *Gustav Vasa* and *Erik XIV*, the play immediately
following, as a unity, and Strindberg himself wanted the plays to form
a group—the Vasa Saga. It is, however, a unity based on rather arbitrary devices: introduction of the same characters, references to historical data, and use of family genealogies. But it is hard to see any genuine thematic connection between the two dramas. In fact, *Erik XIV*
is, as Martin Lamm has already pointed out, without any basic theme
and without any clearly conceived artistic plan. Thus Erik's shifting
role from prince to king does not form an analogy to the education
theme of *Henry IV* and *Henry V*, for the only change that Erik under-
goes is one of title—instead of a madcap *prince* he becomes a madcap
king.

Strindberg's notes on the play show the same ambivalent attitude
vis-à-vis his material that we find in *Gustav Vasa*. His first plan was
for a "Swedenborg drama" with Erik's superstition as a major theme.
Erik was to have gone through a series of religious crises and finally
end as an alchemist and black magician, abandoned and in the end
deposed by his people. The outline of this early idea indicates a much
broader Shakespearean conception than the final version:

Act I: Mourning for Gustav I.
Act II: The Wedding.
Act III: Witchcraft.
Act IV: Sture-murder. Erik is imprisoned (Bulman, p. 146).

But the growing emphasis on the private character of the king which
we noticed in *Gustav Vasa* came to absorb more and more of Strindberg's interest. In *Erik XIV* he abandons his providential view altogether. The public aspect of kingship disappears entirely, and the
drama is reduced to a study of a "characterless character," an amoral
and pathological individual. As a consequence the play is finally con-

ceived on a much smaller scale than the earlier histories, and there is hardly a remnant of the Shakespearean technique of *The Saga of the Folkungs* and *Gustav Vasa*. It is no mere coincidence that *Erik XIV* opens, not with the Shakespearean throng and "chorus" of [the] barber scene [in *The Saga of the Folkungs*] or *Gustav Vasa's* Dalecarlian inquisition, but with the furious Erik, who from his balcony throws nails and flower pots on his councilor and his mistress. Throughout the entire play all the events, with the exception of Göran's love story, are arranged primarily with a view to the effect they will have or the light they may throw on the king's personality.

The analytic temper of the play can be traced back to *Gustav Vasa*. Gustav himself tries to some extent to see his actions in terms of morality, but Prince Erik gives us his whole psychological background. His is the modern dissecting mind that has to explain his unbalanced behavior in terms of various complexes:

> I, alone, abandoned since my mother died; I, hated by my stepmother, by my father and by my half-brother. . . . This lovelessness in which I am born and brought up has become a fire in my soul that consumes me; my blood is poisoned in birth, and I do not believe there is any antidote (*Gustav Vasa*, II, i).

Erik XIV is to a large extent a picture of the consequences of unfulfilled mother love. Erik XIV is a modern problem child in court costume.[9]

The historical dramas immediately following *Erik XIV*, i.e., *Gustav IV Adolf, Charles XII, Engelbrekt, Kristina*, and in 1902 *Gustav III*, are isolated and independent works. Of these the last three deal merely with episodes in the private life of the ruler or with the ruler's personal reaction to political events. But *Gustav IV Adolf* and *Charles XII* show that Strindberg did not surrender willingly to a simplified, non-Shakespearean structure. They are both gigantic efforts to return to the panoramic scale of *The Saga of the Folkungs*. *Gustav IV Adolf* would take six hours to perform, and the action carries us over a large part of Germany during the Thirty Years War. But the king himself, a potential Henry V, seems, as Lamm has pointed out (p. 173), more like a nice gentle schoolboy than a political genius. The outline to *Charles XII* indicates a more spirited and bustling drama than the final, rather static version of the play:

Act I: (a) Lund. In the students' rooms. Students lynched as soldiers.
(b) Market scene. The peasants. The returned prisoners from Siberia. The plague has come from Cracow.

[9] Strindberg thought he could see a similarity between Erik XIV and (an almost Ernest Jonesian) Hamlet. [*Open Letters*, p. 80.]

Act II: (a) Swedenborg.
        (b) At the university. Festival for the king (Bulman, p. 150).

Finally, the three historical dramas of 1908—*The Last of the Knights,
Sten Sture,* and *Earl Birger of Bjälbo*—are weak attempts to return
to a cyclic structure.

Thus Strindberg's historical cycle broke into fragments—although
in one sense he had already completed its pattern in *The Saga of the
Folkungs*—and his individual historical plays gradually lost their
panoramic perspective. This movement is naturally paralleled by a
movement away from Shakespeare. It seems to have been caused by a
continuous encroachment of the modern analytic temper upon a providential attitude towards history (and life) which was largely that of
Shakespeare, and upon a concept of the king as a public man whose
identity is his public office—the true Shakespearean "history" hero.

Taken together, *The Saga of the Folkungs, Gustav Vasa,* and *Erik
XIV* may be said to form a three-act drama of fulfillment and disintegration, with the peripeteia occurring in the second half of *Gustav
Vasa.* In their development from religious ritual and "history" through
pseudotragedy to psychological drama, these plays epitomize a wide
span in the history of the theater; they also indicate the completion of
what Francis Fergusson has called the movement towards chaos in post-
Shakespearean drama (p. 154). *The Saga of The Folkungs* represents
an obsolete attempt to see history *sub specie aeternitatis.* In *Gustav
Vasa* the ambivalent concept of the king gives us a hybrid play of the
same category as *Richard II.* In *Erik XIV* psychology has replaced
morality, and motivation meaningful action, so that the play illustrates
what we could call the analytic fallacy of the modern theater—its self-
conscious preoccupation with the individual psyche to the exclusion of
the more fundamental aspects of the drama—its ritual movement, its
moto spirital.

The Logic of *A Dream Play*

by Evert Sprinchorn

Strindberg's *Dream Play* is customarily lauded for its originality, the power of its dialogue and the beauty of its verse, the opportunity it offers to peer into the strange mind of its creator, and for the welcome contrast its compassionate mood offers to the hysteria of Strindberg's other plays. But those who begin by citing its virtues almost invariably conclude that technical innovations and stage tricks are no substitute for thought and meaning; that subjectivity results in artistic chaos; that verses of such beauty require a more imposing setting; and that, when all is said and done, bursting chrysanthemums are no substitute for the verbal fireworks of Strindberg's sex battles. In a word, *A Dream Play* is technically original, historically important, but utterly incoherent.

Bernhard Diebold, that fine early German critic of Strindberg, distinguished theater poetry from poetry in the theater and esteemed the former as high art when it was an integral part of the play. But the end of *A Dream Play* disappointed him. Chrysanthemums instead of enlightenment: the poet gives up and the prestidigitator takes over.[1] The visual richness of the play makes it extremely difficult to stage adequately and almost as difficult to read. I do not know of any play in world literature which contains so many pictures and images, scenes and characters that are quickly and lastingly imprinted on the mind. But the literary critic tends to overlook the pictures or refuses to examine them with care, preferring to look for meaning where he has always found it before: in the words, in the plot, in the characters.

There is, of course, the semblance of a narrative in *A Dream Play*, but, as Strindberg implies in his preliminary note, the narrative sways rather wildly and threatens at times to plunge completely off the road. In the prologue Indra's Daughter descends from heaven to hear the complaints and grievances of mankind. Incarnated as Agnes, she

[1] *Anarchie im Drama* (Frankfurt am Main, 1921), p. 210.

appears on earth talking to a glazier in front of a growing castle. They enter the castle to release an army officer who is held prisoner there. The Officer is seen next in his parents' home and then at the stage entrance to an opera house, waiting in vain through the seasons and years for his beloved Victoria. A mysterious door with a clover-leaf venthole makes him feel uneasy, and when the police forbid him to open it, he goes to the Lawyer for an injunction. Now the Lawyer meets Agnes and tells her that he is about to be awarded his degree as doctor of laws. In a mimed and danced scene at the church where the ceremonies are held the Lawyer is denied his degree for having defended suffering humanity. The church organ, emitting the sound of human voices, is transformed into Fingal's Cave, as the Lawyer and Agnes decide to unite their destinies. The next scene is a domestic one showing the Lawyer and Agnes married and quarreling bitterly over trifles. The Officer comes to release her from this domestic hell and carry her off to the seaside. Scenes at Foulstrand and Fairhaven present a broad view of society, with the tone varying from the satiric and humorous to the melancholy. The next scene finds Agnes back in Fingal's Cave talking to a poet who had made his first appearance at Foulstrand. To the music of the wind and the waves Agnes reads the Poet's complaint to the gods, and she confesses to him that she has had her fill of earthly life and desires to return to heaven. The scene shifts to the theater corridor for the ceremonial opening of the clover-leaf door which is supposed to conceal the secret of the universe. The learned faculties are gathered there to learn the secret. The door is opened by the Glazier and reveals nothing. In the last scene, outside the castle once again, the Daughter bids goodbye to her companions in life. The castle begins to burn. The whole cast parades by to throw their illusions on the fire. The Daughter enters the castle, and as she ascends to heaven, the golden crown of the castle bursts into a huge chrysanthemum.

There are at least three important motives threaded through this plot. First: "Mankind is to be pitied." Life on earth is generally pretty miserable and someone should let the gods know. Second: "Love conquers all!" Perhaps love can find the way out from this vale of tears. Third: "The secret of the universe." Concealed behind the mysterious door, it must reveal the origin of human suffering, or the meaning of it, or the way to end it.

Tracing these three motives through the play reduces to order some of the apparent chaos of the play. Another pattern emerges from a consideration of the structure of the play. Though Strindberg, trying to capture the fluidity of a dream, designates neither acts nor scenes, there are obviously three separate acts, an act division occurring when there is a distinct break in the flow of merging scenes. Within each act or sequence Strindberg has welded the scenes together by transformations, lighting effects, and other stage tricks to give the effect of dissolving views and uninterrupted action. Lights are dimmed, a wall is lifted away, a bed becomes a tent, an office a church, an organ a cave, and so on, but the flow of the action is unimpeded. (The prologue and the coalheavers scene on the shores of the Mediterranean lie outside the original design of the play. The latter was inserted after the final scenes had been written;[2] the former was written in 1906 when plans were being made for the first production of the play.) The first act or sequence begins at the castle and ends in Fingal's Cave with the Daughter and the Lawyer united. The second act begins in the home of the newly married couple and ends with the Daughter resolving to return to heaven—or with the contrast between the rich and the poor on the Riviera, if the coalheavers scene is kept. The third act begins in the grotto with the Daughter and the Poet seeing visions of drowning humanity and ends at the castle with the Daughter ascending to heaven. A diagram may be of some help:

Acts	*Scenes*		
	(Prologue)		
	1.	Castle	
	2.	Inside the castle	
	3.	Officer's childhood home	
I		4.	Theater corridor
		5.	Lawyer's office
		6.	Church
		7.	Cave
			8. Kitchen-bedroom
II			9. Foulstrand
			10. Fairhaven
			(11. Riviera)
		12.	Cave
III		13.	Theater corridor
	14.	Castle	

In the third act Strindberg has repeated some scenes from the first act. His original intention was to duplicate the form of *To Damascus, Part I,* in which the last eight scenes reverse the order of the first eight. According to Martin Lamm, Strindberg abandoned the scheme.[3] However, if the scenes in *A Dream Play* are grouped as I have indicated—my reasons for doing so will become apparent later—it can

[2] See Martin Lamm, *August Strindberg,* 2nd ed. (Stockholm, 1948), pp. 293, 310.
[3] *Strindbergs dramer* (Stockholm, 1924–26), II, 318.

be seen that Strindberg has simply made subtler use of the cyclical structure.

This arrangement of scenes in both *To Damascus* and *A Dream Play* creates the effect of sinking into a dream and awaking from it. Since, in Strindberg's view, earthly life is an illusion, the deeper the dreamer sleeps, the farther the Daughter sinks into the slough of human existence, achieving complete incarnation as a human being in the kitchen-bedroom scene that opens the second act. Her explorations at the bottom of life occupy this act, and in the third act her ascension begins. This ascension represents an escape from suffering. And when she finally shakes the clay of human existence from her feet and enters the burning castle, are we not to understand that the dream of life is over and that death is an awakening to the higher life promised by the burgeoning chrysanthemum? Such a view, after all, accords rather well with the quasi-Buddhist philosophy expressed by the Daughter in the last act. The secret is that strife is inevitable here on earth and that there is no meaning to the strife. We only delude ourselves by imposing a meaning on it or on our aspirations.

II

But may not the Daughter's explanation be an example of what Freud called secondary elaboration? When the dreamer is about to wake up, he tries to impose a meaning acceptable to his consciousness on the disorganized material of the dream. Such attempts represent invariably the last efforts of the dream-censor to disguise the true meaning of the dream. Not until after he had fashioned nearly all of the play did Strindberg explain to himself and to the Poet what it might mean. On November 18, 1901 he reread his books on Indian religions and adapted some of their teachings to his own use in the final dialogue between the Daughter and the Poet.[4] But Buddha has little to do with the rest of the play. It is much more helpful to invoke Schopenhauer and especially that awakener of modern times, Freud.

Though Strindberg never read a word by Freud, both men were products of the same century and pupils of the same teachers. Both men followed in the wake of Schopenhauer and Hartmann, and both were guided by the pioneering works of Ribot, Charcot, Bernheim, and the host of other philosophers and medical men who were probing the inner life of nineteenth-century man while the followers of Marx and Darwin were exploring his outer life. Strindberg was on

---

[4] See Gunnar Ollén, *Strindbergs dramatik*, 2nd ed. (Stockholm, 1961), p. 398.

the track of the Oedipus complex by 1887. Both men studied hyp-
notism in the 1880s. Freud worked out his "free association" method
between 1892 and 1895, while Strindberg sketched his theory of *l'art
fortuite* and automatic art in 1894. Strindberg began taking notes on
his own dreams in 1893, Freud in 1895. And if the fact that Strindberg's dream plays, *To Damascus* (1898–1901) and *A Dream Play*
(1901), and Freud's central work, *The Interpretation of Dreams* (1899),
were written at virtually the same time is not evidence for the existence of a Zeitgeist, it certainly suggests that great men think alike.

Freud describes at least five techniques by which the reprehensible
thoughts of the unconscious are disguised and allowed to slip into the
conscious mind: secondary elaboration, symbolism, condensation, displacement, and dramatization through regression to visual concepts.
The last is not so much a method to disguise thoughts as it is the
natural method employed by the primitive, unconscious mind to express itself. Pictures and images are employed rather than abstractions and words. For instance, causal connections rendered by the conscious mind with such words as "therefore" and "because" are indicated by the unconscious in the succession of two apparently uncon-
nected scenes.

The visual element is almost as strong in Strindberg's play as it is
in our own dreams, and if we listen to the dialogue with our eyes
closed, we shall never comprehend the play. Let us look at the first
few scenes. The Daughter and the Glazier refer to a prisoner in the
castle. The scene changes to a room in the castle where the Officer,
rocking in a chair, is striking a table with his saber. The Daughter
tells him not to do so and removes the saber from his hands. Sixty
years after Freud, the symbolism of this scene is elementary. The
daughter of the gods is a mother figure in the eyes of the Officer, who
describes her as the embodiment of the harmony of the universe, and
like a good nineteenth-century mother she is telling her son, rocking
in his crib, not to masturbate. This vision of childhood plus associated
thoughts of injustice and the impossibility of escaping from the prison,
motivate the next change of scene, which reveals the nature of the
Officer's prison. In one sense his prison is his childhood home from
whose formative influences he can never escape. He remains a child
in spirit throughout the play. The motive of injustice is developed
when the Officer's mother, evoked by the presence of the Daughter,
reminds him of a childhood theft for which the wrong person was
punished. Now a brewing quarrel between the Officer's parents suggests the disharmony of earthly life, but the Daughter declares that,
though living is difficult, love can smooth the way. This optimistic
declaration is the open sesame to the following scene in the theater

corridor where the Officer waits with unfaltering hope for his beloved Victoria.

Now imagine this sequence of three scenes as a silent film. The Daughter Agnes and fatherly old man outside fantastic castle—close-up of bars on windows—Agnes entering room—Officer rocking—close-up of Agnes removing saber from his hand and shaking her finger at him—pout of displeasure on Officer's face changing to look of admiration and devotion—Agnes urging Officer to escape—Officer shrugging shoulders hopelessly—Officer's mother and father fading in while Agnes and Officer remain on screen—and so on. Filmed this way, the scenes would link together more clearly than they do on the page, for the dialogue often diverts our attention from the basic level on which the play operates. The dialogue is an outgrowth of the visions, not vice versa. That is as it should be, for the play is no more about ideas than the best music is. Hence Strindberg could suggest his *Dream Play* to a composer-friend who was looking for a good musical subject. "But shortened!" wrote Strindberg. "A musical chamber play, with all the philosophizing cut out and only the 'scenes' left. . . . Dramatic-lyrical music, not theatrical-recitative-argumentative." The words function like music to gild the pictures and conceal their meaning, but without the inner tension and beauty they provide, the play would be all the poorer, all depth and no surface.

The visual links are more apparent in the next sequence of three scenes: the theater corridor, the Lawyer's office, the church. Here Strindberg has artfully made the stage properties remain the same throughout while serving different purposes. The linden tree becomes a hat tree and then a candelabrum; the doorkeeper's room becomes the Lawyer's desk and then a pulpit; while the mysterious door becomes the Lawyer's files and then the door to the church sacristy. These three scenes are rigidly grappled together as far as the eye is concerned, and to understand their significance we should think of them as superimposed on one another so as to form one. This is a perfect example of condensation of scenes.

Condensation of characters or its opposite, decomposition of character, is another dream technique that Strindberg consciously and deliberately employs. In his prefatory note he says, "The characters split, double, multiply, dissolve, thicken, fade away, coalesce." The three chief male characters—the carefree, eternally hopeful Officer, who wins the laurel wreath; the harassed Lawyer, who knows only life's pains and responsibilities and who is given the crown of thorns; and the Poet whose moods alternate between enthusiasm and skepticism—are manifestly aspects of one person. Similarly, the Daughter subsumes the characters of the Officer's mother and of the Door-

keeper, whose place she physically takes and whose shawl, incorpo-
rating thirty years of disappointment, she wears. It is only one step
more to see that Strindberg intended that all the men coalesce into
one male and all the women into one female. He seems to have
thought of his play as basically a two-character drama, and in an early
version he listed the dramatis personae under two headings: The
Man and The Woman. Then, finally, remembering the bisexual nature of man, the subjective nature of the play, and the egocentric
nature of dreams, we must allow the two characters ultimately to fuse
into one; and it is absurd to ask, as some cavilling critics have, which
of the thirty characters in the play is the dreamer.

III

The story line of the play takes us on a journey through life in
which the Man grows up to his responsibilities while the Woman
sinks into the mire of earthly existence. In the last part of the play,
as the Woman ascends and shakes the clay from her feet, the Man
becomes a poet seeking a meaning to the strife of existence. This
journey starts at the castle, proceeds through the theater corridor
where the clover-leaf door is the center of attention, and reaches its
first stopping point in the cave. The castle, theater, door, and cave
are the dominant symbols in the play by virtue of their position in its
structure.

The theater introduces us to the notion, basic to the thought of the
whole play, that the world is an illusion and a dream. The idea is
conveyed symbolically here by having us enter the adult world of law,
religion, and learning through the theater. The fact that the mysterious door which opens on nothing is first encountered in the theater
enforces this view.

In the office and in the church the Lawyer is pictured as a Christ-
like sufferer, who takes upon himself the cares and crimes of the world
and receives in return only the contempt of the right-thinking people.[5]
The Daughter offers him a crown of thorns and the consolations of
love and marriage. Love is to conquer all. At this point there occurs
another symbolic transformation. In the church the organ, at which

---

[5] The idea of a lawyer as the embodiment of humanity's miseries may have come
to Strindberg from Balzac, one of Strindberg's favorite writers. In *Colonel Chabert*
there is a passage which reads in part: "There are three persons in our society, the
priest, the doctor, and the man of law, who cannot have any respect for humanity.
They probably wear black robes because they are in mourning for all the virtues,
all the illusions. The most unhappy of the three is the lawyer . . . " (*Oeuvres com-
plètes* [Paris, 1895], IV, 3078).

the Daughter has been playing and from which the voices of mankind have welled up in a profoundly moving kyrie, is transformed
into a sea grotto as the Daughter and the Lawyer decide to marry. The
grotto, the water, and the church are familiar symbols of woman, and
the union of organ and cave is an obvious symbol of sexual intercourse. The association of organ and cave occurs earlier in Strindberg
in his long short story, "The Romantic Organist at Rånö," written in
1888, in which the dreamy organist thinks of the musical instrument
as a gigantic organism which had taken thousands of years to grow,
and compares it first to a cave and finally to his loved one. And the
prototype for this feat of imagination is found in an even earlier
story, "Rebuilding," written in 1884. There the repressed heroine
intoxicates herself with perfume and in a remarkable rapture imagines herself in church, the organ pounding out a *dies irae,* voices
of angels and titans lifting the roof, while flashes of lightning illuminate the words "Crucify the Flesh." After a sudden bolt of thunder,
the organ grows quieter, its pipes become syrinxes, its tunes the
melodies of Pan, Saint Francis becomes Apollo, "and from the graves
beneath the floor could be heard the pounding of the imprisoned beings who wanted to get out, and they shouted, 'The Word is made
Flesh!' "

The second act begins in the kitchen and bedroom of the Lawyer's
home, where Strindberg treats us to a miniature drama of married
life. From this domestic hell Agnes is rescued by the Officer, just as
she had once rescued him from his imprisonment at home. As the
Officer takes her out to enjoy life, the kitchen-bedroom apartment is
transformed into Foulstrand and Fairhaven. The small world gives
way to the large in a myriad of brilliant scenes.

When Agnes has ranged over all of earthly life and seen how fleeting happiness is, how illusory are our hopes, how unceasing the conflict between pleasure and duty, she is ready to begin her ascent to
her heavenly home. But she must start at the bottom, work her way
up, and undergo the final test of existence as a human being: the
repetition of all one's miseries. Here we have another reason for the
cyclical structure of the play.

She returns to Fingal's Cave where the flowing waters, the broken
silver cord, the drowning people, and the song of the wind which is
likened to the cries of newborn babes, all suggest that the scene signifies birth, probably in two senses: the complete coming into the world
of the Daughter, that is, her utter separation from heaven, and the
beginning of her rebirth as a goddess.

Now Strindberg rushes us quickly back to our starting point, back
through the world of illusion, back through the theater corridor and

the pageantry of the door-opening, and back to the reality of the castle. I say the reality of the castle, for if my line of thought is correct, the theater must divide the illusory world from the real.

It takes no doctor come from Vienna to tell us what this castle stands for, with its ability to grow and raise itself, with its crown that resembles a flower bud, with the forest of hollyhocks that surround it, and the manure piles that lie below. It takes all the imagination of a poet to conceive of it as a castle and only an adolescent's knowledge of anatomy to recognize it as a phallus.[6] For the male dreamer the fundamental reality is that represented by the castle. By extension, that reality is equivalent to the id, which Freud postulated as the reservoir of the libido and the basis of the personality. When Strindberg in his preliminary note describes the mind that presides over the dream as having no secrets, knowing no inconsistencies, no scruples, no laws, and neither judging nor acquitting but only narrating, he is giving a beautifully precise definition of the id. Since the id represents the mind in its pristine state before civilization has made its imprint, the castle lies outside society and the Daughter on her return trip must go into the desert to reach it. As the id is the wellspring of all mental life, so the castle is the source of all the action of the play, which flows from it and returns to it. Yet another reason for the cyclical structure.

The fact that the Officer is a prisoner in the castle points in two directions. If the castle is a phallus, the Officer represents the soul or spirit imprisoned in the body from whose peremptory demands it cannot escape.[7] But as mentioned before, the Officer is also the prisoner of his home and his parents, those agents which inhibit the id and which eventually contribute to the formation of the conscience or superego. The transformation of the castle to home and the simultaneous introduction of the theme of injustice show the first step in a process which culminates with the appearance of the duty-obsessed Lawyer.

If we allow the castle to stand for the idea that the only reality is the sensual and unconscious life and that all else is illusion, we can come to a better understanding of the secret of the universe, the search

[6] Source critics point out that Strindberg had in mind an actual building in Stockholm which he could see from his apartment and which he mentions several times in his writings. The fact that a troop of cavalry were quartered there may have begun a chain of masculine associations in Strindberg's mind. As for other uses to which he put the building, there is his poem "My Troll Castle" (written at about the same time as *A Dream Play*), in which the magic castle is built by two lovers on a spring day out of air and mist and the sun of their senses.

[7] "The soul was hurled into the body's prison" and similar statements are not uncommon in Strindberg. . . .

for which is one of the three main motives in the play. And three times it is almost completely revealed: when the door is opened, when the Daughter reads the Poet's lamentation in the grotto, and when the Daughter is about to ascend to heaven. The opening of the door reveals the futility and superficiality of organized knowledge. In the grotto scene the Poet almost stumbles on the secret when in his complaint to Brahma he asks:

> Why are we born like animals,
> We the progeny of God and the scions of man?
> Our spirit demands other vestures
> Than these of blood and filth.
> Shall God's image cut his second teeth—

"Silence!" interrupts the Daughter. "No one has yet solved the riddle of life." Apparently the Daughter is an informed Swedenborgian and like Strindberg knows that in the doctrine of correspondences teeth are a symbol of sensuality.

In the last scene the Daughter herself tries to explain the riddle of the universe to the Poet. Brahma, the original power or potency, was seduced by the world mother, Maja, and out of this sinful union the illusory earth was born. For the dreamer only the male principle is real; the conjunction of male and female ends in illusion. The very structure of the drama supports this view. The castle contains the whole play, while the castle and cave together flank the first and last acts, fencing in both the world of illusion represented by the theater and the social world of the kaleidoscopic second act.

This gives rise to a further thought, a refinement on what I have suggested so far. May not the grotto, the scene of symbolic birth, be the uterus? And may not the theater corridor which separates the castle from the cave be the vagina? We must not hedge in our thoughts with scruples when dealing with the unconscious, which is always more concrete and tactile than the analytical mind. At one time Strindberg seems to have thought of the corridor as having an underground aspect, for in an early version of his play he pictured mushrooms growing out of the walls of the corridor.[8]

If that is so, we might expect to find in the corridor some male symbol or the intimation of a union of male and female symbols. We do not have to look far. Dominating the scene is a single gigantic aconite. With its flowers in a long stiff spike, this is probably a male symbol, providing a reminiscence of the towering hollyhocks of the

[8] . . . Mushrooms are quite relevant to a vagina symbol. In Swedish the word for mushrooms is the same as for sponges, and sponges in the slang of the time denoted a common form of female contraceptive.

opening scene and a harbinger of the profusion of aconites that will surround the castle in the last scene, though its immediate function in the theater corridor is to keynote the scene, its combination of beautiful flowers and poisonous root symbolizing the deceptive hopes and illusions with which life lures us on. The linden tree and the nearby cellar window are intended, I believe, as a visual echo of the castle and cave. The early version of the play ends with the Officer, after having spent his life waiting for his beloved, falling down dead at this cellar window.

IV

The pageant of human suffering that the play offers requires some kind of explanation, and toward the end of the play an attempt is made to provide one. From the unfortunate union of male sexual energy with maternal matter there arose all the contradictory strivings which plague mankind. "To free themselves from earthly matter," says the Daughter,

> the progeny of Brahma seek deprivation and suffering. . . . But this yearning to suffer collides with the craving for pleasure, or love. . . . [The result] is conflict between the anguish of joy and the pleasures of suffering, the torments of remorse and the delights of sensuality.

The conclusion reached by the Daughter is only slightly different from Empedocles' view of life as based on the ceaseless oppugnancy of love and strife and is perhaps even closer to Freud's dualism of Eros and the death instinct. The idea of recurrence expressed by the Lawyer, connected as it is in the play with moral masochism, guilt feelings, and the conception of death as the only liberator, provides an illuminating analogy to Freud's repetition compulsion, from which he derived the death instinct.

In this struggle the woman plays the double role customarily assigned her by Christianity and the Oriental religions. As the embodiment of the reproductive instinct, she is the temptress. But once she has satisfied her instincts and filled her womb, she becomes the redeemer with the power to lift man to heaven on the wings of the hope that he too can be reborn. Sinking down into the earth, the Daughter is primarily the temptress; ascending, she is the redeemer.

The end to the conflict of male and female principles can come only with death. But death in this play has a double meaning, too. As the Lawyer and the Daughter were united through the agency of the organ and the cave, so now the Poet and the Daughter are united by fire in the final moment. The fire suggests sexual excitement, dying signifies orgasm,[9] and the bursting chrysanthemum on top of the castle is ejaculation poeticized.

In the finale all the characters pass in review to throw their illusions on the purging fire. Only the old sensualist Don Juan has nothing to toss into the flames. And when Christina, the girl who spends her time sealing windows—a perfect representation of the inhibitive forces, as is the Officer's mother who is continually trimming the lamp (notice, by the way, how both have the same significant name)—comes to continue her work at the castle, she is informed that there is nothing there for her to seal up.

"Shall I never learn how to kill my flesh?" asks Strindberg in 1895. "It's still too young and fiery. But then it shall be burned up! And will be indeed! But what of the soul? Perhaps up in smoke too!"

So the play ends and the dreamer awakes. For a moment the irreconcilable opposites have been reconciled. If the play had gone on, we would have seen only the scorched hills and the charred tree stumps that greet the Daughter after her marriage to the Lawyer.

V

. . . Every genuine poetical creation must have proceeded from more than one motive, more than one impulse in the mind of the poet, and must admit of more than one interpretation. I have here attempted to interpret only the deepest stratum of impulses in the mind of the creative poet.[10]

So says Freud, and so say I. To stress what I think needs to be stressed I have had to overlook many of my favorite scenes and disregard other symbolic patterns in the work. I have simply endeavored to explain the work on the level which brings the major pattern into view. My concern has been to answer the charge that the play is incoherent and to demonstrate how important the visual element is for an understanding of the play. Far from being chaotic and disordered, the ramblings of a deranged mind, *A Dream Play* is exquisitely constructed; and far from being a phantasmagoria of meaningless scenic effects, it is the most nearly perfect example of theater poetry as distinct from poetry in the theater that the modern drama has to offer.

It would of course be grotesquely wrong to emphasize in a produc-

---

[9] "The highest moment of love resembles death—the closed eyes, the corpse-like paleness, the cessation of consciousness." Strindberg, *Samlade skrifter*, XLVII, 776.

[10] Freud, "The Interpretation of Dreams," *The Basic Writings of Sigmund Freud,* ed. A. A. Brill (New York: Modern Library, 1938), pp. 310–11.

tion the notions I have put forward, as grotesquely wrong as it was for Olof Molander, the pioneer Strindberg director in Sweden, to substitute a cross for the castle in the final scene. Most people, apparently, cannot accept the lesson of the door-opening scene, and they must make life and dreams palatable by imposing on them a higher, sublimated meaning.

VI

Yet an obscure, half-formed thought keeps nagging me, an inconsistency, a snag either in my line of thought or in the fabric of the play. If on one level death is a release from suffering, and if on the other level sexual intercourse provides a relief from the conflicts of life, why should the final scene, with the castle surrounded by beautiful flowers, cause the dreamer such anguish? At that moment, according to Strindberg's preliminary note, waking life, however painful it may be, is a pleasure compared to the tormenting dream. The dream ends beautifully, but the dreamer agonizes!

The advocates of the awakening-to-a-higher-life theory cannot account for the dreamer's anguish without contradicting their own premises. Like the dreamer who sees himself plunging to certain death on the jagged rocks, this dreamer wrests himself from the coil of his dream when he is made suddenly aware that there is no life to come, no *Erlösung,* not even the promise of one. But that point was made quite clearly in the door-opening episode, which did not seem to disturb the dreamer unduly.

Perhaps we have not understood that scene correctly. After the door is opened the cheated public and professors scream at the Daughter and are on the verge of attacking her.

> *The Chancellor.* Will the Daughter be so good as to tell us what she has meant by this door-opening?
> *The Daughter.* No, good people. If I were to tell you, you wouldn't believe me.
> *Dean of the Medical Faculty.* It's nothing but nothing!
> *The Daughter.* Just as you say. But you haven't understood it.

The Daughter seems to be speaking to us as well as to the dean.

Who actually opened the door? The glass-cutter. Why should a glass-cutter open the door? A locksmith was called in scene 4, but the glass-cutter appeared. Who is this glass-cutter? And how did the dreamer return to the scene of the door-opening? I have been arguing that causal links in a dream are revealed by juxtaposing the scenes.

What is the underlying connection here? And why does no one see anything behind the door? In the church that door led to the sacristy; in the office it was the door to the Lawyer's files; and in the theater where it is first seen the Officer was struck by the resemblance it had to the pantry doors he knew as a child. It is not true that there is nothing behind the door. Everything is behind it!

Ah, now the hidden thought that has been disturbing me lies just beneath the surface. Telling us the door contains nothing is a perfect example of displacement, the dream technique by which the ego diverts our attention and shifts the emphasis from what is truly important. The door is a female symbol, and so are the windows the glass-cutter works with. When the Daughter instructs him in the opening scene to put windows in the castle, we have a perfect example of the inversion common in dreams: the glass-cutter is actually putting castles in the windows. As he puts the windows in, the castle grows (see the Officer's speech in the Foulstrand scene). Christina, who seals the windows, would have the opposite effect.

When we first hear of the door, the dreamer in the guise of the Officer associates it with pantries and with food. For the dreamer, the door is not simply a female symbol but a symbol of mother, the provider of nourishment, spiritual and otherwise.[11] In the guise of the Poet the dreamer seeks union with the Daughter in the grotto scene where the birth symbols are so prominent. But what of the vision of Christ among shipwrecked and drowning humanity? That too ties in with the birth symbolism but in a special way. The thought of saving or redeeming life represents an attempt to repay for the act of birth by doing for mother what she did for the dreamer.[12] In this manner the Christ imagery is connected with incestuous wishes.

The Poet entertains such wishes but represses them. Immediately after the Christ vision there occurs a rambling speech by the Poet of which no critic has ever made any sense. The soldiers which the Poet imagines marching over the shadow of a church spire have a sexual significance—the first one to step on the weathercock must die—but before he can become aware of its meaning a cloud passes. "The cloud's water put out the sun's fire," says the Poet. The danger is past for the moment, but the sexual thought remains lurking beneath the surface.

It is during this speech that the scene changes to the theater corridor where the Daughter is already arranging for the opening of the door. This door is no more or less disturbing to the dreamer than the

---

[11] Strindberg always associated food and nourishment with the idea of mother. See my Introduction to Strindberg's *Chamber Plays,* New York, 1962.

[12] See Ernest Jones, *Papers on Psycho-Analysis,* 3rd ed. (New York, 1923), p. 257.

church spire and cross because it concerns the glass-cutter, who is a father figure throughout the play. The door-opening suggests on the bottom level of thought a perfectly proper union of mother and father, while on a more accessible level it foreshadows to the dreamer the impossibility of ever realizing his profoundest wishes.

In contrast, the death by fire at the end is excruciating because it intimates that the Poet-dreamer is taking his father's place. At first the thought is as beautiful as the aconites blooming outside the castle. But like the aconite, the thought has a poisonous root. The Daughter enters the castle—another example of dream inversion—and the submerged Oedipal thought breaks to the surface at the moment of orgasm and death. The veil is rent, and for a second the soul finds release, for a second the eye is blinded by a vision of life without contradictions, and then the dreamer awakes in anguish, feeling but not understanding the enormity of his guilt.

All those questioning, sorrowful faces seen in the burning castle may be condensed into the face of the tormented dreamer. And behind all the unresolvable conflicts that the play sets before us lies the first one that we experience, the one that casts us out of paradise.

"Yes, my friend, the universe does have secrets," says Esther to her lover Max in a novel Strindberg wrote in 1904.

> "But people go about, not like the blind, because they do see, but not understanding."
> "Who you are, who I am, that's what we don't know. But when we were together, I felt as if I were embracing a corpse, which wasn't yours, but someone else's—I won't say whose."
> "And you, you seemed to be my father, and I felt ashamed and disgusted! What is this frightening, secret thing we have stumbled on to?"
> "Now for the first time perhaps mankind will get to know the unsolvable riddles. Suspect them anyway!" [13]

[13] *The Gothic Room, Samlade skrifter*, XL, 243–44.

The Chamber Plays

by Brian Rothwell

"My mind has recently been much occupied with death and
the life after this. Read Plato's *Timaeus* and *Phaedo* yesterday.
Am writing at the moment *Toten-Insel* where I describe the
awakening after death and what comes after that, but I draw
back in horror from revealing the endless misery of life."

The quotation refers to April 1907 and was reprinted in the first
of *The Blue Books* in September of the same year. In these early months
Strindberg wrote four plays as well as the unfinished *Toten-Insel*; *Storm*
(*Oväder*) was finished on the 13th of February, *The Burned House* or
After the Fire (*Brända Tomten*) was finished by the 2nd of March and
was followed by *The Ghost Sonata* and, in May, by *The Pelican*. Strindberg's return to drama after a silence of four years was largely due to
the imminent realization of the plans for an Intimate Theater: August
Falck's company had produced *Miss Julie* for the first time in Sweden
—first in Lund, then in the preceding December in Stockholm, and
success had paved the way for this venture. During the next years
Strindberg was deeply engaged with the art of drama as August Falck's
book (*Five Years with Strindberg*) or the papers collected as *Open Letters to the Intimate Theater* testify. Some of these papers deal with
Shakespeare—thus *Hamlet* is described in terms of a symphony while
in *The Tempest* Shakespeare "questions like the Buddhists the reality
of life"; in other places he describes the aim of the Theater's repertoire
—"the idea of chamber-music carried over to drama"—or talks about
the acting he requires stressing the spoken word—"One can act a scene
in the dark and enjoy it so long as it is spoken well." However, despite
this exaggeration which suggests that Strindberg should have written
radio drama, there is enough to balance it; of the set for *The Pelican*

"The Chamber Plays" by Brian Rothwell. From *Essays on Strindberg*, edited by
Carl Reinhold Smedmark (Stockholm: Beckmans Bokförlag, 1966), pp. 29–38. Copyright © 1966 by The Strindberg Society. Reprinted by permission of The Strindberg Society.

he writes, " 'I should like to live in that room,' I said, though one guessed the tragedy which would here play its last act with the most terrible motif from classical tragedy: innocent suffering children and the humbug mother Medea"; and of the set for *The Burned House* he said, "atmosphere—another word for poetry." Strindberg always demands a large measure of creative collaboration from his producer, his technicians, and cast and it is the potent interplay of aural and visual elements that most impresses me in these plays. The set, the props, the lighting, the use of music or the silent passages of "solo" work—all the resources of theater are used and I want to pick out some of these in the course of the essay and suggest their relation to a few themes and ideas in the plays.

One must begin by making some distinctions between the dramas. It seems to me that there is an increasingly overt religious or mystic view of the world in them; the Gentleman in *Storm,* living in the past and visited by it, is never so "philosophic" as the Stranger who revisits the past in *The Burned House* and neither of these plays presents a dead man on the stage or the interferences of the "powers" as the later plays do. *The Black Glove (Svarta Handsken)* which was added as "Opus 5" in 1909 is separated from the rest by being a "lyric fantasy"—the essential tone distances the death of the old man or the young Lady's madness at the loss of her child, for we know from the start that all will be well. Thus it is within the context of these basic distinctions that I can point to common features.

The proscenium arch of the Intimate Theater was flanked by free imitations of two pictures by Böcklin—the Isle of the Living and the Isle of the Dead. The latter picture was part of the inspiration for the fragment *Toten-Insel* (mentioned in the quotation with which I began) and provides the backdrop to the last scene of *The Ghost Sonata* as the room fills with light and the Student prays that the Lord of Heaven be gracious to the Girl on her journey. This image of the journey appears at the end of *The Pelican* as well; the house burns with all that is old and evil and ugly and Gerda smells the lavender and roses of the linen cupboard and thinks of Christmas Eve while her brother sees the white ferry boat coming to take them in their summer holidays;

> "Hurry up, Gerda, they're ringing the bell on the boat; Mummy's sitting in the saloon . . . no, she isn't there . . . poor Mummy! She's gone; is she still on the shore? I can't see her, it's no fun without Mummy—here she comes! Now the summer holidays have begun!"
>
> (Pause; the doors at the back open and show the red glow which is now very strong. The Son and Gerda sink to the floor.)

Although *Storm* and *The Burned House* end with the thought of a journey neither is so explicitly a journey into life-after-death and neither is accompanied by such strong theatrical effects. Certainly the end of *Storm* as the first lamp is lit and the Gentleman says, "And in the autumn I shall move from the silent house," has the suggestion of death, for earlier he has talked about old age when one balances the books with life and people and he has "already begun to pack for the journey" [1]—but this quiet cadence into "the peace of old age" is very different from the strong positive stress on the journey in the later plays. Again, when the Stranger places his wreath on the ruins, prays and says, "And so, out into the wide world again, wanderer," the suggestion is more of a wandering Buddha than death. *The Blue Books* help us to appreciate the qualities of the "other side" which is continually contrasted with life here where nothing is what it seems and everything falls asunder if you try to hold it. After the journey of death people are instructed in life and learn to accept their "fate," "the task they received, the work they had to get through"; they learn "why they had to do the action they detested; why others were allowed to torment them unjustly." Gradually light and reconciliation spread over the horrors of the past and even the most terrible memories are obliterated. "This was the place of rest or the summer holiday after the first death; and the days were short to them as a feast." The summer holiday to which Gerda and her brother are travelling appears elsewhere in *The Blue Books* in the section. "The Examination and the Summer Holiday." The teacher tells his disciple of old age after the "devastation of evil" (as Swedenborg calls the awakening to self-knowledge and stock-taking of the past) has taken place: one lives more in memory than in the present and, strangely, old age seems like the start of something new—if one has regained faith in the life after death.

> Then you feel as though you were preparing for an examination . . . there is a little exam-fever but also great expectations mixed with dreams of the future which remind you of Christmas, summer holidays, family gatherings where everyone made up their differences, wishes that came true: and there is the scent of freshly plucked birch leaves and the sea-shore, the sound of bells on a Sunday and the organ, the enticements of new clothes and clean linen, a bath in the deep-blue salt water, evening prayer and a good conscience, wife, home, and children after a journey, the fireside in a snowstorm, the first ball and your chosen partner, open-

[1] Leif Leifer's suggestion in a most stimulating article in *Samlaren* 1960 to which I am much indebted. I should also mention Evert Sprinchorn's fine introduction to a translation of these plays (Dover Books) which came to my notice after this essay was written.

ing your saving box and, from start to finish, the examination and the summer holidays.

Here are the Strindbergian positives; the clean linen that smells so fresh in *Storm* when Louise, that "phantom of delight," is working; the bells and Sunday that start *The Ghost Sonata*; happy moments in married life; Christmas and reconciliation as in *The Black Glove* and, of course, the sea—for the Islands of the Dead as Strindberg describes them are very much like his beloved Stockholm's archipelago mixed with the Alps. There is something of a reversion to childhood in these positives—indeed, like the strange wavering between the horrible and the humorous in these plays, there is the continual wavering on the borderline between the childish and the childlike in Strindberg. One remembers that Laura accepted the Captain not as a lover but as a child or the nightmare of the Officer in *A Dream Play* back in his desk at school. In *Storm* the Gentleman fears that Gerda will return and it will be "Begin again, begin again, repeat the old lessons on everything!"—an image from the schoolroom (*bakläxor*). But it is the very simplification, the distorting eye of the child's viewpoint, that gives the intensity to the nightmares—though, once again, that word is less applicable to the earlier plays.

Death is also theatrically present in them all. In *Storm* the Cafe Owner's stories of the deaths in the house and the carriages collecting corpses from the hospital (in a subtle way a variation on the carriages at night to the Fischer's club) keep death present in our minds as do the references to cakes for the wedding or the wake and the wedding carriages and the hearses. In *The Burned House* the ruins are neighbored by the inn, the Last Nail, where the convicts had their last drink in former days, and by the churchyard; we see wreaths for funerals and a bouquet for a marriage and, of course, the hearse driver. In *The Ghost Sonata* we even see the dead man himself and have two deaths behind that ever-present death-screen: in *The Pelican* the smell of carbolic and fir branches pervades the atmosphere and the dead husband (or, at least, the powers) is heard if not seen—and the play ends with deaths. By the time we come to *The Black Glove*, death is, as I said, distanced. The same pattern of growing nightmare ending in lyric fantasy is apparent.

If we look at the set, naturally the use of the house or building demands attention. The house in Östermalm is quiet; underneath in the basement the Cafe Owner bakes his cakes and into this granite stronghold he retires from the troubles above. The Gentleman lives with his memories in the "dignified, the pleasant, the reserved atmosphere

where one does not say everything" but, above, the curtains glow red
where the tenant died in the summer and where Gerda has moved in.
The play moves from outside the house into the Gentleman's flat and
out again just as it moves into his past and memories and out again
into autumn. His memories, "his poems on certain realities," are destroyed for Gerda has come in and there is nothing left,

> *Louise.* But that is deliverance!
> *Gentleman.* Look how empty it seems in there! Like after you've moved
> out . . . and up there, like after a fire!

The house to which he said he was bound by old memories no longer
holds him; the memories go moldy and lose color like badly made
jam. The house is more than a sort of "objective correlative" for his
emotions; it is almost personalized. This is even more true of the revelations from the ruins of *The Burned House*; in both the house gathers
into itself all the past, memories and associations, and in both these
are destroyed. In *The Ghost Sonata* the personalization has gone much
further; the theme returns again and again in the language—Hummel
speculates in houses and people (Johansson makes an explicit relation
between the two), the student saved the child who was not there from
the collapsing house (a variation on his relations with the Girl), and
both Bengtsson and the Student talk of the house having gone moldy
and rotten. In *The Pelican* the House with its deathlike cold (*gravkyla*)
is literally the past; the Mother is asked why she does not leave and says
that the landlord won't let them and they cannot move anyway; she is
locked in the salon with its smell of death because memories haunt the
other rooms. In *The Black Glove* the verse allows even more direct
personalization; the building is a Tower of Babel full of people all
making up the rhythms of "a waltz, a fugue, a sonata," like their pianos.
The house, then, is a theatrical expression of the hold of the past, of
the complexity of human relationships and of the spiritual state of the
actors. There is more to it than this, of course; each play sets up its own
series of references to the image—most complex in *The Ghost Sonata*.
For example when the Mummy meets Hummel again she says.

> "This is what I look like! Yes!—And once looked like that! (Pointing
> at the statue). It is *edifying* to live—I live mostly in the wardrobe so as
> to avoid seeing or being seen. . . ."

Which subtly picks up the personification of building, as well as being a nice example of the use of props to focus our attention on the
past in its relation to the present. In *The Black Glove* the Tower of
Babel becomes (in good Swedenborgian fashion) the ideas of the Old
Man, false schemes to climb up to heaven; in *Storm* it is the citadel of

lies which Gerda built about the Gentleman—a much less integrated motif in that play.

If one thinks of some of Strindberg's early uses of this image of the house and some later ones, the new richness is apparent. For example, the early poem, "Esplanadsystemet," describes a group of young people tearing down old houses; they reply to an old man's dismayed protest that they should build again.

> "This pulling down is to get air and light
> Isn't that perhaps enough?"

The use here is nearly allegorical but in the late *Streetscenes* (*Gatubilder*), describing a street in the morning, an autumn evening and at night, there is much more suggestiveness, many more layers of meaning. The houses lie silent in the morning, men uneasily sleeping and the Norns outside wait to play new games with them; but, where the street rises to a little hill at the end and the morning is appearing, a man comes sweeping the dust which forms a cloud—

> earth and heaven meet in the cloud.

In the autumn evening the houses breathe, full of uneasiness, uncertainty, and fear; at the end of the street is the water and on the other shore a little green island; the sun is setting and the globe on the church tower shines like another sun . . .

> but on the globe there stands a cross.

At night we descend into the blackest of blackness in the cellar where, hidden, the dynamo grinds out light for the whole area. I think these poems underline two things; the richness of the later symbolism and its religious nature—both of which apply very much to our plays. Doubtless some of the inspiration for the new use of symbolism comes from Swedenborg's doctrine of correspondences; one can see in Yeats and Blake, for example, how this pattern of correspondences throughout the universe on the different planes of existence all finally deriving from the Divine, gives an impulse to the symbolic imagination. *The Blue Books* are full of Strindberg's own "correspondences" including the Student's "correspondence" of the leek as a microcosm of the universe. Swedenborg points to a low level of correspondences in human endeavor: ". . . Whatever the industry of man prepares from (the animal, vegetable, or mineral kingdoms) for use, are correspondences; such as food of all kinds, garments, houses, public edifices, and so forth" (*Heaven and Hell*). In this way every act of man is the outcome and expression of the soul to which it bears a more or a less perfect correspondence. If we turn to the use of food or clothes imagery with that

in mind, I think we can fare better than the critics who collect Strindberg's complaints about cold or reheated food without seeing his attitude to them as correspondences and as punishments or warnings from
the "powers."

Obviously the cook with her soya bottle or the Mother with her spices
falsify reality—like the Dyer in *The Burned House* with his colored
hands. But the coldness in the house and the bad food in *The Pelican*
are also physical manifestations of the spiritual coldness, the lack of
love, and the estrangement in the house—like the "poison in the walls"
in *The Dance of Death*. Hummel freezes the Student when he holds
his hand, draining him of strength and warmth just as the Vampire
Cook sucks interest from the lives of others. Hummel too wears a wig
(although this is one of the things he verbally strips from the Colonel)
again falsifying reality: the Son-in-Law in *The Pelican* has stopped
wearing his uniform and is gradually dropping his mask. This theme
of stripping off the clothes or the mask is developed in the two plays
in a number of ways. Most of all one remembers the two banquets in
The Ghost Sonata—the ghost supper itself when Hummel strips the
company and the banquet when the Student's father stripped his so-
called friends and he was carried off to the madhouse. The teacher in
The Blue Books had a similar experience; sometimes he can wake from
his "pleasant sleepwalking": "then I see the company naked, their un-
clean linen through their clothes, their decrepitude, their unwashed
feet, but worst of all, I heard their thoughts behind their words" and
he describes a friend who did what the Student's father did and was
likewise taken to the asylum: "There are many sorts of madness, let
us admit that!" The idea of the world as a madhouse is repeated in
both *The Ghost Sonata* and *The Burned House*. When the Stranger
soliloquizes over the weight from the clock he says:

> Oh little earth; the densest of all the planets, the heaviest, and there-
> fore it is so heavy on you; so hard to breathe, so heavy to bear; the cross
> is your symbol but could have been a fool's cap-and-bells or a straight
> jacket . . . world of illusion and madmen!

There is an echo of Hamlet here, Hamlet who "when he plays the
madman can see how mad the world is" (*Open Letters*). The madman
and the child see in different ways from the adult and, as I said before,
it is the nightmare vision of the child that gives unity and intensity
to *The Ghost Sonata* and *The Pelican*. In the former there is a great
deal of play on seeing: the eyes which hurt after the Student's night of
tending sick and touching corpses and the eyes which can see more
than others as he is a Sunday child; the eyes opened by the poison
which will not let him see beauty in ugliness but do let him see the

sun and "The Hidden One" of his poem. All of this play on seeing is
counterpointed in numerous phrases like "We shall see, we shall see"
and, of course, Hummel with his glasses does not see the Milkmaid
because he is spiritually blind. The Mummy in the wardrobe avoiding
seeing or being seen or the Old Fiancée seeing life in her mirror and
thinking she is not seen, are avoiding reality. There is something similar
in *Storm* where the Gentleman wishes he were blind and deaf like the
Cafe Owner's wife—though later he has to admit that assumed deaf-
ness and silence can be dangerous: but the difference is to be noticed
—the journey into the reality of the past in *Storm* has none of the
feverish horror of the later plays. In *The Pelican,* the imagery is of
walking in one's sleep and then waking to the reality; Gerda puts the
vision of childhood against her assumed sleep—

"You are so vicious, people said to me, when I said that something
bad was bad . . . so I learnt to keep quiet . . . then I was liked for
my good behavior; so I learnt to say what I didn't mean and then I was
ready to go out into life." Life in *The Pelican* is something between a
dream and sleepwalking—one of the rejected titles for the play was *The
Sleepwalkers.* Gerda wakes against her will and the Mother begins to
wake when faced with the reality of herself though she falls asleep
again. *The Burned House* makes use of both images though the conscious sleepwalking of the Stranger is a mixture of knowledge and waiting. More interestingly, he was born without film over his eyes, has
looked enough at the misery of life and turned his eyes inwards to his
own soul. . . .

> *Stranger.* There really is something to see there . . .
> *Wife.* What do you see there?
> *Stranger.* Yourself! And when you see yourself, you die.
> (The wife holds her hands in front of her eyes.)

The truth or reality seems unpleasantly dangerous in Strindberg since
it kills the Girl in *The Ghost Sonata* but here it opens the Wife's eyes
and she is given the good advice to suffer but hope. All of this coming
to terms with the past and with the reality of oneself is again this
strange mixture of Swedenborg and Buddhism. For Swedenborg the
Day of Judgment takes place when a man sees his past life pass before
him and the balancing of the books "reveals a terrible plus on the debit
side." One wakes "as from a dream and can see oneself like a ghost and
one recoils; 'Is that me?' you ask yourself. One discovers things one did
that now seem indefensible and one asks oneself 'How could I?' Yes,
you slid into sin once; another time you were dragged along by the
hair . . . or fell into a trap" (*Blue Book I*). Resignation with hope
("because hope is to believe good of God") seems to be the keynote of

Strindberg religion. The Mummy in *The Ghost Sonata* deals with the
past "through suffering and repentance" and Strindberg wrote in April
about his *Dream Play* which was being rehearsed; "that I revealed the
relative worthlessness of life (Buddhism), its mad contradictions, its
viciousness and disorder, can be praiseworthy, if it gives men resignation; that I showed men's relative (?) innocence in this life which itself
involves guilt, is certainly not bad." Once more the distinctions between
the plays can be made clearer; *The Ghost Sonata*, "questioning like
the Buddhists the reality of life," was subtitled "Kama-Loka; a Buddhist
Drama" in Falck's manuscript and *The Pelican* was at one time to be
called *Purgatory*. This returns to a constant theme in Strindberg since
the *Inferno*; that this life may really be hell or purgatory. Life is perhaps only Maya (Illusion)—the theme is there in *The Burned House*
with its repeated "vanity of vanities": "Suffer! It will pass! This too is
vanity," but in *The Ghost Sonata* and *The Pelican* the suffering is at
once more intense and more purgatorial. In *The Black Glove* the suffering is to cure the heart of the Young Wife and lead her to charity;
in the room of trials testing the patience of the Student, the dirt of
everyday life makes the harp deaf and dumb and death is the liberator.
In *The Pelican* there was no other way to solve the contradictions and
the horror of life than the fire. "Everything must burn to ashes or we
shall never get out of this place."

These journeys into the past or oneself, this waking to new insight
into oneself or life, involve the related problems of guilt and character.
"Crime and secrets and guilt" bind the company at the Ghost supper
together and the Swamp, as the street of *The Burned House* is called,
is where "everyone hates everyone else, slanders everyone else, torments
everyone else" and each person the Stranger meets is bound to him in
some way in the pattern woven by the shuttle of fate. If you try to
disentangle your relations with others and apportion blame you will
just come back to "the rope on the butcher. And the rod on the fire!"
Another part of Swedenborg's correspondence is concerned with this.

> "The work of regeneration is chiefly occupied in making the natural
> man correspond to the rational." "But men, spirits, and angels are so
> full of iniquity that absolute correspondence can never take place to
> eternity, yet the Lord is always making it more perfect."

One has to learn to accept one's Karma (fate): life is according to
the teacher in *The Blue Books*,

> such a web of lies, mistakes, misunderstanding, of guilt and debt, that a
> settlement of the accounts is impossible. . . . Rhadamanthus would never
> be able to disentangle it, but the Crucified could with one word to the
> repentant thief. Today you shall be with me in paradise.

Sometimes guilt and sin seem to be their own punishment; the Son tells his mother he had often said: "She is so evil that it is a pity about her." (The famous sentence of Indra's daughter, *"Det är synd om män-niskorna,"* ["Humankind is pitiful"] perhaps has an overtone of this in it, for "pity" and "sin" are both "synd" in Swedish.) Sin too is not just action but also thought and one can murder with words as Gerda "murdered" the Gentleman in *Storm* or the way the Mother in *The Pelican* murdered her husband. But there is Nemesis, "a punishing justice" where "everything comes back again" (*"allt går igen"*)—a repeated theme from Inferno onwards. In these plays it is often contrasted with the social processes of justice; the Son in *The Pelican* decides not to take his law exam (a subtle hint of the "summer holiday" at the end when their father is free from school and examinations). "I don't believe in law; the laws seem to have been written by thieves and murderers to free the criminal"—which reminds us of the Student's cries over the freeing of Barrabbas—"the thief always has the sympathy!" In *The Ghost Sonata* too, Hummel is thick with the police but he still ends up with the rope around his neck that can remind him of the way he choked the Consul with IOU's. The Police in *The Burned House* may arrest the wrong person but the "net" is not the work of man's hands. Again one is to accept one's fate realizing that one hardly knows oneself (let alone other people) and one must trust that all is finally for the best if one could only see the pattern.

Strindberg, using the illusion of theater to reveal the illusion of life, makes some fine use of theater images. For example, in *The Burned House* when the Wife and the Stranger meet for the first time they find they do not answer the descriptions others have given of them:

> *Wife.* Yes, people are so unjust to each other, and they paint each other—
> each in their own image . . .
> *Stranger.* And they go around like a theater producer giving each other
> parts to act . . .

Earlier in the same play is the idea of life as a theater where certain scenes are set up to be acted out. Something similar is Hummel's command to the Colonel "keep calm now and we can play our old roles again!"—which of course the Colonel does almost too completely; for him illusion has become reality! Both of these examples have a different effect from *Storm* where Gerda admits with shame that she has been on the stage and we hear that the Gentleman hates the stage. Life as illusion—a dream or a play—is underlined by the references in the later plays whereas in *Storm* they are much less involved with the central concerns of the play. The same applies to the comparison of the red curtains in the Fischers' flat to the tabs of a theater behind which they are rehearsing bloody dramas or the Cafe Owner's mysterious. "But dramas have been acted here. . . ."

I have mentioned a few of Strindberg's uses of the set and the props but I should like to point out a few more, for the plays must stand or fall as drama in the theater. Constantly Strindberg focuses the attention on an article of furniture or something in the set to heighten one's awareness of situation or the tension. In *Storm* those red curtains which change from theater tabs to a red cigar at night and finally to a red thundercloud hanging overhead, grow more and more threatening until the storm breaks. In that play too, Gerdas' entry into the room where she lived for five years with the Gentleman is masterly; she appropriates everything to herself including the suggestive carving or painting on the sideboard of the Knight with Eve (—"Eve with the apples in her basket") and the thermometer which "became a symbol at the end" of impermanence or the chess set which emphasizes the loneliness of old age. The telephone waiting to bite like a snake in the last act adds much to the dramatic tension—though less than the hectic scene with the telegraph in *The Dance of Death*. This could be demonstrated over and over again in the other plays; the physical presence of the Buddha with his flower bodies forth the poetry of the last scene of *The Ghost Sonata*; the clock ticks ominously in the silence at the supper; the death-screen is always visible inside the house. In *The Pelican* the evermoving rocking chair "which was always like two chopping-blades when he sat there and hacked at my heart" punctuates the frenzy and the fear of the guilty wife and the sofa on which he died stands covered with a red cloth—"It's a bloody butcher's table," she says and the mysteries of the past have new horrible overtones added to them. Indeed the relationships and the past are never sorted out in these plays—the numerous entanglements and allusions cannot be given logical and causal coherence by even a hundred readings—and so some of these uses of the props are powerfully suggestive.

This is also true of the silent passages where the character reveals him or herself in action. The Gentleman's long silences in the second scene where he plays chess with himself, wanders up and down, exclaims "The peace of old age! Yes!" and then sits drumming on the table, lighting matches and blowing them out, looking at the clock, and so on, reveals more of his tiredness with the peace of old age than words; it is too a magnificent lull before his dialogue with his brother that ends with the entry of Gerda—furioso! (Strindberg is, in my opinion, a master of "rhythm" in the construction of his plays). In *The Ghost Sonata*, Hummel's wanderings around the room, greedily fingering objects or arranging his wig, is another solo vignette challenging the actor. The most difficult one is in *The Pelican* when the Mother prepares to jump out of the window (incidentally something that has been mentioned before about her), knocks on the door prevent her, she closes the window but there is no one outside the door, though it opens; the Son can be heard inside but the roars are from the garden in her imagination— they *are* her husband; she hides; the wind comes again, the papers fly and a flower pot crashes to the floor; she puts all the lights on (like the Captain in *The Dance of Death*), the rocking chair moves as she goes round and round the room finally throwing herself on the sofa. As elsewhere in the play it is the "powers" that are warning her; later the "three knocks" will stop her when she is talking about the dead man and earlier the stage has been empty while similar things have happened. This scene certainly does demand much "creative collaboration" from the company! Easier, because more stylized, is the mimed scene by candlelight in *The Black Glove* when the child is being taken. There music underlines the action—as it does in the Old Man's lyrical memories in the same play. Music, again as a stimulant to memory or a concomitant of the action or mood, is used in *Storm* and *The Pelican* as well—the waltz with its associations of the past in the first case and of the Mother's attraction for the Son-in-Law in the other and the Chopin *Fantasie Impromptu* to punctuate the Gentleman's loneliness in *Storm* and to add to the storm at the start of *The Pelican*.

The chamber plays will probably always be "caviar to the general" and the demands they make on the performers and the theater are not small. The strange religious-mystical view of the world which I have sketched is probably very foreign to most of us and only superlative production could save them from laughter but I am more and more convinced that they could be strong theatrical experience and that their distorting vision provokes uncomfortable but salutary reassessment of oneself and life. *The Ghost Sonata* has been the most produced and the most influential but the other plays demand attention and they are mutually illuminating—from the carefully modulated tone of the *Storm* to the nightmare visions of the later plays and the final lyric fantasy of *The Black Glove*, where the poetry and the themes of reconciliation and love form a lighter and more graceful world.

Chronology of Important Dates

1849   (January 22) Johan August Strindberg born in Stockholm, the fourth and eldest legitimate child of a grocer (later shipping agent) and a former servant girl and waitress. Eventually twelve children in the family, seven of whom live to maturity.

1853   Father goes bankrupt; later attains a degree of financial recovery.

1862   Mother dies.

1863   Father marries his housekeeper.

1867   Passes Matriculation exam and spends autumn semester at Uppsala University.

1868   Supports himself by substitute teaching in elementary school in Stockholm, and by private tutoring.

1869   Studies medicine briefly and fails as apprentice actor. Writes first three plays (two of which have been preserved: *The Freethinker* [*Fritänkaren*] and *Hermione*[1]).

1870   Returns to Uppsala to study humanities. *In Rome* [*I Rom*] produced at the Royal Theater.

1871   Receives small grant from King Charles XV's private purse. Grant terminated next year upon the king's death. Spends first of several successive summer stays in the Stockholm archipelago.

1872   Leaves Uppsala without a degree. Prose version of *Master Olof* [*Mäster Olof*].

1872–74   Holds various jobs as journalist in Stockholm, including the editorship of a trade journal for the insurance business.

1874–82   Works as assistant in Royal Library, and studies sinology. Contributes to newspapers and periodicals.

1875   Meets Siri von Essen Wrangel, a married actress of Finnish extraction.

1876   First visits Paris. *Master Olof* in verse.

1877   Marries Siri von Essen after her divorce from Baron Wrangel.

---

[1] Strindberg's works are listed under the year in which they were completed. In most cases, this (or the year following) was also the year of first publication.

1878   Daughter dies shortly after birth.

1879   Achieves fame with *The Red Room* [*Röda rummet*], a satirical novel about writers and artists in contemporary Stockholm.

1880   Karin Strindberg born.

1881   First performance of *Master Olof* (prose version). Greta Strindberg born.

1882   *Lucky-Per's Journey* [*Lycko-Pers resa*], a romantic-satirical fairy play, influenced by Ibsen's *Peer Gynt*. *The New Kingdom* [*Det nya riket*], a miscellany of satirical pamphlets.

1883   Leaves Sweden. Lives abroad (France, Switzerland, Bavaria, Denmark) until 1889.

1883–84 *Poems* [*Dikter*] and *Sleepwalker Nights in Broad Daylight* [*Sömngångarnätter på vakna dagar*], two volumes of verse.

1884   *Married* [*Giftas*], I, a collection of short stories about married life. Returns briefly to Sweden to stand trial for alleged blasphemy (actually, more likely, for outspoken treatment of sex) in one of the stories. Acquitted, but great nervous strain. Subsequently has difficulty finding publishers. Suffers penury and sense of persecution. Visits Italy. Hans Strindberg born.

1885   *Married*, II, a more openly antifeminist collection of stories.

1886   First two volumes of *The Son of a Servant: The Growth of a Soul* [*Tjänstekvinnans son: en själs utvecklingshistoria*] a thinly disguised autobiography. *Comrades* [*Kamraterna*] (originally entitled *Marauders*), first naturalistic play.

1887   Last two volumes of *The Son of a Servant* (vol. IV not published until 1909). *The Father* [*Fadren*]. *The Natives of Hemsö* [*Hemsöborna*], a local-color novel set in the Stockholm archipelago.

1888   *Life in the Skerries* [*Skärkarlsliv*], island short stories. *Miss Julie* [*Fröken Julie*]. *Creditors* [*Fordringsägare*]. *A Madman's Defense* [*Le plaidoyer d'un fou, En dåres försvarstal*], the story of his first marriage, originally written and published in French. Corresponds with Nietzsche, shortly before the latter's insanity.

1889   Strindberg's Scandinavian Experimental Theater in Copenhagen, modeled on André Antoine's Théâtre Libre in Paris, opens and almost immediately closes. Writes *The Stronger* [*Den starkare*] and three other one-act naturalistic plays. Returns to Sweden.

1890   *By the Open Sea* [*I havsbandet*], another island novel, about the psychological disintegration of an intellectual superman.

1891   Divorces Siri von Essen.

1892–96 Enters second exile. Leads bohemian life among artists in Berlin (the circle gathering in the Zum schwarzen Ferkel tavern). Later stays in Paris and Austria. Paints, conducts chemical experiments.

1892   *The Bond* and five other one-acters, last plays before the Inferno period.

1893   Marries Frida Uhl, an Austrian writer, on the island of Helgoland. Honeymoons in London.

1894   Kerstin Strindberg born. Separates from second wife.

1894-97   The Inferno crisis. Travels restlessly (Paris, Austria, Sweden); suffers mental and spiritual anguish, periodic paranoia, hallucinations; converts to Swedenborgian mysticism; retires temporarily into monastic seclusion; studies occultism, alchemy, theosophy; writes little.

1895, 1896 Two separate voluntary stays at nerve clinic in Ystad, Sweden.

1896-99   Residence in Lund, Sweden, interrupted for a few months in 1897-98 by last visit to Paris.

1897   The Inferno books: *Inferno*, a subjective autobiography (in French) of the years of crisis; *Legends* [*Legender*] (originally including *Wrestling Jacob* [*Jakob brottas*], the author's metaphysical self-vindication in monologue). Second divorce.

1898   *To Damascus* [*Till Damaskus*], I, II, first expressionistic play. *Advent*, a mystery-morality.

1899   *Crime and Crime* [*Brott och brott*] (appearing with *Advent* under the common title *Before a Higher Court* [*Vid högre rätt*]). First series of history plays: *The Saga of the Folkungs* [*Folkungasagan*], *Gustav Vasa*, *Erik XIV*. Settles in Stockholm.

1900   *Gustav Adolf. Easter* [*Påsk*]. *The Dance of Death* [*Dödsdansen*], I, II. *The Bridal Crown* [*Kronbruden*], a folklore play.

1901   *Swanwhite* [*Svanevit*], a fairy-tale play. *To Damascus*, III. *A Dream Play* [*Ett drömspel*]. Further royal histories: *Charles XII* [*Karl XII*], *Queen Christina* [*Kristina*]. Marries Harriet Bosse, a young Norwegian actress, and for the next several years devotes most of his *Occult Diary* [*Ockulta dagboken*] (begun in 1897) to his relationship with her. Makes last trip abroad (Denmark, Berlin).

1902   *Gustav III*, last of the royal plays. Anne-Marie Strindberg born.

1903   *Alone* [*Ensam*], last of the autobiographies.

1904   *Black Banners* [*Svarta fanor*], a virulently satirical *roman à clef* (published in 1907). Third divorce.

1906   *The Roofing Feast* [*Taklagsöl*], an experimental novella. *The Scapegoat* [*Syndabocken*], a short psychological novel.

1907-12   Writes philological and cabalistic works and various polemics on religion and politics, including four *Blue Books* [*En blå bok*, etc.], collections of brief, miscellaneous essays.

1907   The Intimate Theater (Intima teatern) opens in Stockholm,

Strindberg's own small, experimental stage under the management of the young actor-director August Falck. *Storm* [*Oväder*], *The Burned House* [*Brända tomten*], *The Ghost Sonata* [*Spöksonaten*], *The Pelican* [*Pelikanen*]—all "chamber plays" written for the Intimate Theater.

1908   Moves into apartment in "the Blue Tower" in Stockholm, his last home.

1908–9   *Open Letters to the Intimate Theater* [*Öppna brev till Intima teatern*], essays on drama (mainly Shakespeare) and theater. Last history plays. *The Black Glove* [*Svarta handsken*], "opus 5" of the chamber plays.

1909   Last play, *The Great Highway* [*Stora landsvägen*], a pilgrimage play like *To Damascus* and *A Dream Play*. Engaged briefly to Fanny Falkner, a nineteen-year-old art student, whom he tries to make into an actress.

1910   The Intimate Theater closes.

1910–11   Is involved in the "Strindberg feud," a newspaper controversy over his return to political liberalism.

1911   Signs contract with Albert Bonnier's publishing house for the publication of his collected works. Achieves financial security.

1912   His sixty-third birthday is publicly celebrated, and he accepts a "people's gift" of nearly 50,000 *kronor* (about $12,000)—"my anti-Nobel prize" according to Strindberg himself, who had quarreled with the secretary of the Swedish Academy.

(May 14) Dies from cancer of the stomach.

Notes on the Editor and Contributors

OTTO REINERT, the editor of this volume, teaches in the English and Comparative Literature Departments at the University of Washington. He has edited several drama anthologies and has published articles on drama and other topics both in this country and in his native Norway.

ERIC BENTLEY, born in England, was from 1953 to 1969 Brander Matthews Professor of Dramatic Literature at Columbia University. He preceded Robert Brustein as drama critic for *The New Republic*. In addition to translations of and introductions to the plays of Bertolt Brecht, his many publications on modern drama include *The Playwright as Thinker* (1946), *Bernard Shaw* (1947; revised edition 1957), *In Search of Theater* (1953), and *The Life of the Drama* (1964).

ROBERT BRUSTEIN has been Professor of English and Dean of the Yale School of Drama since 1966. Since 1959 he has been drama critic for *The New Republic*. The most important of his books on modern drama are *The Theatre of Revolt* (1964), and two collections of reviews, *Seasons of Discontent* (1965), and *The Third Theatre* (1969). In 1964 he edited a selection of Strindberg's prose and plays.

MAURICE GRAVIER taught at the French Institute at the University of Stockholm from 1937 to 1940. Since 1955 he has been Director of the Institute of Scandinavian Studies at the University of Paris (the Sorbonne.) He has done extensive translations of Scandinavian and German literature. In 1949 appeared his *Strindberg et le théâtre moderne*.

WALTER JOHNSON is head of the Scandinavian Department at the University of Washington. He has translated and edited Strindberg's history plays and written the definitive critical and scholarly study of them, *Strindberg and the Historical Drama* (1963).

R. JAMES KAUFMANN is Professor of English at the University of Texas in Austin. A specialist in intellectual history, he has written books and essays on Renaissance drama and on modern culture.

PÄR LAGERKVIST is the most eminent living Swedish author—novelist, short-story writer, playwright, and poet. Among his novels are *The Dwarf* (1944), *Barabbas* (1950), and *The Death of Ahasverus* (1960). His plays include *The Man Who Lived Twice* (1928) and *The Executioner* (1933). He is a member of the Swedish Academy. In 1951 he received the Nobel Prize for literature.

MARTIN LAMM (1880–1950) was Professor of Literature at Stockholm University and a member of the Swedish Academy. He is the author of *Strindbergs dramer* (1924–26), *Strindberg och makterna* (1936), *August Strindberg* (1940–42; revised edition 1948), and *Det moderna dramat* (1948; translated as *The Modern Drama*, 1952).

BRIAN ROTHWELL is a young English Strindberg scholar at St. Catherine's College at Cambridge University.

EVERT SPRINCHORN is Professor of Drama at Vassar College. Among his many publications on Scandinavian drama are an edition of *Ibsen's Letters and Speeches* (1964) and translation-editions of Strindberg's plays and prose, with substantial critical introductions.

BIRGITTA STEENE teaches English literature at Temple University. She has written a study of Ingmar Bergman's films for the Twayne World Authors Series. Her book on Strindberg, *The Greatest Fire*, will appear in 1972.

VICTOR SVANBERG has now retired as Professor of Swedish Literature at the University of Uppsala. His publications, chiefly on nineteenth-century literature, emphasize the relationship between literature and society.

RAYMOND WILLIAMS is a Fellow of Jesus College at Cambridge University. Among other books, he has published *Drama from Ibsen to Eliot* (1952; revised as *Drama from Ibsen to Brecht*, 1968), *Drama in Performance* (1954; revised edition 1968), and *Modern Tragedy* (1966).

Selected Bibliography

I. Strindberg's Works

A. IN SWEDISH

Brev. Edited by Torsten Eklund, with an introduction by Martin Lamm. 11 vols. (in progress). Stockholm: Bonnier, 1948– . Strindberg's letters from 1858 till November, 1896.

Dramer. Edited by Carl Reinhold Smedmark. 3 vols. (in progress). Stockholm: Bonnier, 1962– . The published volumes include all the plays written before 1889.

Samlade skrifter. Edited by John Landquist. 55 vols. Stockholm: Bonnier, 1912–20. The standard collected edition, but not inclusive or always textually reliable.

Skrifter. Edited by Gunnar Brandell. 14 vols. Stockholm: Bonnier 1945–46. Includes just about all the important works. Good, brief commentary.

B. IN ENGLISH

The Chamber Plays. Translated by Evert Sprinchorn et al. Introduction by Evert Sprinchorn. New York: Dutton, 1962.

A Dream Play and The Ghost Sonata. Translated by Carl Richard Mueller, with an introduction by Robert W. Corrigan. San Francisco: Chandler, 1966.

Eight Expressionistic Plays. Translated and with prefaces to the pilgrimage plays by Arvid Paulson, introduction and a preface to *The Ghost Sonata* by John Gassner. Toronto: Bantam Books, 1965. *Lucky-Per's Journey, The Keys to Heaven, To Damascus,* I–II, *A Dream Play, The Great Highway, The Ghost Sonata.*

Five Plays. Translated by Elizabeth Sprigge. Garden City, N.Y.: Doubleday Anchor, 1960. *Creditors, Crime and Crime, The Dance of Death, Swanwhite, The Great Highway.*

From an Occult Diary: Marriage with Harriet Bosse. Edited and with an introduction and notes by Torsten Eklund, translated by Mary Sandbach. New York: Hill & Wang, 1965.

[Historical plays.] Translated and with introductions by Walter Johnson. 5 vols. Seattle: University of Washington Press, 1955–59. *Queen Christina, Charles XII, Gustav III* (1955). *The Last of the Knights, The Regent, Earl Birger of Bjälbo* (1956). *Gustav Adolf* (1957). *The Vasa Trilogy: Master Olof, Gustav Vasa, Erik XIV* (1959). *The Saga of the Folkungs, Engelbrekt* (1959).

Inferno, Alone, and Other Writings. Edited and with an introduction by Evert Sprinchorn. Garden City, N.Y.: Doubleday Anchor, 1968.

Letters of Strindberg to Harriet Bosse. Edited and translated by Arvid Paulson. New York: T. Nelson, 1959.

A Madman's Defense. Translation based on Ellie Schleussner's version, *The Confession of a Fool,* revised and edited by Evert Sprinchorn. Garden City, N.Y.: Doubleday Anchor, 1967.

A Madman's Manifesto. Translated by Anthony Swerling, with an Introduction by Børge G. Madsen. University, Ala.: University of Alabama Press, 1971. The first English translation based directly on Strindberg's original version in French.

Miss Julie. With a preface by the author. Translated and with an introduction by Evert Sprinchorn. San Francisco: Chandler, 1961.

The Natives of Hemsö. Translated by Arvid Paulson, with an introduction by Richard B. Vowles. New York: P. S. Eriksson, 1965.

Open Letters to the Intimate Theater. Translations and Introductions by Walter Johnson. Seattle: University of Washington Press, 1966.

Plays. Edited and translated by Michael Meyer. 1 vol. (in progress). New York: Random House, 1964. *The Father, Miss Julie, Creditors, The Stronger, Playing with Fire, Erik the Fourteenth, Storm, The Ghost Sonata.* This promises to be the standard edition of the major plays in English.

The Red Room. Translated by Ellie Schleussner. New York: Putnam, 1913.

Seven Plays. Translated by Arvid Paulson, with an introduction by John Gassner. New York: Bantam Books, 1960. *The Father, Miss Julie, Comrades, The Stronger, The Bond, Crime and Crime, Easter.*

Six Plays. Translated by Elizabeth Sprigge. Garden City, N.Y.: Doubleday Anchor, 1955. *The Father, Miss Julie, The Stronger, Easter, A Dream Play, The Ghost Sonata.*

The Son of a Servant: The Story of the Evolution of a Human Being. Translated and with an introduction and notes by Evert Sprinchorn. Garden City, N.Y.: Doubleday Anchor, 1966. Part I of Strindberg's autobiographical tetralogy.

A Strindberg Reader. Compiled, translated, and edited by Arvid Paulson. New York: Phaedra, Inc., 1968.

Three Plays. Translated by Peter Watts. Baltimore: Penguin Books, 1958. *The Father, Miss Julie, Easter.*

To Damascus. A Trilogy. Translated by Graham Rawson. New York: Grove Press, 1960. First published in London, 1939, by The Anglo-Swedish Literary Foundation.

Twelve Plays. Translated by Elizabeth Sprigge. London: Constable, 1963. *The Father, Miss Julie, Creditors, The Stronger, The Bond, Crime and Crime, Easter, The Dance of Death, Swanwhite, A Dream Play, The Ghost Sonata, The Great Highway.*

II. Biography

A. IN SWEDISH

Brandell, Gunnar. *Strindbergs Infernokris.* Stockholm: Bonnier, 1950. Neither factual biography nor literary analysis, but a study of the psychology of Strindberg's spiritual crisis in the mid-1890s.

Falck, August. *Fem år med Strindberg.* Stockholm: Wahlström & Widstrand, 1935. By the manager-director of the Intimate Theater, 1907–10.

Falkner, Fanny. *August Strindberg i Blå tornet.* Stockholm: P. A. Norstedt & soner, 1921. Strindberg's last years described by the woman who almost became his fourth wife.

Hedén, Erik. *Strindberg: liv och diktning.* Stockholm: Bokförlaget Nutiden, 1921. German translation by J. Koppel, *Strindberg: Leben und Dichtung.* Munich, 1926. Still the fullest biography. Assumes direct relationship between life and work.

Smirnoff, Karin. *Strindbergs första hustru.* 2nd ed. Stockholm: Bonnier, 1926. A vindication of Siri von Essen, Strindberg's first wife, by their eldest daughter.

Svedfelt, Torsten. *Strindbergs ansikte.* Stockholm: Nordisk rotogravyr, 1948. A virtually complete iconography.

Tranströmer, Gösta. *August Strindberg, 1849–1949.* Stockholm: Åhlén & Åkerlund, 1948. A pictorial biography with brief text.

B. IN ENGLISH

Mortensen, Brita, and Downs, Brian W. *Strindberg: An Introduction to His Life and Work.* Cambridge: Cambridge University Press, 1949, 1965. A reliable and readable guide, of more than just biographical interest.

Sprigge, Elizabeth. *The Strange Life of August Strindberg.* London: Hamish Hamilton, 1949. Undocumented and insistently empathic, but supersedes earlier biographies in English.

Strindberg, Frida Uhl. *Marriage with Genius.* Edited by Frederic Whyte. London: J. Cape, 1940. The memoirs of Strindberg's second wife. Abridged.

III. Bibliography

Bryer, Jackson R. "Strindberg 1951–1962: A Bibliography." *Modern Drama,* V (December 1962), 269–75. Continues Esther Rapp's bibliography (below).

Gravier, Maurice. *Strindberg et le théâtre moderne. I: L'Allemagne.* Lyon and Paris: IAC [Imprimerie Artistique en Couleurs], 1949, pp. 171–79. Extensive and discriminating.

Gustafson, Alrik. *A History of Swedish Literature.* Minneapolis: University of Minnesota Press for The American-Scandinavian Foundation, 1961. Pp. 601–9; biography and criticism; pp. 651–54; Strindberg in English translation.

Lindström, Göran. "Strindberg Studies 1915–1962." *Scandinavica,* II (May, 1963), 27–50. A judicious survey of Strindberg scholarship in Sweden and abroad. Calls for a new complete scholarly edition and a definitive biography.

Rapp, Esther H. "Strindberg's Reception in England and America." *Scandinavian Studies,* XXIII (Feburary, May, August, 1951), 1–22, 49–59, 109–37. An annotated chronological list of translations, books, articles, productions, and reviews before 1950.

Rinman, Sven. "Bibliografi: Strindberg." *Ny illustrerad svensk litteraturhistoria.* Edited by E. N. Tigerstedt. Stockholm: Natur och kultur, 1957. IV, 421–29.

Vowles, Richard B. "A Cook's Tour of Strindberg Scholarship." *Modern Drama,* V (December, 1962), 256–68. Identifies issues and areas of interest in recent Strindberg studies.

IV. Criticism

A. IN SWEDISH, FRENCH, AND GERMAN

Berendsohn, Walter A. *Strindbergsproblem.* Translated from German by Knut Stubbendorf. Stockholm: Kooperativa förbundets bokförlag, 1946. Substantial essays on Strindberg's psychology and art.

Brandell, Gunnar. "Der moderne Strindberg." *Merkur,* XVIII (1964), 21–33. On Strindberg's expressionism as an anticipation of contemporary absurdism.

* ———, ed. *Synpunkter på Strindberg.* Stockholm: Aldus/Bonnier, 1964. A collection of essays from 1912–62, mainly by Swedes.

* Gravier, Maurice. *Strindberg et le théâtre moderne. I: L'Allemagne.* Lyon and Paris: IAC [Imprimerie Artistique en Couleurs], 1949. Strindberg's influence on German drama.

* Denotes a selection included in whole or in part in this volume.

Jolivet, Alfred. *Le théâtre de Strindberg.* Paris: Boivin et Cie, 1931. A good general study.

Lamm, Martin. *August Strindberg.* Rev. ed. Stockholm: Bonnier, 1948. (1st ed. in 2 vols. 1940, 1942). Discussion of Strindberg's whole canon in the context of his life. Particular emphasis on the nondramatic writings. A basic study.

━━━. Strindbergs dramer. 2 vols. Stockholm: Bonnier, 1924, 1926. Younger Swedish critics have supplemented and modified some of Lamm's views and challenged his biographical bias, but this remains the standard critical discussion of the plays in Swedish. Deserves translation.

━━━. *Strindberg och makterna.* Stockholm: Svenska kyrkans diakonstyrelses bokförlag, 1936. On Strindberg's metaphysics. Stays away from psychopathology.

Leifer, Leif. "Den lutrende ild. En studie i symboliken i Strindberg's kammerspill." *Samlaren,* LXXXI (1960), 168–94. A provocative but difficult essay on the chamber plays.

Linder, Sten. *Ibsen, Strindberg och andra.* Stockholm: Bonnier, 1936. The long title essay is a useful comparative study of the two Scandinavian playwrights.

Ollén, Gunnar. *Strindbergs dramatik: en handbok.* Rev. ed. Stockholm: Radiotjänst, 1961. Facts about composition, sources, plots, publication, and productions of all Strindberg's plays. Brief but sound critical comments.

Rinman, Sven. "Strindberg." *Ny illustrerad svensk litteraturhistoria.* Edited by E. N. Tigerstedt. Stockholm: Natur och kultur, 1957. IV, 31–144. A full, informative, balanced, and incisive discussion in the best European tradition of literary history.

Svensk litteraturtidskrift, XII (1949). Centennial issue with tributes by world authors.

B. IN ENGLISH

Adler, Henry. "To Hell with Society." *Tulane Drama Review,* IV (May, 1960), 53–76. A spirited defense of (mainly) *A Dream Play* against Kenneth Tynan's charge that Strindberg's dramatic visions are socially irrelevant and therefore negligible.

Allen, James L., Jr. "Symbol and Meaning in Strindberg's *Crime and Crime.*" *Modern Drama,* IX (May), 1966, 62–73. On the ambiguities of the play's imagery of guilt and atonement.

Andersson, Hans. *Strindberg's Master Olof and Shakespeare.* Uppsala: Lundequistska bokhandeln, and Cambridge: Harvard University Press, 1952.

Bentley, Eric. "August Strindberg." In *The Playwright as Thinker.* New York: Harcourt, Brace, 1946, pp. 135–53. Still a valuable assessment of Strindberg's place in modern drama.

● ———. "Strindberg, the One and the Many." In *In Search of Theater*. New York: Knopf, 1953, pp. 134-43.

Borland, Harold H. *Nietzsche's Influence on Swedish Literature*. Göteborg: Wettergren och Kerber, 1957.

● Brustein, Robert. "August Strindberg." In *The Theatre of Revolt*. Boston: Little, Brown, 1964, pp. 85-134. A slightly revised version of "Male and Female in August Strindberg," *Tulane Drama Review*, VII (1962), 130-74.

Bulman, Joan. *Strindberg and Shakespeare: Shakespeare's Influence on Strindberg's Historical Drama*. London, J. Cape, 1933.

Dahlström, Carl E. W. L. *Strindberg's Dramatic Expressionism*. 2nd ed. with the author's essay "Origins of Strindberg's Expressionism." New York: B. Blom, 1965. (1st ed. Ann Arbor, Mich.: University of Michigan Press, 1930.) The essay added in the 2nd edition first appeared in *Scandinavian Studies*, XXXIV (1962), 36-46. Finds expressionistic elements in Strindberg's naturalistic plays.

Freedman, Morris. "Strindberg's Positive Nihilism." *Drama Survey*, II (Winter, 1963), 288-96. Also in *The Moral Impulse: Modern Drama from Ibsen to the Present*. Carbondale: Southern Illinois University Press, 1967, pp. 19-30. The "moral progression" in Strindberg's plays is "from the bitterness of personal anger to the hopelessness of the universal."

Gassner, John. *Masters of the Drama*. 3rd rev. ed. New York: Dover, 1954, pp. 388-96.

———. *The Theatre in Our Times*. New York: Crown, 1954. Pp. 170-76: "Strindberg and the Twentieth Century"; pp. 177-81: "Strindberg: 1950 Centenary Productions"; pp. 208-11: "Strindberg, Ibsen, and Shaw."

Gustafson, Alrik. "Strindberg and the Realistic Breakthrough." In *A History of Swedish Literature*. Minneapolis: University of Minnesota Press for The American-Scandinavian Foundation, 1961, pp. 243-75.

———. "The Scandinavian Countries." In *A History of Modern Drama*. Edited by Barrett H. Clark and George Freedley. New York and London: Appleton-Century, 1947, pp. 1-75.

———. "Six Recent Doctoral Dissertations on Strindberg." *Modern Philology*, III (1954), 52-56. On recent Strindberg studies in Sweden.

Haugen, Einar. "Strindberg the Regenerated." *Journal of English and Germanic Philology*, XXIX (1930), 257-70. Strindberg's earlier dramatic world of sin and hatred is redeemed by Christian charity, humility, and resignation in *To Damascus, III, Easter*, and *The Ghost Sonata*.

Hildeman, Karl-Ivar. "Strindberg, *The Dance of Death*, and Revenge." *Scandinavian Studies*, XXXV (November, 1963), 267-94. On the real-life models for the characters in the play.

Hoy, Cyrus. "Beyond Tragedy." In *The Hyacinth Room*. New York: Knopf, 1964, pp. 280-303. On the religious imagery in the post-Inferno plays.

Huneker, James. *Iconoclasts*. New York: Scribner's, 1905, pp. 139–62. One of the first intelligent and sympathetic appreciations in English.

Johannesson, Eric O. *The Novels of August Strindberg: A Study in Theme and Structure*. Berkeley: University of California Press, 1968. The only extensive treatment in English of Strindberg's fiction.

———. "The Problem of Identity in Strindberg's Novels." *Scandinavian Studies*, XXXIV (February, 1962), 1–35.

* Johnson, Walter. "Strindberg and the Danse Macabre." *Modern Drama*, III (May, 1960), 8–15.

———. *Strindberg and the Historical Drama*. Seattle: University of Washington Press, 1963. A substantial study by the author of the definitive translations of the historical plays.

* Kaufmann, R. J. "Strindberg: The Absence of Irony." *Drama Survey*, III (1964), 463–76.

Klaf, Franklin S. *Strindberg: The Origin of Psychology in Modern Drama*. New York: Citadel Press, 1963. A Freudian interpretation of Strindberg and his plays.

Krutch, Joseph Wood. "Strindberg and the Irreconcilable Conflict." In *"Modernism" in Modern Drama*. Ithaca: Cornell University Press, 1953, pp. 23–42. Strindberg's main contribution to modern drama has been his view of man as unredeemably irrational.

* Lagerkvist, Pär. "Modern Theatre: Points of View and Attack." Translated by Thomas R. Buckman. *Tulane Drama Review*, VI (Winter, 1961), 20–31.

Lamm, Martin. "August Strindberg." In *The Modern Drama*, translated by Karin Elliott. Oxford: Oxford University Press, 1952, pp. 135–51. A brief but comprehensive chapter on "the most daring and poetically greatest experimenter in modern drama," by Sweden's most eminent Strindberg scholar.

———. "Strindberg and the Theatre." Translated by Thomas R. Buckman. *Tulane Drama Review*, VI (November, 1961), 132–39. Mainly on the staging of the chamber plays.

Lucas, F. L. *The Drama of Ibsen and Strindberg*. New York: Macmillan, 1962. Pp. 301–463: "Strindberg", pp. 464–78: "Strindberg and Ibsen." A traditional humanist's attack on Strindberg's life and work as sick and evil. Eccentric and vulnerable.

Lyons, Charles L. "The Archetypal Action of Male Submission in Strindberg's *The Father*." *Scandinavian Studies*, XXXVI (August, 1964), 218–32. Northrop Frye–inspired.

Madsen, Børge Gedsø. *Strindberg's Naturalistic Theatre: Its Relation to French Naturalism*. Seattle: University of Washington Press, 1962. A study of influence.

May, Milton A. "Strindberg's *Ghost Sonata*: Parodied Fairy Tale on Original

Sin." *Modern Drama,* X (September, 1967), 189–94. On the allegorization of folklore motifs.

Milton, John R. "The Esthetic Fault of Strindberg's 'Dream Plays.'" *Tulane Drama Review,* IV (March, 1960), 108–16. The plays are evidence of Strindberg's failure to resolve his inner conflicts by art.

* *Modern Drama,* V (December, 1962). Strindberg issue, edited by Robert Shedd.

Paulson, Arvid. "*The Father*: A Survey of Critical Opinion." *Scandinavian Studies: Essays Presented to Dr. Henry Goddard Leach on the Occasion of His Eighty-Fifth Birthday.* Edited by Carl F. Bayerschmidt and Erik J. Friis. Seattle: University of Washington Press, 1965, pp. 247–59.

* Smedmark, Carl Reinhold, ed. *Essays on Strindberg.* Stockholm: J. Beckman for The Strindberg Society, 1966. Twelve essays, mainly on the plays, by American, British, French, and Swedish critics.

Sprinchorn, Evert. "Strindberg and the Greater Naturalism." *The Drama Review (TDR),* XIII (Winter 1968), 119–20. In naturalistic staging and acting Strindberg sought selective realism, the significant detail, not petty verisimilitude.

* Steene, Birgitta. "Shakespearean Elements in Historical Plays of Strindberg." *Comparative Literature,* XI 1959, 209–20.

Steiner, George. *The Death of Tragedy.* New York: Knopf, 1961, pp. 298–300. Two provocative pages on Strindberg as a filmic playwright, outside any tradition, whose drama "is not primarily an imitation of life, but rather a mirror to the private soul."

Styan, J. L. *The Dark Comedy.* 2nd ed. Cambridge: Cambridge University Press, 1968. Pp. 68–73: "Strindberg's Naturalism"; pp. 118–24: "Strindberg's Dream Plays."

———. "Tempo and Meaning." In *The Elements of Drama.* Cambridge: Cambridge University Press, 1960, pp. 158–62. Close analysis of a short scene in *The Father.*

Valency, Maurice. "Strindberg." In *The Flower and the Castle: An Introduction to Modern Drama.* New York: Macmillan, 1963, pp. 238–362. One of the liveliest and fullest critical discussions in English of all of Strindberg's major plays. Occasionally controversial.

Vowles, Richard B. "Strindberg and the Symbolic Mill." *Scandinavian Studies,* XXXIV (May, 1962), 111–19. Traces a single motif through several plays.

Williams, Raymond. "August Strindberg." *In Drama from Ibsen to Eliot.* London: Chatto & Windus, 1952, pp. 98–125. A non-biographical approach to Strindberg's changing dramatic styles, represented by *The Father, Miss Julie, To Damascus, Easter,* and *The Ghost Sonata.* An important study.

* ——— "Private Tragedy: Strindberg, O'Neill, Tennessee Williams." In *Modern Tragedy.* Stanford: Stanford University Press, 1966, pp. 106–20.

Winther, Sophus K. "Strindberg and O'Neill: A Study of Influence." *Scandinavian Studies*, XXXI (August, 1959), 103–20.

World Theatre, XI (Spring, 1962) Strindberg issue, ed. René Hainaux. Essays by John Gassner, Siegfried Melchinger, Maurice Gravier, and Raymond Williams on Strindberg in, respectively, the American, German, French, and British theater.

Young, Vernon. "The History of Miss Julie." *The Hudson Review*, VIII (Spring, 1955), 123–30. Discriminating praise of Alf Sjöberg's film *Miss Julie*, with some fresh perceptions on Strindberg's play.

TWENTIETH CENTURY VIEWS

European Authors

BAUDELAIRE, edited by Henri Peyre (S-TC-18)
SAMUEL BECKETT, edited by Martin Esslin (S-TC-51)
BRECHT, edited by Peter Demetz (S-TC-11)
CAMUS, edited by Germaine Brée (S-TC-1)
CERVANTES, edited by Lowry Nelson, Jr. (S-TC-89)
DANTE, edited by John Freccero (S-TC-46)
DOSTOEVSKY, edited by René Wellek (S-TC-16)
EURIPIDES, edited by Erich Segal (S-TC-76)
FLAUBERT, edited by Raymond Giraud (S-TC-42)
GIDE, edited by David Littlejohn (S-TC-88)
GOETHE, edited by Victor Lange (S-TC-73)
HOMER, edited by George Steiner and Robert Fagles (S-TC-15)
IBSEN, edited by Rolf Fjelde (S-TC-52)
KAFKA, edited by Ronald Gray (S-TC-17)
LORCA, edited by Manuel Duran (S-TC-14)
MALRAUX, edited by R. W. B. Lewis (S-TC-37)
THOMAS MANN, edited by Henry Hatfield (S-TC-36)
MOLIÈRE, edited by Jacques Guichardnaud (S-TC-41)
PIRANDELLO, edited by Glauco Cambon (S-TC-67)
PROUST, edited by René Girard (S-TC-4)
SARTRE, edited by Edith Kern (S-TC-21)
SOPHOCLES, edited by Thomas Woodard (S-TC-54)
STRINDBERG, edited by Otto Reinert (S-TC-95)
TOLSTOY, edited by Ralph E. Matlaw (S-TC-68)
VIRGIL, edited by Steele Commager (S-TC-62)
VOLTAIRE, edited by William F. Bottiglia (S-TC-78)

TWENTIETH CENTURY VIEWS

British Authors

(continued on next page)

(*continued from previous page*)